# CADENZA

*Erich Leinsdorf*

# CADENZA

## A MUSICAL CAREER

*Illustrated with photographs*

HOUGHTON MIFFLIN COMPANY BOSTON 1976

A portion of this book has appeared in
*Musical America.*

*Library of Congress Cataloging in Publication Data*

Leinsdorf, Erich, date
  Cadenza : a musical career.

  Includes index.
  1. Leinsdorf, Erich, 1912–    2. Conductors
(Music) — Correspondence, reminiscences, etc.
I. Title
ML422.L28A3    785'.092'4[B]    76-3553
ISBN 0-395-24401-3

Printed in the United States of America

W 10 9 8 7 6 5 4 3 2 1

"... the story of my life
And the particular accidents gone by
Since I came to this isle."

PROSPERO,
in William Shakespeare's *The Tempest*

# Preface

Overtures are usually last to be composed. How else can one be sure that all important tunes get quoted and grandly underlined?

It is the same with prefaces. It was only after writing many hundred pages of this autobiography that I knew what my main themes were. If compelled to capsule principal aims into one sentence I should introduce what follows as "Representing My Views and Recollections Without Censorship."

A person who wishes to stay in public life must edit what he says or he must allow others to tone down and rephrase opinions, ideas, and statements, lest a personal truth in unpalatable form make trouble. There arrives a moment in a man's career — if it has not been wholly inconsequential — when he wants to say what he really feels and thinks.

Autobiography is well suited to such a purpose if three principal pitfalls inherent in that genre are avoided. First there is the "Apologia Pro Vita Sua," then "Get Even with the Bastards," and finally "Mellow Memories of Overripe Age," all of which I have aimed to avoid. I feel no need to apologize. If any bastard got the better of me I blamed myself and have no further need for getting even. Mellow I am not and while some of my memories are bathed in a glow I believe that — in many respects — the Golden Age is with us right now, at least for the professional who performs music. If one does not overestimate the significance of the small cabals, my profession is honest.

The attempts at "corriger la fortune" lead either nowhere or not very far.

Perhaps there is a difference between my definition of success and that of simpler minds to whom money and notoriety spell fulfillment. Ultimately each of us faces only the Self, whom we cannot cheat. In the long run a performer's fate is decided by the public and no stacked deck of cards wins but a short round.

People who stand up in public to do something have a motivating drive that differs from individual to individual and from generation to generation. Social mobility has changed much since I was a child, when a musical career was still one way for making the upward step. A boy who did not have the means to attend school beyond age fourteen was better off playing the cello in a coffee house from five to seven and from nine to midnight than becoming an apprentice to a small tyrant shopkeeper or craftsman.

Having been born a couple of years before the War of 1914 began I had the great benefit of a general schooling, which combined new democratic principles of the republican postwar era with old-fashioned very high standards of individual teachers. A combination of inherited background and acquired knowledge made me desirous to hold myself fully responsible for the way my life turned out. I am not equipped to argue what free will is or what tricks our psyche plays on us, but I insist that when I moved it was on my own initiative and not as a chessman in somebody else's hand.

Even in my teens I resisted efforts to that end. I broke off relations with my superlative teachers rather than let them do the moving around. I am sure that this strong desire to run my life in my own way has made me overly sensitive to well-meaning counselors and friends.

Such stubborn insistence on self-management implies — it is safe to assume — that I don't need a few hundred pages to start any apologia now.

Neither do I wax Olympian when I disdain any desire or intention to "get even" with anybody. Whenever I felt that urge I wrote letters that were not posted. The writing itself did it and I got rid of whatever resentment gnawed in my bowels.

My calendar says Evening. Some of my ideas and concepts have proved illusory and the human condition appears to me as most melancholy — but I feel that I have retained my capacity to be enthusiastic, optimistic, indignant, pessimistic, and never mellow. That mood has eluded me so far and it has not been on my palette in painting the past.

My major conflict has been an instinctive anti-Establishment feeling while my every interest tied me to the most established groups of the Establishment.

What I cannot tell truthfully I have not mentioned and what I have written down is — to my best recollection — my truth.

## Curriculum Vitae

For those who like data and statistics: I was born on February 4, 1912, at home in Kochgasse 21, Vienna VIII, to Julius Ludwig Landauer and Charlotte, née Löbl. My mother was thirty-eight and in spite of this, her first pregnancy, refused to go to a modern hospital, lest by negligence of the maternity ward the baby be exchanged with that of other parents. The delivery was difficult — it was a breech birth — and to make things worse the obstetrician had only nine fingers. For the rest of her life my mother had to be treated regularly as a result of the botched-up job, which did not prevent her reaching the age of eighty-six. My father died from the aftereffects of an early illness, aged forty-one, a few days before my third birthday. I have no recollection of him. After his death we moved to an apartment around the corner in Haspingergasse 4, where we lived until our respective travels to the United States. "We" includes my mother's older sister, Henriette, called Tante Jetti, who remained unmarried and lived with us from the first day I remember. She and my mother were inseparable, sharing their domiciles from birth to death.

I went to a kindergarten also around a corner, to a music school around two corners, and to a public school less than five minutes' walk from home. From 1922 to 1930 I attended a school called Reform–Real–Gymnasium and was graduated in a ritual called erroneously *Matura*.

In 1937 I settled in New York, though at the time it was by no means obvious that I would remain in the United States for thirty-three years. In 1939 I married Anne Frohnknecht, daughter of an American mother from Albany, New York, and a German émigré father from Frankfurt am Main. There was an older sister, Margaret, who married the writer Arthur Kober in 1941. From my marriage to Anne there were born five children: David Immanuel in 1942, now a lawyer and County Commissioner in Colorado; Gregor Jonathan in 1944, now a young tycoon in the metal trade; Joshua Franklin in 1945, who writes poetry and prose and has tried to make Eugene McCarthy President of the United States; Deborah Hester in 1948, a medical doctor; and Jennifer Gabrielle in 1952, a nursing student. Our marriage was dissolved in April 1968.

Later the same year I was married to Vera Graf, a violinist, born in Montevideo, daughter to Pablo and Margarita, who were both émigrés from a region of Hungary that has been disputed between several states and is now Yugoslav territory.

# Contents

# Illustrations *following page 146*

# PART I

# Viennese Beginnings

# Crossroads

In the late fall of 1967 I went through a crisis that was not the first but the meanest of my life. Neither my personal nor my professional existence seemed tolerable any longer.

While my wife and I, after the ups and downs of many years, had seriously discussed separation in 1965 we decided then — like so many — to try a while longer and avoid the pains of splitting up after more than twenty-five years.

My workload as conductor of the Boston Symphony was nothing short of mad, and my protests to trustees and management had been of no avail. One hundred and three concerts each year, active direction of the Berkshire Music Center, some thirty recording sessions to produce ten LPs annually, rehearsals, tour travels, appointments, correspondence, my own study and preparation for an ever-increasing repertoire, plus abrasive labor relations had brought me in five years too frequently to the brink of complete exhaustion. If that was the price of holding a top post — I had come to feel — let others bid for it and do it if they wish.

Only six years earlier I had been overjoyed at being asked to a position considered among the most prestigious in my profession, and now I could only hope to get out with my health still intact.

Why had I so confidently accepted a quantity of work that to the best of my knowledge my predecessor, Charles Munch, could not and would not attempt? What had made me so cocksure? I suppose that it was simply competitive arrogance on my part, the desire to prove myself stronger than the next man, and lack of an adviser who might have warned me. With a capable manager behind me I doubt that Boston's administration would have got away with such abuse.

Now, in November 1967, numb with chronic fatigue, I discovered that the spirit of competition may be the needed philosophical foundation for a free-market economy, but for the individual human being the urge to be overly active is, at best, a delusion and at worst a psychological illness. Since I knew myself to be afflicted by it, this was now the time to overhaul my life. As I struggled with the decisions how to do this and that, as I sat up late at night rummaging in the recesses of my mind, I recalled scenes that were filed away but never forgotten.

There was the illness and death of Mitropoulos. After finishing one grueling eight-week stint with the New York Philharmonic, he had a heart attack and landed in hospital within two days of the final concert. Having little else to live for he returned too soon to the orchestra and to the Met, for the inevitable second attack and further hospitalization. As if on a suicidal mission he undertook in 1960 to prepare the Third Mahler Symphony with the orchestra of Milan's La Scala and died during a rehearsal, perhaps through shock from the proverbial chaotic conditions of Italy's musical world.

There are always romantic tale spinners who will proclaim this to be an heroic end. To me it is a sorry finale for a distinguished and good man. Even the obituary in the *New York Times* mentioned, with more accuracy than delicacy, that all the unparalleled kindnesses to players did not obtain for Mitropoulos their best efforts. There is, alas, no relation between human empathy and musical good behavior.

I dreaded sickness, not only as we all do, but particularly in the form of inner fatigue, which is of deadening effect to a performer who must be at his freshest each time before the public.

Another of my memories went back to 1954 when I attended a performance of *Don Giovanni* in the outdoor riding school of the Salzburg Festival theater. Furtwängler conducted. That he was ill I knew from a number of questions his wife had asked me in reference to his planned forthcoming American tour. She was worried about transportation between cities to make things as easy as possible with obvious concern for the conductor's health. His hearing had become worse, more noticeable in opera, where he betrayed hesitancy as to when the harpsichord had concluded the cadence and the orchestra should be cued to come in. This was not the man of my early years in Vienna when we students stood in back of the stalls entranced by his personality and his music-making; this was a shell of his former self.

Upsetting as the performance had been to me, I felt saddest during the curtain calls when I could see the great man standing in the doorway awaiting his turn for a bow. To be pulled out for his ovation seemed as important to the aging, infirm giant as if he were a debutante and the future depended on the reception. Goethe wrote in a marginal note that "Actors and Musicians live off the crowd's applause." Can these clapping noises conceal fading alertness, waning control, and a deteriorating hearing? Are there no friends and relations who will prevail upon a man of stature that the time has come to contemplate rather than act?

In that summer I was especially susceptible to such a melancholy experience as it took place a mere four months after another hero of mine, Toscanini, had laid down his baton under bewildering circumstances that have remained unclear to this day. My knowledge came from a marginal involvement. On a Saturday evening in early spring I received a phone call from Ernest La Prade, administrator of music and the orchestra at NBC. It was a discreet inquiry asking if I could and would, in case of need, conduct the next day's NBC Symphony concert, an all-Wagner program. To my question if Maestro was un-

well, La Prade replied somewhat vaguely that the recent death
of Mrs. Walter Toscanini, the daughter-in-law, had greatly
affected the eighty-seven-year-old man. I noticed that the lame
reasoning covered something else that was not for discussion,
and simply expressed my hopes that all would be well, especially
since rehearsals had been done and I was not eager to take on a
program, though of well-known pieces, without proper preparation. But I did agree to "stand by" and next evening, which
I spent watching a performance at Juilliard, I left my seat location with the switchboard like a good medic. Not being disturbed in my enjoyment I assumed that all was in order until
Monday's morning paper carried a detailed report of a breakdown in the continuity of the Venusberg Music, which had
always been a Toscanini war-horse and favorite selection. Radio
listeners had noticed that at some point in the piece a recorded
First Symphony of Brahms intruded and replaced the Wagner
strains, then after seconds or minutes shifted back to the original program, a thoroughly confusing and crass event. A day
later, Toscanini's retirement was announced to the public.

From the three bits of factual information and from later
tales by orchestra members I concluded that in rehearsal for
that concert memory lapses had greatly disturbed Maestro.
Hence his reluctance to conduct the program. He never used
scores while performing and would not have known how at
that stage of his life. Judging from the musicians' reports on
how the Venusberg Music fell apart, the memory lapses must
have recurred at the concert. The readiness of NBC with a
recording — albeit a strange choice to pick Brahms — was further proof that the mishap was no surprise. Ambulances stand
by wherever accidents appear probable.

In the wake of Maestro's resignation and retirement from
active conducting the NBC Symphony was disbanded in a high-
handed manner. David Sarnoff was fully rewarded through
enormous publicity for having had the most famous living conductor with a specially created orchestra but after seventeen

years of it the corporation was tired of the expense and for them it was not a day too early when Maestro declared himself out. NBC's high command had tried sometime earlier to induce Maestro to resign.

Not as drastic and dramatic, yet equally superfluous and anticlimactic, was one of Bruno Walter's final appearances. On Good Friday afternoon in 1960 he conducted Verdi's Requiem Mass at the Met, replacing the traditional *Parsifal,* which Met general manager Rudolf Bing disliked. I was at the time attached to the Met management and attended, for my pleasure and in line of duty, the performance in a proscenium box next to John Gutman, assistant Met manager. Chorus and solo quartet were placed on stage while the orchestra played in their customary position in the pit.

Walter during that particular season had still given wonderful concerts with the New York Philharmonic at Carnegie Hall, yet age had taken physical vigor out of his arm and his beat was weak. With only instrumentalists this need not be detrimental, but vocal participation demands from the conductor above all other things a decisive signal. Without that choruses will flounder.

Rarely have I perspired as much as I did during that short afternoon. Many were the moments when it was touch and go if the music would continue at all or break down in total chaos. Experience and good will on both sides avoided any involuntary halt and the work staggered on like a wounded war-horse. Walter himself knew how things had gone, judging by his comments as we went backstage to pay our respects. His remarks could not cover the fact that it had been as sorry and superfluous an embarrassment as was ever visited on a great man in his old age — for no other reason than unwillingness to admit a purely physical weakness that made choral works too strenuous.

What shoddy commodity is success if it has no bearing on wisdom and maturity? I was always a hero-worshiper and I always got bitterly disappointed when I had to witness the pathetic, the undignified, the ridiculous. Needless exposure of natural deterioration, particularly in an admired person, enrages and mortifies me.

These sad endings intruded into my own consciousness only at a time when I had troubles with myself and tried to find a balance.

Standing at my own crossroads, I felt that the forces that had driven me for so long would be my ruin if I did not resolve my conflict and decide on my future course. In the decline of my great and admired models I had seen the human condition and I was frightened by what I had seen. I had led a life so heavily weighted on the side of work and career that all else was shortchanged.

Among my many lucky breaks I count the timing of this great crisis. I was not yet fifty-six when it happened. After I rearranged things I began to feel the urge of writing and of sharing what I had discovered with others.

With the story of my life I shall attempt to sketch the changes in music over the past fifty years. When I was ten the Vienna Philharmonic would make an extraordinary trip to South America that took three months. Fifty years later the Berlin Philharmonic would play the same number of concerts in Japan within a period of eighteen days. In many other ways, what had been extraordinary has become commonplace and vice versa. It was a matter of course in my youth that a new production of an opera would feature identical casts for a considerable run of repeat performances. Not so today. For three shows a star collection is assembled to be spelled then by nonentities to the vexation of the luckless subscriber who holds tickets for the fifth repeat.

Great music festivals, Bayreuth above all, were events at which the best artists performed without thoughts of monetary profit. Today the shrine of Wagner functions like a machine every summer and exhibits as a matter of fiscal convenience and of artistic conviction beginners rather than masters.

Radio, Microgroove and tape, television and jet planes have caused some of these changes, which at times resemble upheavals. Young men with hunched backs are seen entering the concert halls in increasing number. There is nothing wrong with them — the cause of their deformity is a tape recorder, smuggled in to produce pirate issues of the musical program.

As I wrote this I had been entertained after hours by a book on multinational conglomerates. Surprisingly enough I found in it some disturbing parallels with twentieth-century composition. The author of the book describes the remarkable character and abilities of a chairman whose major preoccupation consists in eliminating the surprise element from his business. His subalterns will perhaps avoid the chancy ups and downs, but their better initiative toward finding new paths, albeit with mistakes, must be stifled.

I wonder if the trend toward systematizing musical composition through total serialization may not come under the same heading?

In this memoir my emphasis will be on such topics rather than on the questionable adventures of who slept with whom. While the horizontal element is of crucial importance in composing music, the vertical assures us of harmony. No decent method will neglect one over the other.

## Youth

I do not have complete recall of my childhood. World War I began when I was two years old and before I turned three my father died of an illness the nature of which my mother

withheld from me. We lived in one of the better petit-bour-
geois districts of Vienna together with my aunt and a maid,
Ella.

The war to us meant poor food. Once in a while my mother
sent Ella to her native village in Moravia from where she
returned with butter, eggs, and, most precious of all, a goose.
On many a grim winter day Ella and I would race after the
bread wagon to catch a second loaf in a store where they didn't
know us as having already purchased one. The bread itself was
wretched and God only knew what went into its making. Regularly we developed boils on our fingers, which meant trips to
the doctor, who lanced these otherwise harmless water bubbles.
Once the war and shortages ended none of us developed these
sores ever again.

As long as Ella was with us, she took care of me, and I tried
later to reciprocate by teaching her how to read. I did not suc-
ceed. Though she was illiterate, her intelligence was quite evident and her loyalty to us beyond reproach. Many times she
would take me ostensibly for a healthy walk and to my joy we
attended instead military funeral processions, which started at
a nearby hospital. Ella treated these rituals like a precious entertainment, defying my mother's strict orders not to take me.
Her suggestion to conceal the nature of our outing found me
most willing, yet once in a while my tongue slipped and my
mother issued a renewed ukase against such festivities.

My early experience of these somber, yet colorful pageants
gave me a keener understanding of many a march movement in
Mahler's works. When I rehearse the opening of his Fifth with
musicians, who are obviously too young to have known these
WWI ceremonies, I recount my excursions: sitting on Ella's
shoulders to look over the crowd's heads, the man on horseback
wearing a black coat of mail, the brass band playing the dirges
off-pitch to the steady beat of muffled drums.

I emerged from the war years with some slight lung trouble
for which the doctor blithely suggested trips to higher altitudes.

My mother dismissed these councils as financially impossible but took me for the afternoon on good-weather days to an outdoor café, situated in a moderately elevated spot on the outskirts of Vienna. The city's location at the eastern end of the Alps provides ideal excursions to hilly regions by streetcar. This was quite sufficient for my lung trouble, which since then has never reappeared.

Our tram terminal was called Türkenschanzpark. The legacy of the Ottoman siege was still very much present in Vienna, in names, monuments, and above all in the superlative coffee. In the garden where my lungs were to benefit was a pavilion, with a small orchestra giving forth all kinds of fare. After my ice I would leave the table and stand behind the conductor, fascinated by the whole procedure. A special favorite of mine was a cornet solo, played from somewhere in the garden, outside the music shed. I am sure it was not Beethoven's Third *Leonore* but some sentimental selection of which I recall only the mystery of the player's whereabouts.

Like many Viennese my mother spent a considerable part of her life, winters and summers, at the coffee house. Sometimes she met friends and acquaintances there, but every day of the year, she was joined after office hours by Tante Jetti. Theirs was such a symbiotic relationship that all who knew them foresaw that the surviving one of the siblings could not last long. And they were right. My aunt passed on less than seven months after my mother's death in 1960, of no clearly diagnosed cause.

Modern fresh-air-minded friends kept telling my mother how dreadful it was for a little boy of four and five to be cooped up in a smoke-filled place for several hours a day, watching card games, chess games, billiard games or looking at questionable illustrated periodicals instead of being outdoors with other children. My mother let them talk; she wanted to have her little son under her own eyes. She had no intention to fidget over my safety and in hindsight I cannot fault her.

*

The worst memories of my childhood were our regular trips to the cemetery where my father's grave was. Even now, over sixty, I have a moment of ill feeling each time I pass the Central Cemetery on the way from or to the airport of Vienna.

First came the interminable rides on the tram through the ugliest proletarian district of the city. Then the search for the grave. As often as we went, I do not remember a single time when we didn't have trouble finding the spot. As soon as we finally arrived at our destination my mother cried a lot, which embarrassed me. I could not understand why it took the actual arrival at the gravesite for her to start howling. Perhaps my own imagination was already alive to the futility of death rites and later ritualistic mourning. Flowers, stone monuments, candles, prayers, tears, and the lot never had any meaning for me. I do remember my dead keenly, with a sharp undiminished sense of loss, without ever making the pilgrimage to a grave.

Aside from these sorry excursions my preschool years were pleasant. I did have company of children, the most memorable being a girl named Bronia, who had lice, which I got from her. My head was shaved, my mother forbade me further association, and yet, ironically, after more than half a century I recall no early playmate except little louse-infested Bronia.

My father's relatives did not mean much to me emotionally. My grandmother and several aunts and great-aunts were all physically ugly and mentally uninteresting. The duty visits on which my mother insisted had to be suffered, but it was clear that she too did not care much for the in-law group.

It was disappointing to her when I was not allowed by law to enter first grade in 1917. Though I was five years and seven months, the deadline was a birthday on or before December 15, all of which meant waiting for September 1918. That "lost" year was later made up when I jumped fifth grade, not an unusual thing, and in 1917 I was put into a French kindergarten and a neighborhood music school. The kindergarten gave me my first chance to imitate a teacher, in this instance an overwrought lady whose every other sentence was a larmoyant "je suis très nerveuse," which I recited each day upon returning home, to the vast amusement of my household. At the music school I absorbed the customary easy tunes, which I played with both hands on the treble keys while the teacher supplied the harmony. Soon I began to browse through volumes of sheet music left by my father. He had been a devoted amateur who bought the tunes and overtures and potpourris of musical selections that he had heard and liked. There were many dozens of pieces bound in hard covers, a curious lot that, assorted alphabetically, contained next to a facilitated piano arrangement of Wagner a military march by Waçek. Without fear or judgment I plowed through this odd mixture from cover to cover, making at first a wild mess of it, but acquiring by degrees that most important ability for a musician: how to read music.

The nonmusical inheritance from my father had been, with wise council of trusted friends, invested in War Bonds, a move more patriotic than prudent. In 1918, with the war lost, we had nothing except the modest salary of my aunt, a clerk in an insurance company, who shared what she made with us. Later on the impoverished Austrian Republic granted a small monthly payment to my mother, which terminated when she left for the United States.

Soon after the Armistice in November 1918 we got the first shipment of food parcels from the United States. We queued on a very cold afternoon for some hours in front of a beautiful baroque *palais*, eventually receiving a splendid basket of food, with a large tin of corned beef the outstanding item. Meat had been more than scarce and that same evening the four of us did away with the contents of the tin can. It was such an overdose after a long dearth that none of us ever could face corned beef again.

After more normal times returned we went once in a while to a restaurant. Vienna is full of inexpensive eateries where well-cooked meals can be had and I liked public places already from my years in the coffee houses. The one drawback to these outings was the necessity to order — as we called it — from the right side of the menu. The finger went up and down the price list and stopped at the lowest quotation, which was the main course to order. I confess that my most acute feeling of accomplishment in life comes when I read the menu in a restaurant and can ask for any dish without consulting the price list. I laugh at this and yet it has become some sort of ridiculous yardstick.

Among the many cousins in my mother's family there was one, named Clara, who was married to a shoe manufacturer. My father also had been in the shoe business, traveling for a big firm, but this cousin's husband was of a different breed and made a fortune in the postwar era. The evening conversations at home hinted darkly at black-market operations. They acquired a house with garden in Perchtoldsdorf, a village outside the city limits, reachable after a long but delightful tram ride. We were invited frequently and at times, when they spent part of their summer in Italy, my mother and I lived for a few weeks in the house.

I adored the place, particularly my own exploratory walks to the station house of a small branch railroad line. There I could sit for hours, though few trains came through. It was heaven for me to walk around the small room, studying the timetables on the walls and planning my own trips all over the railroad net as listed on the posted sheets. It greatly stimulated my imagination and the desire to travel, which, though amply fulfilled in my life, has never diminished. The charm of moving from place to place, the fascination with timetables — now of airplanes — is with me today as it was my dream then.

\*

When I was eight I was taken to a serious piano teacher, who was the wife of the composer Paul A. Pisk. She was connected with a private conservatory where I received a scholarship. My mother was able to accomplish this relief from having to pay in every single instance of my schooling, be it public school or private instruction.

My first year at the conservatory was concluded with one of those notorious student recitals, but I was spared a solo performance. I played the piano in an arrangement of Haydn's Toy Symphony, which was conducted by an older student, Mosco Carner, who has become a well-known musicologist in England.

After three years Mrs. Pisk declared that a man's guidance was of the essence. I was, due to my home setup, totally immune to female authority, and she proposed to have her husband, the composer, speak to one of his pianist friends, a well-known splendid teacher, Paul Emerich. I was accepted and was taught for five years, without monetary compensation, in a most unusual manner. Emerich was not a virtuoso, geared to the brilliant display of high pianism, but at all times first and foremost a sophisticated musician, opening up to me the encyclopedic vistas of music for chamber groups and ultimately leading to the orchestra. He had many students who were regularly presented in musicales held in his spacious apartment. In 1927, the Beethoven centenary year, we performed not only all the piano music but also every chamber work with piano and the concertos. For the pieces with string instruments, Emerich's sister, a cellist with whom I took lessons too, recruited the necessary talent.

For most of the sonatas I was understudy. One wildly hysterical Russian girl was so unreliable that I had to be fully prepared, and, indeed, when she got a crying fit in the first movement of Opus 31, No. 3, Emerich calmly said, "Erich" and I went to the piano and played the sonata.

What I liked best was my monopoly on accompanying the concertos on the second piano. It was great fun to produce the illusion of an orchestra, not being held strictly to the printed text and, last but not least, not having to practice as one must for a piano part. I had caught on that there are several ways of using the keyboard. No arranger can convey through the printed notes how to produce the sounds that will be orchestral rather than pianistic. Notes are added, others omitted, bass lines are doubled in octaves, leading instruments are stressed, horns and flutes are imitated by different touch; one might even sing a line that may be more than ten fingers can handle. It's a special kind of playing, which I got the knack of early and which undoubtedly led me a good part of the way from the concert grand to the operatic rehearsal studio.

Emerich, while pleased with this, also wanted me to become his shingle as a full-fledged concertizing pianist. For that his ambivalent attitude toward the virtuoso composers, Liszt, Rachmaninoff, even Chopin and Schumann, stood in the way. I suppose this was one of the reasons why Emerich never "produced" a real pianist. But we had other advantages, unknown to piano players in general: we had to play the entire Bach and the whole of Debussy, but also, alas, Reger, with whom Emerich had studied.

By 1930 we had had many acid arguments over my neglecting the pianistic element in favor of operatic and orchestral music. It ended by Emerich's throwing me out in anger, and I never attempted to go back. He had been not only a fine teacher, but very good to me, seeing to it that I took up a stringed instrument and going back to Pisk with the request that he take me on for theory and composition. He put it very wittily, saying that Pisk, in return for having recommended me as piano student, should now reciprocate the favor and teach me counterpoint and harmony and all the technical know-how of writing music.

It was almost a forgone conclusion that the ever-widening horizons of music beyond one instrument would lead me away from the virtuoso career, but Emerich still took it all very badly when it happened. I wished that the legitimate parting of ways would not spill over into the personal sphere. There were recriminations, with terms such as "lack of gratitude" and "selfish indulgence" filling the air, which must have prompted me to say things far too abrasive to be justified or excusable. I was quite aware at eighteen that this was the reverse side of getting tuition free. One always pays in other coin and it is mostly pain.

I have been considered all my life to be the robust type. While this is correct I have feelings of extreme sensitivity to many overtones. Anyone who has received the classical treatment of the impecunious develops an extra antenna as a matter of course. I remember too well after decades what humiliation can be connected with a so-called gift. I have found that those born to affluence are less generous with money than we who have received charity. Poverty is a state of mind and much praise to my mother for never making me feel "poor." Impecunious — yes. Hand-me-down suits notwithstanding, free lessons to the contrary, she managed to instill the idea of the quid pro quo, and, indeed, my teachers made me do plenty of jobs; I was aide, secretary, porter, handyman, and jack-of-all-trades. I never minded but I registered. This I kept all my life, registering, even if I pretend not to notice, and I suppose I am overly touchy to every tiny nuance of behavior.

Pisk, as a teacher, was a thorough classicist to whom counterpoint was the beginning and end for a composer. His own masters were Franz Schreker and Arnold Schönberg, whose ideas he tried to amalgamate in his own writing, which was mostly delicate in fabric without being as frail and pointillist as Webern's. He arranged for three students to take lessons together — a wonderful way of training us to be critical. Creativity, alas, cannot be taught.

We studied and analyzed *Wozzeck* but were never allowed to neglect chorale harmonization and the three-part counterpoint. Toward the contemporary schools of composition we were expected to be as clannish and as intolerant as any member of the second Viennese school was brainwashed to be. The Trinity was Schönberg, Berg, and Webern, who were infallible, and the rest did not count. This type of mental limitation was not my way, and it led later to my own defection. I was not a joiner, neither of clubs nor of schools. I believed passionately in individual judgment, right or wrong, orthodox or revolutionary. On that point I have never yielded.

Pisk also provided me with all my first professional opportunities until in 1934 his own backing disappeared. He made his living by writing criticism for the *Arbeiter Zeitung,* the organ of the Social Democratic Party. His boss, David Bach, a pompous man who never let one forget that he was a friend of Schönberg's, kept the big events for himself, the opera premières and important concerts, while my teacher had the many recitals and chamber concerts to report on. Vienna's music life took place in five concert halls, which made it impossible even for two men to be at every event. Thus I, from age thirteen, became a ghost critic, attending three or four nights a week the least attractive and most insignificant concerts. I admit I was, as any critic must be, highly critical. Honor to Pisk that he never printed my negative comments.

Included in this comedy of the teen-age critic was a strange coincidence. My mother's not so secret plans for me had focused above all on a journalistic career. Her sense of practicality had told her that Uncle Emil's position as editor of the conservative *Neues Wiener Tagblatt* would be of considerable help, and in her own dreams she saw me as its first-string music critic.

It came differently, probably through my tasting the blood

of public performance early in life. I was fifteen when I took my first plunge as a paid piano player, hired, through the good offices of my teacher, to accompany a dance group in one of Vienna's housing projects. Pisk, with his job for the Social Democratic Party paper, was in deep with the very active and significant Arts Council of the party, which gave me nearly all my opportunities to earn money and show my varied musical and organizational abilities up to the political disaster in 1934.

In the spring of 1930 my class graduated from the Viennese equivalent of high school, and then the lack of any concrete plans became acute. For the preceding three years I had earned some much-needed money and done a number of diverse musical odd jobs, which taught me more and prepared me better than master classes and seminars. Yet they were not a career, even without any foreknowledge that the entire source of my employment would disappear in four years' time.

It was during the previous winter that I had come to the parting of ways with Emerich. The musical portion of our agreement, stripped of personal acrimony, is still valid and represents even now, forty-odd years later, my musical philosophy.

I did not find it appealing to practice a piece for piano several hours a day for several weeks when I could absorb the musical content within a very short time. It was clear, even to Emerich, who was no virtuoso-type player, that the Schnabel repertoire would never guarantee a career to anyone else. I would not have minded working on great music, but it seemed a waste of my energies to tame my ten fingers to master the acrobatics of Liszt et al. I had acquired through my voracious sight-reading the ability to recognize musical patterns instantly, and it was only natural and logical that music which goes round and round in repetition of a simple motif could not interest me for long. All the people who came to Emerich's musicales and all of Pisk's friends were highbrows who looked down their collective noses on the lion-maned keyboard demons who were still the vogue. Moriz Rosenthal, Ignaz Friedman, and Vladimir de Pachman were as legendary and as madly successful as their total musical offering was shallow. This kind of mental orientation was obviously not going to turn me into a concert pianist. My sense of practicality also had registered that the recital as a viable form of concert activity was very much on the decline.

A young man like myself had much better chances after 1945. Then the revival of Baroque music and the increasing cultivation of chamber music offered more diversification to an instrumentalist. In 1930 it was recital and teaching, and those were not my long suits.

During my years with Pisk I began to regularly attend performances at the opera and much of Vienna's rich fare of orchestral concerts. Up to age fourteen my principal interest had been the theater, which was of superlative quality and played such a vast repertoire that I saw more different Shakespeare plays at the Burgtheater than have been produced in New York over the past thirty-five years. As my main musical interest shifted I acquired opera scores and scores from the symphonic repertoire, stood in line for many hours, and taught myself score-reading and -playing instead of practicing Czerny and Chopin.

Vienna was ideal for observing the greatest masters among conductors. Furtwängler, Kleiber, Klemperer, Walter, and a host of local celebrities whose performances were certainly good enough to give me the full grandeur of the great symphonies on first impact made every visit to the two halls, Musikverein and Konzerthaus, an event. The opera, which had become somewhat lazy after Richard Strauss left as co-director, got an uplift when Clemens Krauss took over the reins and began, with the help of his associates from Frankfurt, to restudy the repertoire and produce new works. (If I am somewhat skeptical when I read of the Mahler revival in the nineteen sixties and hear other claims of publicity seekers, I remember that in the late twenties and early thirties there was not only a Verdi renaissance at the opera but cyclic performances of the Mahler symphonies. The Seventh under Krauss and the Sixth under Webern are still very much present in my mind. It was, in short, part and parcel of the remarkable artistic and intellectual vitality that the Weimar Republic promoted across the borders.)

There was, in Vienna, always the ridiculous going hand in hand with the sublime. *Wozzeck* was one of the opera director's greatest deeds, and it was kept in the repertoire in spite of half-empty houses. I saw and heard it fourteen times in two seasons.

At the first night, the story goes, a young man visited Frau Baronin Pollak von Parnegg, our Mrs. Malaprop, in her box to ask how she liked it. "Very interesting," she allowed, "but rather unsuitable for a première."

When school was done in June 1930 I did not feel that it was the end of a prison term. I had been treated with much consideration to my active professionalism in music since 1927. I have good memories of many teachers, stayed friends with one of them, whose death was a great personal loss to me, and have no negative reactions when I pass my school building nowadays.

My mother, Viennese to the core, wished me to attend University and obtain the title Doktor. It was the custom that every reputable person in Austria should carry at least that distinguished prefix, which is used before the names of not only medics, but lawyers, teachers, clergymen, or anyone, including businessmen, who had attended four years of University-cum-graduation. To become a doctor of law one only needed to pass several exams, for which private cramming courses were available. This created a galaxy of *Doktoren* who had never attended any classes.

Not knowing exactly what I preferred, I enrolled at the Music Department of Vienna University without enthusiasm, not having any inclination toward the career of the scholar. What I liked much better was the traditional "Maturareise," a trip of several weeks to experience the "world" as a crowning of twelve years attendance at school. Instead of any grand tour my mother, who had saved for it, let me take part in a master class the Mozarteum in Salzburg held for eight weeks each summer.

I was accepted as a scholarship student and found the experience rewarding in more than one sense. The head of the Mozarteum was Bernhard Paumgartner, who loomed large to an impressionable youth. He had made a lifelong study of Mozart, and what with the increasing publicity for the Salzburg Festival, he was considered an expert interpreter of the town's musical patron saint. Like most "specialists," his was a happy mixture of good promotion and a genuine feeling for Mozart's unfathomable and inexhaustible genius. He was a natural musician, a good speaker, and, in order to hold on to a position of consequence in Austria, surely a good politician. His active participation at the annual festival was, by international standards, marginal. Every summer he conducted the C Minor Mass at St. Peter's and the outdoor serenades in the court of the bishopric.

For the master classes in 1930, which extended beyond the five weeks of the festival's duration, he had secured two other conductors for the bulk of instruction, Meinhard von Zallinger, an amiable and pedantic German, and a very young man, only four years my senior, who was both teacher of score reading to us and disciple to the older Zallinger, who had much more experience and coached the younger man whenever the occasion arose. That was Herbert Karajan, at the time without the little v between his names. During the winter he was conductor in Ulm and in July 1930, before the festival, he conducted performances of *Tosca* at the Salzburg Landestheater, a beautiful, small house that served the local population. While Karajan rehearsed *Tosca,* Zallinger sat behind him, giving from time to time whispered advice and direction.

Forty years later, in Lucerne, I chatted with Karajan, who

checked into the hotel while I was checking out, and we rummaged a little in the past. He had not kept track of the lady who sang Floria Tosca on the earlier occasion, so I reminded him that she was Helen Gahagan, a lady who was later married to actor Melvyn Douglas and whose political career was damaged beyond repair by one Richard M. Nixon.

It was a fruitful summer for me, especially as I discovered that my orchestral conducting was not so hot and that I needed more exercise and experience. My principal problem, and that of most young conductors, is a nervous clogging up of the capacity to hear. Rehearsing an orchestra means to diagnose instantly what goes wrong, to decide which wrongs warrant stopping and interrupting the flow of the music, and, if a halt is decided on, to state in the briefest and clearest language the alternative or the correction. I have found in my life that the ability to keep an open ear is altogether a rare quality and not limited to musical conductors. Wide-open attention is incompatible with personal preoccupation; the latter handicaps simple conversation just as it blocks the abilities of the nervous musical leader.

Besides stimulating teaching the summer in Salzburg brought me more and better opportunities for work and travel. Zallinger, who was engaged as conductor of the opera in Cologne, had noticed that I played well and recommended me to one of its tenors, Gotthelf Pistor, who came to Vienna on an extended guest appearance in the early spring of 1931. Pistor needed a coach to learn the long and difficult tenor part in Schönberg's *Gurre-Lieder,* which he had to perform in Cologne later that season. He liked working with me and invited me to drive with him back to Germany, where I had never been. Thus I saw not only a good part of the country but was taken to Bayreuth as the singer's private coach.

There I had the unique opportunity to watch at close quarters many rehearsals under the direction of Toscanini and Furt-

wängler. Considering the history of the Wagner festival between 1933 and 1974 I would say that 1931 may have been
the last time when the scores of the master were the primary
concern of the festivals' performers and of the artistic directors.

When, in September 1930, I entered the Music Department
of Vienna University as a student I had no clear concept of the
curriculum and its impact or meaning. I was expected to get
a doctor title, and music history and musicology seemed as good
an avenue as any. The department had acquired a first-class
reputation under the leadership of Guido Adler, who was the
prime mover and editor of a grandiose publication in many volumes, *Denkmäler der Tonkunst in Österreich*. It is a monument
indeed. Adler had retired, but there was still a fine faculty of
important musicologists, Alfred Orel, Robert Haas, and Rudolf
von Ficker. I took several courses and one seminar, which for
that semester was devoted to compositions for use in schools.
The democratic trends of the Weimar Republic had inspired
important composers, such as Hindemith and Weill and Hans
Eisler, to write works of educational and entertaining quality
for instant use by musical beginners.

In the first session of our seminar the teacher, discussing a
Hindemith opus, wished for a demonstration on the piano and
asked for volunteers. We were at least two dozen students, and
I, a freshman, felt that I would wait and see rather than pipe
up like an eager beaver. But no hands were raised, so I finally
got up and offered my services, went to the platform, and
played what the teacher had wanted. It was rather simple, I
was thanked and sat down.

Next week the same scenario. I waited in vain when volunteers were asked for, then played and sat down. By the third
week the teacher simply called on me, and all my fellow students looked quite happy that the threat of having to exhibit
their own pianism was past. I had acquired a monopoly, and
since I did nicely the teacher brought longer and more demand-

ing scores for discussion and demonstration. Once I went through an entire Weill school opera entitled *Der Jasager*.

For a brief period this was an ego boost, which was not what the doctor ever would have prescribed for me. But, success is success and we take it when we get it. One of my colleagues, a girl with whom I walked from classes, enlightened me that most of our group, herself included, were theoreticians without ambitions of performing. Library work, program notes, teaching, and perhaps criticism were the branches for their future, and even if some of them had fluency on an instrument, it would by now be rusty through disuse, which accounted for the reluctance of one and all to play.

These explanations and my own observations made me decide to discontinue my university career, to the discontent of my mother, who saw the doctorate evaporating. Before the Christmas recess I made my rounds to say Farewell and Adieu, to the evident distress of the seminar instructor, who was losing his demonstrator. He even hinted that I could expect the easiest exams with all the credits that would accrue to me for my valuable collaboration. I professed gratitude but kept to my decision and left. Between 1945 and 1967 I collected four honorary degrees in the United States, two of them while my mother was still alive, and she was as proud of them as if I had really been doctored.

My three months at the University's Music Department were by no means a total loss. I learned *Stilkritik* (critique of style), which serves me well in guessing the composer of a work unknown to me onto which I may stumble when turning on the radio in the middle of a selection.

At the beginning of 1931 the question "What Now?" faced me again. My need for more practice in orchestra-conducting narrowed my options ultimately to choosing an institution with a large student orchestra. Thus I went for a two-year course to the State Academy of Music, which then had the best possible student orchestra, an active opera department, and, head-

ing these, a well-known very able conductor, Oswald Kabasta.
He was typically Austrian, with a cherubic countenance that
concealed but for a brief first acquaintance his fierce ambition.
Whatever his character, he was an excellent musician and conductor. While no love was ever lost between him and me, I
learned a good deal through — rather than from — him, and I
was impressed by his own performances as well as by his ability
to hold down several jobs at the same time.

Kabasta's way of discharging his manifold duties was as dis-
honest as that of his latter-day colleagues who hold on to equally
incompatible positions. Somebody is always shortchanged, and
in his case the Music Academy was rarely graced by his presence,
which meant that the student conductors were in charge of
orchestra sessions. Without the supervision of a faculty member
these usually turned into bedlam, but I somehow managed to
hold my own with the unruly youngsters. Once, when Kabasta
was present and stayed on after dismissing the orchestra to give
us a critical postmortem of the rehearsal, he wondered why,
among the several conducting disciples, I had been the only one
to keep order and get anywhere; my fellows explained that
nature had endowed me with such a loud voice that I could
bellow down any noisemakers. This undeniable asset led to a
diploma after the two-year course was done.

Graduation was also marked by a public concert in the beautiful Musikvereinssaal, my part being orchestral accompaniments to the Concerto in A by Liszt and the first movement
of Brahms's Violin Concerto. This conductorial debut was also
my last Vienna appearance until I conducted there after the
war under the auspices of the United States occupation army
during the grim winter of 1946–1947. After that second round
it took another hiatus — this time of twenty-six years — until
conditions were propitious for the prodigal son to reappear in
his hometown.

None of this could be on my mind in 1933. I felt that finally
school had ended and that I was no longer a boy.

I was twenty-one and all was well, except that the German situation made it impossible for me to follow the established route for a young apprentice conductor. It was customary for graduates to present themselves to one of several talent agents who, in turn, would introduce the young hopefuls to visiting general music directors coming to Vienna for replacements in such posts as assistant conductor, chorus master, or for any other musical position. The more talented would by steps or by leaps move from the smaller towns, like Magdeburg or Osnabrück, to larger places and then from subaltern positions in larger houses to leading assignments in smaller theaters until the cream of the crop reached the several pinnacles in Berlin or Munich or Vienna. This well-oiled channel through which many generations of musicians went and which brought out most of the great names we admired was now shut to me and to all who did not qualify to pass the test of racial Aryan purity.

Knowing the course of history now, it is easy to sneer at some of my colleagues who then tried to chisel their way around these obnoxious new laws. I was closely acquainted with a very fine musician, son of an English mother and a German-Jewish father, who told me — a few years later — a ghastly tale of his and some singers' endeavors to buy by very shoddy means their undisturbed continuation in Germany.

They were engaged in Dresden, where Fritz Busch was general music director. In 1934 the local Nazi cell leader collected signatures from the Dresden Opera's personnel to force Busch's resignation. He was completely untainted by the severest criteria of Nazi racism, yet he and his family had been known Social Democrats and fine citizens of the Weimar Republic, representing the very best German liberal tradition. My friend and others with similar fears for their jobs signed the petition but, to keep a good seat on the fence, sent flowers with affectionate reassurances to Mrs. Busch. The flowers were returned, Busch later was ousted, and so were all the petition signers whose pedigrees were found wanting.

Patriotism of this kind is not limited to Europe or to the Nazi era. In 1942, after the United States had entered the war, the patriotic fervor of a North Carolina basso landed Ezio Pinza temporarily at the detention camp for enemy aliens on Ellis Island. The pretext had been a Pinza comment admiring some action of Mussolini's that was overheard and passed on. The southern patriot had his day in the sun, singing Mephisto on the Met's spring tour, which led the Cleveland *Plain Dealer* to tag him "the poor man's Pinza."

Back to 1933. The years between my "debut" and my departure from Vienna were personally most rewarding and professionally haphazard and yet singularly successful, not only for the moment but as a sendoff for my subsequent American career. Eight months after my graduation Austria was the scene of a bloody civil war, the end of parliament, the establishment of a Fascist one-party system, and the elimination of the Arts Council that had provided me with every bit of earned income for seven years. Fortunately I had by then other sources of employment, albeit very temporary. Since my summer in Salzburg I had learned Italian, and as a result I was asked from time to time by members of the Vienna Staatsoper to help them in their preparation for roles in Italian.

Coaching singers can be delightful and it can be hell. It depends on the patience and personality of both participants, singer and coach. Never having been endowed with the character of Job I could not bear singers who needed all the time simply to learn notes.

A singer at best is half artist and half athlete. For most vocalists the placement of the singing voice, its "production," is like ballet, a matter of daily classes. I never mixed into that most delicate and difficult part of the training and kept to musical and interpretive questions.

While always alert to poor pitch or other vocal abuses, my real work consisted in getting the singer to the meaning of words and music.

Coaching singers for their performances in opera or concert, often with renowned conductors, I had to allow for other musical ideas to prevail. In such instances I noticed that I had already formed strong convictions that made this kind of preparation for others tedious. It clearly spelled that I would be happier if my concept of a work could be fully realized, and that meant simply my own responsibility and my own conducting instead of being handmaiden to others.

In my general progress I was helped most by my orchestral piano playing, by my uninhibited way of singing cues in a raucous voice, and by my ability to be of considerable assistance in three languages. Many of Vienna's singers, whether students or members of the opera, came originally from the depths of the Balkans, where international languages did not form part of the school curricula.

Every story has one pivotal character, and in my own fortunes it was Luise Helletsgruber, a pretty, second-line soprano of the Vienna Staatsoper, who had been my very first "major league" coaching client. In 1934 she led me, unaware she was a dea ex machina, to several of my greatest opportunities.

She was a member of the first Glyndebourne Festival Company, where she sang Donna Elvira in *Don Giovanni* and Dorabella in *Così Fan Tutte* in Italian. She was so well prepared that she recommended me to her colleagues when they needed a coach for an Italian role.

One day she greeted me with the exciting news that the opera management had cast her as Nedda in *Pagliacci,* a great event for her, marred by the lack of adequate rehearsal possibilities. She would take some dramatic histrionic instruction from a great stage director, Wilhelm von Wymetal, who between travels to New York's Metropolitan Opera seasons was in Vienna then and had agreed to spend some time with her on Nedda with me accompanying on the piano. Witnessing and learning how Wymetal went about teaching a role to a singer was a great experience for me, so much so, that I feel more than forty years later the benefits of having been exposed at the outset to such a man of stature instead of making do for years with the minor talents in provincial theaters.

He insisted that a singer must never rely on the prop department, especially where personal objects, like combs, fans, daggers and pins were involved. His small apartment seemed tiny compared with a large stage, yet he could show in a limited space many things no singer would ever forget: how to stand when ostensibly singing to a partner without directing the voice toward the wings, where the sound got lost; how to move the body both effectively and gracefully; how to pose to show joy or force or suffering or vengeance — all this was the essence of his own past as actor and director. There were many patterns in technique, comparable to the standard steps of ballet yet fairly unknown to most of Wymetal's colleagues whom I have watched since.

After he had finished with Nedda-Helletsgruber he kept calling me directly whenever he coached other singers. Most memorable to me were the sessions with Maria Müller, who journeyed to Vienna solely for lessons to act Tosca. She had been one of my favorite singers since I heard her first in 1931 under Toscanini in Bayreuth, and it was very exciting for me to play for her coaching sessions.

Wymetal also asked me to play for his own preparation, and that was the best of all my assignments. At that time he was studying Verdi's *Don Carlo* for a new production in Rome and wanted me for long afternoons when he planned the timing of the big chorus scenes and I had to go, in stages, over the entire score again and again. He would ask me to point out the more difficult vocal portions in order not to make singers run about when they needed their breath for other purposes.

Simply stated I learned in those afternoons what staging an opera meant. Wymetal, who was also a great gentleman, treated me as a friend and asked me each time after our working hours to stay for dinner. When I left his apartment I always found an envelope with a most generous fee in the pocket of my overcoat. We had never spoken about a price, but he was, after all, an artist and not a businessman, so my trust was well rewarded. The dinner was served by his housekeeper, who, obviously more than an employee, sat and ate with us after seeing to our needs. One evening, while she removed the dishes, Wymetal announced in his most formal stage manner that he had seen fit to legalize his relations with the lady, principally to get the better of his landlord, who had refused to guarantee to the housekeeper the continued lease after Wymetal's passing. As Widow Wymetal, she could never be thrown out of the apartment.

Also around this time Helletsgruber informed me that the forthcoming Salzburg Festival would feature a new production of *Don Giovanni* — no longer *Don Juan,* as it was called in Vienna — in the original Italian, with herself as Donna Elvira, Bruno Walter conducting, and Herbert Graf as stage director. Another Viennese, the basso Karl Ettl, was cast as Masetto, and he came to me for coaching. From him I learned that the staff of the Vienna Opera — which went *in corpore* to Salzburg each summer — contained no one who knew Italian. That gave me the cue I needed and I wrote to the general administrator of the festival, Dr. Erwin Kerber, offering my services as a bilingual musical assistant. I had ascertained that the cast would be a mixed one, with Helletsgruber, Ettl, Emanuel List as the Commendatore, and Lotte Schöne as Zerlina representing German-trained artists, while the genuine Italian element would be impersonated by Dusolina Giannini as Donna Anna, Ezio Pinza as Don, Virgilio Lazzari as Leporello, and Dino Borgioli as Ottavio.

To my surprise I received by return mail a letter-contract for a two-week engagement as unspecified assistant. The two weeks were the period of rehearsals for the opera. My agreement ended on the day after the dress rehearsal and before the première. From that moment on, with my Italian tutor I fervidly studied da Ponte's libretto as if Dante had been its author. When I landed in Salzburg a few days before the appointed time I knew the text and the music as well as anyone could ever know them.

I was fully aware that this was a giant step directly from obscurity into the arena of international music. My first day was a big letdown. Walter, holding piano rehearsals with the cast, showed me in no uncertain way that he needed my assistance like the proverbial hole in the head. I turned pages while he himself played the piano and gave his ideas to the singers. Later on I realized that Walter's way of preparing an opera made anybody else's assistance not only unnecessary but even unwelcome such was his very personal manner with his singers.

A couple of days later staging sessions began, with Graf and Walter always present, but I was still a fifth wheel because the regular musical staff from Vienna did everything. My turn came for the first time when the rehearsal pianist had to go to the men's room and I accompanied for ten minutes. I also had to translate one or two messages from the Italian singers to the Viennese singers.

Dusolina Giannini, an Italian American from Philadelphia, was the only cast member fluent in both languages. The three men from Milan spoke not a word of German, while the other four knew no Italian whatever. Graf and Walter could make themselves understood, but real trouble started only in relation to the prompting. (For all staging rehearsals the presence of a prompter is essential. This is equally true for plays as it is for opera.)

For *Don Giovanni* the first prompter of the Vienna Opera had been assigned, on the criterion that he was the only one who could pronounce the Italian text. Yet as soon as he opened his mouth to help the singers, the Italians got confused and continually made mistakes. Earlier, around the piano with Walter, they had seemed dead sure of their roles. Pinza especially lost his temper each time he made an error. After several miscues resulting in unpleasantness he stopped and came over to me, asking me to tell the prompter that he invariably brought the words too early. I tried to pass on the complaint, but no improvement was noticed. At lunch break, Borgioli, the calmest and in many ways the most educated of the singers, kept me with him for a full briefing of the problem. Italian opera functioned in fact with two conductors, one in the pit and a subaltern one in the prompter's box, whose responsibility included all musical cues for the voices on stage. In the non-Italian opera houses the chief conductor cues stage and orchestra, while the prompter merely whispers the text in advance of actual lines.

After we returned for the continuation of rehearsals I recounted the whole explanation to the Viennese, who promised to try, but doubted his own ability, not being a trained musician and never having given musical cues. He tried but was singularly unsuccessful and irration was, if anything, more pronounced than in the morning. Later I proposed to relieve the poor prompter, who was losing his nerves, and when I simply spoke the first syllable of a new phrase in exact tempo and rhythm, as if it were a preparatory beat ahead of the actual cue, the whole machinery suddenly ran as if it had been lubricated, without kinks or further stoppages. While Pinza and his confreres encouraged me with bravos, the German-speaking contingent began to flounder, having learned the text mainly by rote and therefore needing much more help with sentences than the Italians, to whom it was their own language. I juggled both systems for a while, treating the Germans and Italians as each of them was used to being prompted, but when I wanted to yield my place to the regular prompter he was firm in his refusal to continue, having understood that this type of bilingual tightrope was not his long suit. He was most polite but intransigent in his stance.

Then Pinza asked me pointblank if I would take this task, though in our latitudes no maestro ever descended to the lower depths of the prompter's box. I assured him that I should be happy to do any kind of job that was needed and that I could perform, except that my contract ended with the dress rehearsal. That, Pinza assured me, he would fix with "il dottore Kerber," as long as I was game — and was I game! It meant that I could stay on for the entire duration of the festival, what with the repeat performances spread over several weeks.

Neither Pinza nor anybody else could have known how much this meant to me, a windfall and a confirmation that I was getting on, after a discouraging start, when I had felt absolutely superfluous. It was a fine feeling to be needed, and to make things complete Kerber called me, full of compliments for my attitude toward performing a task that should have been, by the stuffy standards of professional pride, "beneath my dignity."

I never deceived myself that it was musical talent but realized it was my Italian and my willingness to try something new that made this grand chance possible.

Walter wrote a charming dedication in my own score of *Don Giovanni* and further proved his appreciation by engaging me as his assistant for the 1935 Maggio Musicale Fiorentino, a great and important festival in those years. Mozart's *Die Entführung aus dem Serail* was the work, but no amount of study could have kept me busy for eight months of unemployment in Vienna. It is not easy to go back to a mixed bag of singers for private coaching after having tasted the blood of the real thing.

It was curious that in 1934, a year of civil war in February and the murder of Chancellor Dollfuss in July, my own professional fortunes prospered so spectacularly. I was on the road to the kind of career of which I dreamed, unaffected, even aided by, the sad political events in my own country.

Luck is, in my own private philosophy, not the goddess Fortuna swooping down in a cloud, the horn of plenty in her arm, the ropes of the cloud being held by a couple of stagehands on the light bridge above. It is rather constant alertness to both pitfalls and opportunities. I have always gladly admitted that I had plenty of good fortune, but thought of it in terms of having recognized a moment of promise and a threat of danger. Looking back, as if from the hilltop outside the town I left behind, I see quite clearly that in 1934 I literally grabbed several chances and two years later had the sense to leave my hometown for good, though actual political disaster was still eighteen months away.

In November 1934 I met Toscanini, who had begun to guest-conduct the Vienna Philharmonic Orchestra after bursting onto the musical scene of Austria a few years earlier, first when La Scala visited and later when he led a tour of the New York Philharmonic Orchestra. Since 1933 he had appeared with our own orchestra, and from the first meeting with him I knew that he would influence me more profoundly than any of the other great musicians whom I had met and worked with. My connection with him spanned two decades, and I am sure we shall not see his likes soon again.

## Toscanini

As I had much free time I often sat in rehearsals of orchestras, particularly when important conductors directed. Since the summer in Salzburg I was known to the officials of the Vienna Philharmonic, a difficult lot in general, but somehow agreeable to my requests for permission to be present at their rehearsals. One of the programs for Toscanini's guest stint during that fall consisted of Beethoven's Ninth Symphony, to be preceded by Zoltan Kodály's *Psalmus Hungaricus*. The concert was to be repeated a few days after Vienna in Budapest, from where a chorus came to sing the two works. The soloists also were Hungarian, except the basso Richard Mayr, without whom no Ninth would have been complete. I watched with great interest a purely instrumental rehearsal on a Wednesday, which was to be followed by complete ensemble sessions Thursday and Friday.

During intermission I saw the president of the Philharmonic, the bassoonist Hugo Burghauser, frantically telephoning and betraying great distress. When I spoke to him, mainly to say "thank you" for the privilege of being allowed in rehearsal, I asked why he was so upset. "Find me a pianist who will play tomorrow at ten the *Psalmus* by Kodály for the piano rehearsal which Maestro wants with Rösler [the tenor soloist]. Nobody knows the piece and if they knew it they are all petrified of Toscanini." "Herr Professor," I said (always use titles in Vienna), "I know the piece and will be glad to help out." "How can you know this piece?" He did not believe a word I said. "Nobody at the opera knows the piece, it is dreadfully difficult to play on the piano, and Maestro is not known for his patience, and I don't want any upset." Words to that effect. I then detailed to the understandably skeptical man that in 1932 I had, for three months, played it every Tuesday evening as rehearsal pianist for the choral society of the Social Democratic Arts Council and since Anton Webern had been our chorus director he could be pretty sure that it had been thoroughly studied, hence my acquaintance with the work. Burghauser glared at me incredulously but, needing somebody badly and wanting to have a solution to his problem, he agreed that I should report next morning at ten to the green room of the Musikverein. After the end of the morning's rehearsal I went home and practiced all afternoon to restore the tricky chords of the *Psalmus* score to my fingers.

When I arrived next morning, a bit early as is my wont, I was by no means first on the scene. Richard Mayr was already present, obviously tense and nervous. He was one of Vienna's all-time favorites, which in that enthusiastic city meant that he could do no wrong. He was, by any yardstick, a superlative singer and actor, whose Ochs, Pogner, Gurnemanz, and a host of other roles were memorable experiences to behold. In concert too he belonged to the special category of artists who are equally at home in oratorio and lied. It was natural for him to feel apprehension, as the legendary ruthlessness of Toscanini even with accomplished celebrities was well known. No one in Mayr's class cares to be chided and made to feel like a student.

We had never met, and as I introduced myself he took me for Toscanini's regular assistant and began at once to protest that after thirty years of singing the Ninth in *his* way he could not change and if Maestro wanted it another way he would have to get another basso. I assured him that I, too, was new to working with Toscanini, but that I, resident of Vienna and regular opera fan, was his, Mayr's, most ardent admirer. Whether that was any help or not I don't know, but a few moments later Maestro and the three other soloists arrived, the short introduction to the recitative of the solo was played, and Mayr sang. Toscanini sat on my left, looking up through his thick lenses at the beautiful countenance of the singer, and as soon as Mayr had finished the main part, Toscanini tapped him gently on his arm and said very simply but with much conviction, "Bene, Bravo."

And that was it for Mayr's solo, the passage was never again repeated that morning, nor was it different in the orchestra rehearsals. Toscanini had understood what caliber artist Mayr was. I had this same experience time and time again: Maestro left well enough alone, never fussing over minutiae when the overall concept was there. Used as I was to the tempi of German conductors, it was also most astounding to me how fluently he took the tempo of the fearsomely difficult final quartet portion. Toscanini, perhaps because of his Italian background, was most keenly aware of vocal problems, and his way with that passage eliminated all terror for the singers. Nobody ran out of breath.

The Ninth was over fairly soon, three singers left, and only Rösler, Maestro, and I remained for the raison d'être of my presence, Kodály's *Psalmus*. Toscanini once again simply sat and listened, at times making an ever so slight gesture to correct a tempo, but not stopping us at all. After we finished, he complimented the tenor and I got "bene" several times for the rendition of the difficult accompaniment. A few phrases were discussed and repeated and by eleven o'clock the rehearsal was over. Rösler left but I stayed and decided then and there to tackle a major subject that was on my mind:

"Maestro, I read in the papers that you have agreed to conduct two operas next summer in Salzburg and if you do not bring with you any of your permanent assistants, I am happy to offer myself for any kind of work you will need done." To my infinite surprise Toscanini said that he had no assistant, it was years since he had been at La Scala, and his only operatic activity since had been Bayreuth in 1931. He would welcome my helping him.

After he left, Burghauser expressed his satisfaction that all had gone so well, and from that moment on I did not have to do much, because the gossip took care of elevating my short hour of piano accompaniment to a far more imposing status. When the Hungarian chorus arrived, it was immediately arranged that I must play the piano for the chorus rehearsal. Burghauser had one single idea: to keep any upset away from Toscanini. Having seen that I did nothing to upset him, he pushed me into every conceivable spot where trouble might develop.

A few days later I went to see Kerber. He was fully briefed on the entire venture with *Psalmus Hungaricus*, and I had no difficulty getting a verbal commitment for the entire 1935 festival as assistant to both Toscanini and Walter. This verbal understanding between Kerber and myself was never followed up

by written contracts, either for that year or the next two summers. No fixed sum was established, and whenever I asked for
an advance Kerber wrote a few words on a piece of paper and
I took from the cashier what I needed. On those occasions he
always said that he was proud of my confidence, but at the same
time apprehensive that this blind trust put him under an obligation to be far more generous than he wanted to be. And he
was. As with Wymetal, I was dealing with a great gentleman.

The speed with which I advanced from a one-hour rehearsal
accompanist to Toscanini's sole assistant was one of the typical
happenings that gave Vienna its reputation. Intensive interest
and wide participation can parlay a fortuitous incident into a
grand discovery. This happened many times, but woe to those
who do not justify their rocket treatment. Their downfall and
undoing will proceed as speedily and with as little justification
as their dizzy promotion; worse, it will be accompanied by
sadistic expressions by word of mouth and in print, as if to
take revenge on the poor victim for his failure to respond. This
was Vienna and it has not changed. A beautiful place to visit —
as tourist or as professional guest — not a place to remain in.

The two operas that I now had to prepare were *Fidelio* and
*Falstaff*. To make my own work both more interesting and
more taxing I decided to play all rehearsals from the orchestral
scores, using my own piano arrangements as we went along.
*Falstaff* was surely Toscanini's single greatest favorite. It also
brought to the fore his worst behavior. The famous temper
tantrums were in ample evidence during *Falstaff* rehearsals.
There was no comparison between his ways at the *Fidelio* sessions, where he acted like a mellow father, and his manner at
the *Falstaff* rehearsals. In the Italian work he felt as if he had
an authentic mandate, as if the great composer had charged
him with supervising his most minute nuances and all his intentions. Toscanini had known Verdi, and there was an extra
dimension of personal involvement that was not as obvious in
his labors for other composers.

He knew *Fidelio* as intimately as *Falstaff*, he stood in all the staging rehearsals with the libretto, he knew every line of the prose dialogue in German, but his manner of making observations and corrections was totally different. It was more conciliatory, almost as if he had always some question as to the ultimate validity of his comments. He was also slightly uneasy with the production and its director, Lothar Wallerstein, who himself had left his more authoritarian manner behind and tried very hard to get along.

For five years Wallerstein had been the real artistic head of the Vienna Opera, not in title but in every other way. Clemens Krauss, who had brought him from Frankfurt, abandoned Vienna in 1934 for the greener pastures of Hitler's Germany, and Wallerstein's position was weakened by the uncertainty of who would fill the chair of the Viennese opera director. He also was an artist and wanted to work well with Toscanini. Yet no love was lost between the two, and it was for Toscanini one thing to conduct a brand-new *Falstaff* production and another to lead an already much-performed *Fidelio*. If all went well, Lotte Lehmann had to be thanked. She, like Mayr, a favorite in Vienna, had been a memorable Leonore since the Beethoven centenary in 1927. By 1935 her latent vocal problems with the top had become noticeable, particularly in the aria *"Abscheulicher! wo eilst du hin!"* and Toscanini, also an admirer and friend, wanted to spare her anxiety and attempted to provide relief. First he proposed to transpose the entire piece, and I was assigned to read through it with the orchestra in a special rehearsal on the day of the second repeat performance. Transposing Beethoven was one of "those things" no German conductor would ever dare do, hence no printed material existed such as is available for other, more traditional key changes in *Faust, Il Trovatore,* or *La Bohème,* where the alternative versions come together with the original from the publisher.

After performing the aria transposed, Maestro felt, as we all did, that the recitative had suffered in the lower key, particularly Leonore's phrase *"Da leuchtet mir ein Farbenbogen,"* which came off poorly in B major. There are for musicians mental associations connected with key signatures, and what the "Farbenbogen" (rainbow) expressed was so much C major that in the half-tone lowering of the piece a wondrous moment seemed to fade into insignificance. To remedy this and still help Lotte, Toscanini then devised a clever transitory harmony that left the entire recitative in the original key and yet transposed the aria into E flat. There were plenty of raised eyebrows over such interference with Beethoven. Beyond the purists' concern, it was a radical change of something very fundamental. In classical works, opera as well as symphony, there is a big arc connecting the entire score, and in the case of *Fidelio* the key of E is represented by the opening overture and Leonore's aria, the central emotional moment of the long first act.

While the whole enterprise was open to legitimate criticism, I found it a document for Toscanini's approach to a complex masterwork. It disproved several legends. He was a pragmatist and not a stickler for the printed dot on the i. And it showed that he went to great length to accommodate an artist whom he admired and appreciated. It was a much more pointed proof of my first impression about his tempo for the quartet in the Ninth. I have tried, especially when the frailty of the human voice was involved, to follow Toscanini's example rather than the German idea of theory first and let the human being adjust to it.

Maestro also could be a superlative psychologist, though I am sure he never read Freud. The première of *Falstaff* was a performance of unmatchable perfection. Yet, for the eve of the first repeat, some five or six days later, I was asked to call the cast of ten together for a brush-up rehearsal with piano. I looked forward to another chance to play from this wondrous score, and we all assembled, ready to go, in the charming old University classroom that served as our practice hall. For a full hour Maestro and the ten singers just sat around while old stories

were swapped. "Do you recall Reggio Emilia when we did . . ."
and "Wasn't it strange when the impresario at . . ." So it went
until Toscanini with the kindest greetings all around dismissed
the *Falstaff* cast. I remained to find out what kind of a rehearsal this was supposed to be and asked him, knowing by then
full well that he loved to be asked questions and was always
ready to explain and elucidate. "It is important," he said, "to
remind the cast of tomorrow's show that each of them can set
a schedule of rest and of refreshing the memory for the 24 hours
preceding the performance according to their needs. Since all
went well at the première there was nothing for us to rehearse
or correct."

His rehearsal technique was a great surprise to me. The legend that he rehearsed more than anybody else was contradicted
by facts and data. Since it was in circulation, other conductors,
Walter not excepted, asked for far more time than they had
been allotted in previous years when Toscanini was not around.
Kerber, with the task of organizing the whole big schedule, and
I were perhaps the only two people who knew that Maestro's
demands of rehearsal time were most reasonable and often more
modest than those of his colleagues. What evidently nobody
noticed was the incredible efficiency of his preparatory work,
a result of his lucid overall concept and his unwavering tempi.
My greatest surprises came in the following summers when he
revived operas with a most amazing minimal time for orchestra-
stage rehearsals.

His mental image of the complete work was so clear that he
could prepare each part of an opera separately in such a way
that at the first general rehearsal there was little need to stop
for major corrections. This is by no means a virtue common to
conductors, who frequently get so carried away by the sound of
the orchestra that they forget the tempi that were taken in
piano rehearsals. It is quite usual to be faster at the piano and
slower when the orchestra plays. Toscanini had neither of these
vagaries.

I still profited from such unique experiences thirty-nine years later, when I went through a general stage rehearsal of a revival after a lapse of more than two years, albeit with the same musicians, without prior orchestral reading sessions, stopping only once for a correction to the chorus. To the happy and astonished members I recounted later when and where I had first seen such a demonstration.

During that memorable 1935 summer I made a foolish mistake that hurt me for many years. I was so obviously taken up with the preparation for Toscanini's operas that my time with Walter shrank to the irreducible minimum. This was selfish on my part, but I felt that I learned more from Toscanini and that I was actually more needed. It was most unwise of me to demonstrate such partiality, for whatever reason. Walter, who had been kingpin in Salzburg prior to Maestro's joining the roster, felt upstaged, and there was no good interest of mine served by underlining this.

While the two men were on excellent speaking terms, embracing one another with great outbursts of "*Caro Amico*" and such, they disapproved of each other's interpretations most eloquently when they were with their own group of intimates. Using the tags and slogans of literature, the one was a classicist while the other approached music as a full romantic. Like all generalities this is only superficially correct; it gives, however, a picture of a hotly debated musical issue.

Later, much later, I noticed that there was also the usual party line of cliques, political and artistic. In 1974 Oskar Kokoschka said in an interview that he would not and could not "do" Toscanini, who had "a metronome in place of a heart." This is to me purely an expression of musical partisanship without meaning, a throwback to the unnecessary divisions that identified people one hundred years ago as either Wagnerian or Brahmsian. As it appeared to me, in the terminology of the "clique," Walter was one of the apostles of Bruckner and Mahler, while Toscanini was relegated to the opposition camp.

The inclusion of *Die Meistersinger* in the program for 1936 was another first for Salzburg and for me the high point of my involvement. The international significance was Toscanini's conducting Wagner outside Bayreuth, which he shunned since Hitler was in power. Several weeks before the festival I selected singers for the small roles, including an experimental David, whom I found in an operetta theater and who then studied his role with me. I also went through tense days with Charles Kullmann, the tenor singing Stolzing, who, with incredible stoicism, did not begin to study his long and difficult part until the end of June. When he arrived in Salzburg and sang for Toscanini, after only seventeen days of study, I was more nervous than he, but I also noted then the superiority of American musical talent.

The major crisis that summer developed around the role of Hans Sachs, for which the bass-baritone Friedrich Schorr had been engaged. It was not clear to me how Schorr was originally selected. I assumed that Maestro knew him well from New York, where the singer had been for many years the top interpreter of Wotan and Sachs. The casting must have been approved on the advice of friends because as soon as we began to rehearse with Schorr it became obvious that Toscanini disliked everything the singer did. Schorr, set in his ways, did not give an inch, or could not fall in with the conductor's suggestions, and the atmosphere became heavy with tension.

After each rehearsal, when we were alone, Toscanini gave vent to his concern and kept explaining to me Schorr's total unsuitablity for Sachs. After this had gone on for too many days, considering that a festival's schedule cannot be postponed, Toscanini told me that he would write a letter to Schorr, asking him to withdraw. This he did, and it became a disagreeable cause célèbre, since a world-famous artist cannot be simply dismissed, no matter what euphemism of "withdrawing" or "indisposition" is used for public explanation. As I was the only other person who witnessed the crisis between the two men, my own relations with Schorr later in New York were marked by lack of ease, though I never spoke of the rehearsals I had attended before the crisis.

Schorr's replacement was a lesser-known German, Hans Herman Nissen, whom Toscanini liked. He spoke to me appreciatively of the man's beautiful smile. A smile was of the highest value on Toscanini's list of a singer's qualities and abilities. At the time I found this stress puzzling until years later I discovered that a face that lacks a natural smile has few other expressions either.

To work on three operas, such as *Fidelio, Falstaff,* and *Meistersinger,* prompt *Don Giovanni,* and be present at all Toscanini's rehearsals and performances gave me a very taxing workload, one that cemented a close and cordial relation with Maestro. That I had alienated Walter never dawned on me until many years later I found out that he had objected to my being engaged as guest conductor for the New York Philharmonic, where his influence was decisive at a time when it hurt me.

In 1936, however, Toscanini translated his own feelings for me into deeds that gave me the start and sendoff toward my whole American life and career.

Toscanini could not, or pretended not to, understand why I was not a member of the musical staff at Vienna's opera house, and he interceded with the cabinet minister in charge of the state theaters. We all met in September in Vienna, where the Salzburg production of *Fidelio* was given with the identical cast. I was invited to lunch with Toscanini, who had learned that his recommendation was not strong enough to win the political game the Austrian government was playing at that time between Mussolini and Hitler.

More important was my discovery that hall acoustics influence tempi. I noticed that the two *Fidelio* performances in Vienna were from start to finish a tiny bit broader than the eight I had heard from the same performers in Salzburg. At our luncheon with my heart in my mouth I asked Maestro if he was aware of that acoustical influence on tempi. He thought for some time until he allowed that this was not only possible but probable and that he was not conscious of any voluntary slowing down. This erased the legend that he never varied his tempi.

Shortly after Toscanini's Viennese visit ended, I made my way to Kerber, who had become the administrator of Vienna's opera house, and heard from him in no uncertain terms that I could not expect to be hired. He put it in his own inimitable language: "Leinsdorf, if the rosary hung down from your fly I could engage you." I thanked him and told him with my regrets that the price seemed too high for my taste and left. I wrote to Toscanini that within a few days I would get a lift from friends who were driving to Milan and that I would be in touch, hoping for a winter of work in Italy, where his influence was enormous.

The *galleria* in Milan, a set of high-ceilinged arcades between the Cathedral and La Scala, with coffee bars, restaurants, and shops of all kinds, was then also the absolute center of Italian opera. If an impresario planned to take a troupe to Japan or to organize a six-week *stagione* in Bologna, all transactions, casting, engaging, promising, and breaking promises took place right there around the small coffee tables.

Opera in Italy was so centralized that not only the live talent came from Milan but all accessories as well. The publishing houses were in Milan, and here orchestrations and rare instruments, such as tuben and bells, were rented; the shops who owned costumes and sets would furnish everything to the many theaters, which could not dream of having their productions specially designed and executed, and in the *galleria* I, too, landed within a week several engagements that spelled for me a busy and productive winter. I departed from Milan for Bologna soon after these successful transactions had been made; I spent several weeks in that most attractive city, ate incomparably well, conducted, prepared, did all sorts of things, and yet felt that the volcano was about to erupt. Some musicians, with whom I spent a good deal of time, listened very privately to the Spanish Republican radio; they discussed the threatening situation interminably, and these ominous sounds of the world of affairs made a troubling contrast to my otherwise carefree days.

After Bologna I was engaged for another *stagione* by the Teatro Verdi in Trieste, where I asked my mother to join me for the Christmas holidays. She had been most unhappy with my decision to leave Vienna, a departure which I considered a permanent adieu to my native city, while she felt that my progress in the glamorous international set of music was spectacular and quite sufficient. While we were together in Trieste the dilemma of what to do next year was solved by a cable from New York; it was signed by Miss Constance Hope, whom I had met in 1935 at the Salzburg home of Lotte Lehmann, for whom she was doing publicity. Miss Hope was offering me a contract as assistant conductor with the Metropolitan Opera Company, commencing in November 1937. Without any hesitation I cabled my acceptance. It looked to me like manna must have appeared to the hungry in the desert.

In February 1937 I met Toscanini in Rome. Trieste was finished, I had a few weeks of free time before my next *stagione* in San Remo began, and there was the additional reason of a most attractive soprano from the roster of the Trieste Opera whom I followed to her hometown, Rome. Toscanini stopped en route from Tel Aviv, where he had conducted the Palestine Orchestra, then in its first stages as a cultural assembly of the finest instrumentalists ousted by Nazi Germany. Maestro, ever since 1933 in a position of public protest against the German dictatorship, had, with this visit, expressed once more his political convictions. Now he was in a hurry to reach Milan, where an emissary from David Sarnoff and the National Broadcasting Company had arrived to submit plans for a new symphony orchestra, formed especially for him. He was as pleased and excited by this prospect as anyone could be. It was obvious that he wanted to return to New York, less than a year after having given up his post with the Philharmonic there.

Later, when I met in New York the complete cast of characters around Toscanini, I noted that Samuel Chotzinoff, music critic of the *Post*, brother-in-law of Jascha Heifetz, and fervent admirer of Maestro, took full credit for bringing the prodigal conductor back to the States. I had been present in Rome when Maestro spoke of the plan and at that time the doorman of the Astor Hotel could have collected his signature of agreement.

Toscanini's return to New York yielded for Chotzinoff a life-long post as a major executive with NBC, and his fierce loyalty lasted until Maestro and the broadcasting company came to the parting of ways. Then, as Irving Kolodin of the *Saturday Review* put it, "the corporate star outshone the individual star." Chotzinoff, like several of the coterie I had met in Salzburg, made my own relations with Toscanini more distant within three years of my arrival in New York. The atmosphere of a court has never been one in which I breathed easily. As long as I had a firm working schedule with Maestro I was not part of his social life and did not come, but for fleeting instances backstage, face to face with the assortment of jesters, bodyguards, intellectual jugglers, and simple thurifers.

Many years later when I again visited him from time to time at his home in Riverdale, I understood that he too had been saddened by the diminishing closeness of our relationship. His favorite topic was music, and he relied upon the few truly musical friends and companions who were capable of understanding what subtle problems of music gave him pause.

I am getting ahead of my chronology. There was still the important "last" summer of Salzburg before history made return and continuation impossible. For the 1937 festival Toscanini had taken on a fourth opera, *Die Zauberflöte*, while the other three would still be repeated on and on.

Even with all his great efficiency of re-rehearsing the works of previous summers, he was then seventy, and the sheer quantity of four operas, with perhaps a total of sixteen performances within a five-week festival, loomed large.

*Die Zauberflöte*, for other reasons, showed for the first time, even to the most devoted admirers, that there were limitations to Toscanini's interpretive insight. The work has become part of Austrian folklore and, like any music and play that has entered the category of popularity in its deepest meaning, Mozart's opera is loaded with traditional ways and nuances that the dramatic urge and personal dynamism of Maestro swept away with a blast. Some cast choices proved disappointing, particularly a young Hungarian soprano, whom Toscanini chose for the Queen of the Night, rightly saying that the terrific utterances of the offended mother demanded a strong voice instead of the customary piping high coloratura. Alas, our troubles with this soprano never ended, even after her second aria was lowered by a whole tone, which disturbed Mozart's balanced sequence of key relationships without providing any other improvement.

Beyond that, the overall approach to the work was totally alien to us. It is idle to speculate if Toscanini perhaps knew better what the composer had wanted in 1791. Time has a way with great works, and they are often changed beyond recognition.

Toscanini, being revered beyond words, was treated with full honors, and whatever disappointment was felt remained muted and polite. It is quite possible that he himself had sensed the gap between his ideas and their fulfillment on that occasion. Years later he said to me quite bluntly that he did not have a very comfortable feeling with Mozart and that Haydn was closer to him, because he could spot here and there the human hand of imperfection, while the infallibility of Mozart seemed awesome and superhuman. And yet, he criticized the Dies irae of Mozart's Requiem as lacking the frightening terror of the Day of Judgment; he felt that this was more suitably composed by Verdi.

I did not have much time to contemplate these problems just then. I had, in addition to playing all of Toscanini's piano rehearsals, which I reserved jealously for myself, to do the chores of the chorus master, who had been upset by some run-in with Maestro the year before and therefore refused to appear in Salzburg in 1937. That meant I also had to prepare the chorus for the Ninth, which Furtwängler conducted. The great man embarrassed me quite a bit, when after one of our rehearsals he asked pointblank what Toscanini had against him. I was twenty-five, loyal to Maestro, and not endowed with a ready standup diplomatic dictionary. I could merely mumble something neutral and meaningless.

Thirty years later I would have said, without taking anything away from my admiration, that Toscanini was not happy with other stars on the same firmament, but then the same applied to Furtwängler himself, who had a very hard time in the 1940s and 1950s digesting the rising Karajan's position. If I had understood these human foibles in 1937 there would have been no good purpose in getting older. But then some residue of these encounters, a horse sense that recognized early how shallow the reserves of great artists could be in the human equation, made me per chance mold my own life to be less one-sided and to have more to fall back on after the applause has died away.

While I had made preparations since October 1936 to leave Austria, it was a moment of heartache when I bade adieu to Kerber at the close of the 1937 festival. He spoke cheerfully of the 1938 season and my return, but I could not suppress the ever-present "if." Everybody in my acquaintance knew of the Met contract in my pocket, and I felt that in my own homeland I had gone actually much further than I had considered possible four years earlier. There were ahead of me eight weeks of free time, which I spent at home in Vienna, studying the Met repertoire and detaching myself gradually from my native city and a few personal affiliations that could not survive a prolonged absence.

The seventeen years between Toscanini's first night at NBC and the sad Sunday evening in April 1954 surely need special treatment in a separate book. There is a tremendous story still to be told, not only about musical events but also about the curious cross relations between radio, television, commercialism, recording, industrial prestige, and tax write-offs. For that a sociologist with much musical knowledge is needed.

When the entire Toscanini family arrived in December 1937 at their usual New York domicile in the Astor Hotel on Broadway between 44th and 45th streets, I could hardly wait to see Maestro, who was always available. He answered the phone himself when I called and asked me to come up as soon as I was free. The Met, my place of work, was only six blocks away, and five minutes after my final rehearsal I was at the Astor. That seemed splendid and augured well for the unbroken continuity of our close relationship. Yet soon after this first brief visit things became increasingly uncomfortable for me. Maestro was very outspoken and made no bones that the Met had to burn down if America was to have decent opera. As a brand new Met member I was embarrassed whenever these outbursts occurred, which was most of the time. There was no way to debate rationally a subject with a much older man of overwhelming authority who had every right to his strong views and who did not have the tact to avoid causing me obvious and acute discomfort. I could neither defend the artistic policies of the Met nor did I care to sit by and tacitly agree with summary death warrants for an institution that was at present my life line. Other Met members sat by obediently and then ran back to Met general manager Edward Johnson to mend their fences.

The feeling of closeness to Maestro was fading. I did not miss any opportunity to have musical contact: I played Brahms's *Liebeslieder-Walzer* with an NBC staff pianist at a time when I was full conductor at the Met just to manifest my constant admiration and desire to make music under Maestro's direction. Finally I had to conclude that one is either an adulating assistant or disciple and stays in this role forever, or one goes to a different platform, which spells the end of all pseudofilial relationships. Since I lost my father so early in life I could never be sure what a natural filial relationship was, and I am even less certain how in one individual the filial and paternal can be combined. I had to lead my own life, which meant my exit from Toscanini's inner circle.

He never hesitated for an instant to ask me to visit when I rang him up, and one of my fondest memories is of a New Year's Eve party at Riverdale, when there were skits and high jinks and later some old movies shown by his son, Walter, who gave a running commentary, identifying the personages in these films. While he explained Maestro often mumbled something to himself. I moved my chair closer to his and understood after a while that each time Walter commented that someone shown was now dead, Toscanini said, "*Stupido*" — obviously meaning that people who die have conclusively proved that they are stupid. Perhaps this is necessary if one is to live until nearly ninety.

It is very difficult to discuss the qualities of a gigantic musical performer. Posterity cannot take mere panegyric on trust, and I recognize that much of what I say must remain unsatisfactory, since the live presence of such a great personality is essential to any kind of a true portrait. The recorded output of performances will confuse more than enlighten, because style and manner of musical interpretation have changed, like everything else.

In March 1967, I was one of several conductors interviewed before a television camera for Toscanini's centenary. On the twenty-fifth, his birthday, I could watch the edited product. Eugene Ormandy and I spoke in the conventional terms of highest praise without saying much that would explain Maestro's art. George Szell gave, as a specific example, Toscanini's tempo for the second movement of the Seventh Symphony by Beethoven, which became seminal, influencing all but a handful of stubborn traditionalists to restudy and rethink the entire tempo question in Beethoven. What could a young person, especially a nonprofessional, get out of all this?

The unfathomable is, and will always be, personality. Toscanini was, to start with, a beautiful man on the podium. He was elegant even in rehearsal, attired in a specially made jacket like Chou En-lai's chemise. In concert he appeared rather old-fashioned and conducted with a simple clear orthodox beat. This extreme simplicity of the visible was a perfect mirror of what one heard. The great line of a work's form came first for him. Detail was subsidiary, which, paradoxically, means that it is most difficult to pinpoint memorable moments or unforgettable effects, of which the renditions of more romantic conductors, say Furtwängler, abounded. Toscanini's effects appeared greatest after their conclusion, when everything had fallen into its perfect place and proportions seemed ideal. In drama it would mean that secondary roles never stepped beyond their passing importance. To use another art for comparison, I would say that in his last twenty years Toscanini considered design more important than color. His way with L'Après-midi d'un faune was not memorable because here form can't make up for the lack of decadent indulgence. He was so healthy and robust that the twilight of romanticism, Bruckner or Mahler, had no appeal for him. After one single essay with Bruckner's Seventh in New York, he never touched the composer again, saying that his music showed that he had never had a woman.

My first encounter with Toscanini's music-making was over the radio, when he brought the New York Philharmonic to Vienna in 1929. The lucid, crystal-clear orchestral texture was new, not only to myself but to most Viennese, used as we were to a thicker and more cozy musical approach.

No conductor was more universally admired by musicians, critics, or the lay public. The only group immune to his radiance were the "moderns," composers and their champions alike; the lack of affection was cordially reciprocated, Toscanini having stopped going along "with it" around the end of World War I. Of living composers he performed only those whose style was a throwback to the nineteenth century, the Pizzettis, Respighis, and of course Richard Strauss. His startling discoveries included some Haydn symphonies, Rossini overtures, and odd pieces, such as Mendelssohn's Reformation Symphony, which have rarely again come to life as they did under his guidance.

His way with the giants, the Ninth, the *Missa Solemnis*, the Verdi Requiem, or any of the big classic symphonies, seemed to me more dignified and less given to overemphasized effects than performances of many another distinguished conductor.

I know that deep down he had more confidence in the genius of a great composer than many of his confreres, their pious assurances notwithstanding. He studied all the time and re-examined the scores, of which he knew every dot and dash. He added pencil marks to indicate to his librarian what needed more emphasis. Jimmy Dolan, who held that post at NBC, came on stage to add last-minute touches as late as a moment before Maestro entered from the wings. The bland assertion that he played only what was printed needs, like any generalization, much elaboration and explanation.

He was aware, as he often told me with considerable emphasis, that composers mark both what to do and what not to do. This is incomprehensible to all who are unaware of performance technique during a composer's life. Toscanini read scores with an imagination and knowledge that made things clear to him while the same text remained puzzling and problematic to others. Imagination is not contagious and can't be taught. Therefore, the greatest imitators of Maestro came to grief by misunderstanding his sources and his mental processes. His much-publicized precision was an accurate reflection of inner clarity.

Whether in symphonic or operatic music, he was always concerned first and foremost with the grand design. I never had the good fortune to hear "live" any of his performances with La Scala's ensemble. I am sure that those were the days when his famous tantrums took place. From his Salzburg days on, he chose casts of musicianly singers, even if their total equipment was less than first-rate. He wanted to perform Verdi unmarred by vocal vagaries and by the individual vanity that increases with a singer's vocal prowess. I have little doubt that *La Bohème, La Traviata,* and *Aïda* as he presented them during his NBC years were authentic interpretations. There was a classic balance of freedom and control, a lack of excess yet the most vigorous dramatic thrust, none of which is commonly associated with performances in opera houses. Perhaps even Toscanini could not have duplicated his NBC concerts of Italian opera in stage performances.

In my years at the Met I saw what devastating inroads Toscanini had made upon the egos of maestri who battled the inertia of established singers to get at a larger concept, who rode roughshod over vocal necessities, and who never achieved anything but a rocky improvisation in lieu of a Toscaninilike mastery.

Perhaps the fittest conclusion to this probably unsatisfactory assessment of the great man is an old platitude: "Quod licet Jovi non licet bovi." "What is allowed to Jupiter ain't permitted to the ox." In many respects the "Old Man" was Jupiter.

## 1937, First American Friends

During the prefestival period in 1937 Maria Reining, our Eva in *Meistersinger* — after Lotte Lehmann had resigned from

the role due to some nasty mail that considered her too matronly
— asked me to drive to St. Gilgen with her for a visit with
"important Americans." She, too, had plans to be in the States
later that year and wanted us both to meet these "immensely
rich" people whom she herself had not seen. An art dealer friend
of hers arranged for this get-together with the idea that it never
hurt to have acquaintances in a new environment. So I went
along, also for the purpose of playing for Reining, should the
occasion arise for her to sing a little.

In St. Gilgen we were greeted by an impressive man, about
fifty, with a beautiful child of two riding on his shoulders. This
was Charles Marsh. A moment later a young lady of perhaps
twenty-five appeared, she too quite tall and very handsome, obviously mother of the little girl and noticeably pregnant. We
became friends very fast. This was not an illusion. They remained my friends, Charles until he died and Alice, the handsome lady, still on close terms with me as I write this.

At the time of that "last" summer, when I felt that there
were great changes ahead, their appearance in my life was symbolic. They seemed to represent the best America had to offer.
That was not merely the exaggeration of an impressionable
twenty-five-year-old to whom the United States loomed large
and omnipotent. People like Charles and Alice are the best in
any country under any circumstances, and the only sad part is
that the terrible equalizing powers saw to it that neither of them
stayed happy for long.

I felt acutely uncomfortable because the false friendships and
open resentments of "great" men did not at all tally with my
own concept of wanting great artists to be equally great people.
If great artistry and talent plus continued success do not lead
to security, strength, and therefore honesty, what good is the
whole talent and the whole success? Rather than correct my
preconceived notions, I shelved my uncomfortable feelings of
misgiving and remained still tied to my illusions.

## New York

The *Normandy*, on which I had booked a berth in a second-class cabin, sailed November 3, allowing me a few days in Paris, where besides enjoying myself I wanted to have some words with the Met agent for European singers, Eric Semon. I wanted to know as much as possible about the constellation that I would find, and since I knew nothing whatsoever, some advice or at least description of the prevailing "winds" would be helpful.

I left Europe with much gratitude in my heart for this timely chance to escape from a future that appeared rather grim. Notwithstanding my political acumen, which proved to be quite correct, I was in every other respect an unspoiled young man. Looking back thirty-seven years later, it is hard to know whether my contemporaries in school, University, and Music Academy were more or less naive than I, but I am quite sure that my own sons were infinitely more aware of life when they turned twenty-five.

Perhaps too much of my total energy had been spent in pursuit of musical study and the opportunities to earn a little money and advance myself.

Personal alliances, friendships, and affairs of the heart were all results of professional contacts. There was an overlap between emotional attachment and musical collaboration that completely deceived me as to the true nature of a balanced life. I am quite certain that I am not the only person whose lopsided development led to ultimate vexation, but since I do not know anyone else's inner life as I know mine, it would not do to pontificate.

It did take me thirty years from that fall when I departed for America to muster my courage and admit that there is some-

thing oddly worrisome about success. I had seen and registered
the jealousies among several of the most successful men in my
chosen profession. I did not miss the cattiness and envy the
admired giants of my youth had shown on close inspection.

Though Semon had no stake in me and no percentages in my
contract he was happy to let me know how he viewed the 1937
situation. During the Depression years the opera season in New
York had been shortened to a mere fourteen weeks. In 1935,
early in February, the Met had a windfall when a Norwegian
soprano, then an understudy for the great Frida Leider, went on
as a last-hour replacement and became an instant sensation in
*Die Walküre.* That was Kirsten Flagstad, whose emergence
changed the Met's predominantly Italian repertoire to one with
a much greater Wagnerian emphasis. With other splendid
singers on the Met's roster, *Tristan und Isolde* and *Die Walküre,*
followed closely by *Lohengrin* and *Tannhäuser,* became as
popular as any hit show. Artur Bodanzky, a veteran conductor for the Met since 1915, had conducted all German
opera until the increase of these performances overtaxed his
uncertain health. In need of a younger man to shoulder part of
the burden, he had engaged in the summer of 1936 Maurice
Abravanel, sight unseen, on the highest recommendation of
Bruno Walter, whom Bodanzky met each summer in a Swiss
resort.

It took only a few weeks of the 1936–1937 season for the
Met's high command to conclude that Abravanel's engagement
did not solve the problem of Bodanzky's overwork. That was
the moment when I received the cabled offer to join the musical
staff in the fall of 1937.

Abravanel's option for a second year had been taken up by
the Met, yet my engagement showed that a saw had been applied
to cut off the branch on which he sat. But Semon very kindly
kept assuring me that it would have happened under any circumstances and that I should never feel guilty. The Met was a
very tough house for conductors, especially at a time when eco-

nomic stringency allowed for only scant rehearsing. He assured me that my success was at that moment of general interest and importance to the Met so that I could consider this a most favorable constellation.

This was a valuable briefing and proved entirely accurate. The Met has remained a tough soil for conductors and I have had occasion to witness how excellent men, with fine reputations, simply could not "prevail" in that particular environment. Not to prevail means that one's design and plans cannot be carried out and that the conductor is dragged along the path of routine and customary ways.

In opera it boils down ultimately to the delicate but decisive relation between conductor and leading singers. The Met has always been a star theater that passed up the very best on the way up, waiting until they had reached the top and become box-office draws. This was policy.

When established singers finally arrived at the Met it meant that they were also set in their ways — as I had noticed with Schorr in Salzburg — and some of them, having waited long years for the opportunity, were bitter and intransigent and very difficult to handle. This was the artistic material with which a conductor at the Metropolitan had to cope. I felt the auspicious situation, but I left my kind adviser in Paris with some apprehension in my heart as well. I knew that the sum total of my conductorial experience was small and hoped for the best. Other impressions took over as I embarked on a mean and stormy crossing, arriving in New York on November 8. I was met at the pier by Miss Hope, who had engaged a room in an old brownstone house on West 85th Street, where I was taken in a taxi. While unpacking, I heard above my head a fine pair of hands practicing Beethoven's Fourth Piano Concerto, which I considered a good omen for my first hours in the New World and decided to investigate.

The door upstairs was ajar and through the opening I spotted a young man in shirt sleeves. I walked in and met the pianist

Zadel Skolovsky, perhaps four or five years younger than I, very pleasant and most kindly disposed. It was the natural thing for us to become friends, living in the same house, going round the corner for meals, exchanging information, with him telling me much about American music life of which I knew nothing and, best of all, having a faithful companion throughout this first, quite exciting and difficult winter season.

I was much impressed by Zadel, whose pianistic dexterity was great, and since I had never been even close to acquiring the big virtuoso fingers, I overestimated his chances. My musical expectations for him did not materialize. I was overly impressed by his potential and didn't reckon with a lack of personal and artistic growth that kept him running with the field, finally relying on teaching to make ends meet.

On my second day I went to introduce myself to the Met and vice versa. The outside of the house was plain ugly and located in an absurd neighborhood, the garment district, where I saw during luncheon hours the oddest assortment of humanity standing around talking and waiting until the bell called them back to work. What the Met's exterior lacked was more than made up for by the grand, horseshoe-shaped auditorium with its aura of history created by the mystical residue of great events, great personalities, and great stories.

I met the high command of the opera association, a troika consisting of Edward Johnson, Edward Ziegler, and Earle Lewis. Johnson, ex-tenor and urbane public relations man, was nominally boss with the title of general manager, while Ziegler, an assistant general manager, was the man whose decisions stuck. He was in appearance as much as in fact éminence grise, older than Johnson, far more educated than befits an opera executive, and honest beyond the shadow of a doubt. In contrast to this quality in Ziegler, the other assistant general manager, Earle Lewis, was rumored to be susceptible to gifts. He was a cherubic-looking man, and if his whispered suggestions about imaginative casting were proof, he did have a number of favorites among singers.

I was one of three assistant conductors for the German repertoire. Karl Riedel and Hermann Weigert were my colleagues, the former an old hand, stoic, relaxed, and battle-scarred from insults and invectives hurled at him by his boss, Bodanzky. When he laughed at being called something scatological, his uppers would fall down with a clicking sound that sent him into more spasms of hilarity. To this somewhat fatigued Viennese, Weigert was a complete contrast, more German than the Germans, pedantic but extremely competent, and quite responsible for having prepared the novice Flagstad for eight major Wagnerian roles. I was being looked over by these colleagues as any newcomer would be examined, especially in a situation where an incumbent like Abravanel is on the way out.

Finally I got the chance of saying "good day" to Bodanzky, whom I had never met before. A tall, hook-nosed man, resembling some lean bird, he could be and was in private conversation the perfect charmer. Witty, urbane, fed up with his work, and only excited by his card games, skat and bridge, which he mastered superbly, he welcomed me with great warmth and asked immediately if I was prepared to conduct the repertoire, which for the 1937–1938 season consisted of eight Wagner works plus *Elektra, Der Rosenkavalier,* and *Salome.* The last-named was not assigned to any of the German conductors but to Ettore Panizza. Only *Lohengrin* and *Tannhäuser* were Abravanel's. Already at this purely social introductory visit Bodanzky advised me that I would very soon rehearse with the orchestra to give him the chance of judging how "ready" I was.

During the Depression years costs at the Met had been drastically cut, and among the items most radically affected were rehearsals. It was par for the course to allot one three-hour rehearsal per act to the long Wagner works and that was it. Some operas were revived after the long hiatus of nearly seven months between seasons without getting any general stage rehearsal. Such was the case with most of the Wagnerian music dramas during that season.

The orchestra gathered on a Monday morning, one week before opening night at the very end of November. Bodanzky took the first day for brushing up *Rosenkavalier,* which had been out of the repertoire for a few years, and then told me to be ready by Thursday to run through act one of *Die Walküre* with the orchestra alone. Bodanzky was not like so many older men who unconsciously lay traps for their potential successors while claiming to need them. He was always most helpful, he never played tricks, he truly wanted someone to spell him on short notice when he felt ill or tired. To be treated in such a positive way made me feel extremely grateful to my chief. What I did not like was his open admission of boredom with work and his attempt at humor during the first rehearsal, when he voiced his hope that this might already be the last day of the season with vacation following. (In 1937 I measured every conductor by the yardstick of Toscanini, who was never bored and who never spoke of fatigue.) I could not understand how this great repertoire, perhaps the greatest challenge to a conductor, could cause anyone a feeling of tedium.

Later, when I got Bodanzky's whole story from friends, I realized that he was quite ill and held on to the unloved Met for money. He, like many high-living Americans, had been badly burned in the crash. Still, for me, at age twenty-five, this was depressing and seemed an incongruous picture, the superimposition of Wall Street upon the great scores of music.

The Met orchestra, reflecting the whole company ethnically, was predominantly Italian, with a small sprinkling of older Germans and perhaps three recent émigrés in the string section. Whenever Bodanzky was displeased he used a choice vocabulary of Viennese invective that, I was told and soon noticed, he lavished with gusto on poor Riedel. I became a little apprehensive, since I had never taken abuse in any form, either from schoolteachers or in my professional contacts, and I had no intention of being called names. It was from the day of my first rehearsal that I made doubly sure how I would be treated.

Bodanzky was not endowed with any meanness, just with short patience and a long dictionary. He had a most infectious ear-to-ear grin and was always ready to apologize.

That he came to the Met as successor to Toscanini and was still there twenty-three years later made me study him even more attentively. The only major post he had held prior to the Met was at Mannheim. For me it was then quite puzzling to find a conductor who appeared basically a capable routineer yet had a worldwide reputation and a powerful position in New York. Up to World War II it was perhaps easier for authoritarians to assert themselves, since their freedom to hire and fire could cow all but the most reckless "employees." The changes in this respect have been nearly revolutionary since the war ended. As a result of reform movements by unions and musicians, the power of conductors has been curtailed to the vanishing point, and therefore the crop of maestri who hold sway in the second half of this century must be musically better equipped than their colleagues of yore; there can be no more reliance on fear as a substitute for real musical authority.

The "39th Street Roof Stage" where I began my American career was a square room on the sixth floor and barely large enough to accommodate the huge Wagnerian orchestra. The ceiling had been hung with crisscrossed heavy chord to cut down on loudness in this comparatively small space. Bodanzky introduced me and then sat down right behind me. I started with the opening storm music and, with very few corrections, went ahead at a good clip. About one fourth of the way into act one I found a wrong note in the *celli*. Discovering an uncorrected misprint in music from which musicians have played — and to make it worse, under the man who sat right there watching — is like accusing a predecessor of bad ears, laxity, or incompetence. In this particular case the issue was quite subtle.

It was a mistake in voice leading without causing a clashing dissonance, simply a wrong note and not a false one. Since I had studied from a pocket edition of *Walküre* that had that chord correctly printed I knew I was right. Bodanzky, very surprised, got up to look, first at the score, then at the cello parts, both of which had the same error. I explained to him my view — he agreed and sat down again while the cellists wrote the corrected note into their parts.

This small incident was for me a big break. It brought instant attention and respect from the orchestra, and it meant that I would never hear a harsh word from my chief.

While that had been a great Thursday morning for me, my contractual duties for the opera were a little less exciting and continued without change for quite a while. I was first and foremost an assistant conductor, which is an English-language euphemism for coach and rehearsal pianist. Being the newest of the staff, I got, logically enough, the least interesting assignments. Weigert kept the coaching of principal roles for himself, the secondary roles went to Riedel, and what was left came to me. For backstage services Riedel, who had the better conducting hand, would attend to the band in the third act of *Rosenkavalier,* Weigert would be with Flagstad for the backstage "Ho-yo-to-ho!" and I would sit in the cistern with Jokanaan and warn him when his next cue came around lest he go to sleep.

I became pianist for the most time-consuming of all rehearsals, the staging of *Rosenkavalier* under the guidance of Leopold Sachse.

In the 1930s conductors complained that the Met was stingy with orchestra rehearsals, but there were always minimum quotas of time. Stage directors got literally nothing that would enable them to do any kind of reasonable work for the histrionic part of the operas. Sets were old and often so tattered that even the best tricks of the chief electrician could not conceal

the seaminess of canvas. A careless motion would rock any
palace, a false step could create waves in Wotan's mountains,
Hunding's hut needed another mortgage to pay for repairs, and
Tristan's ship would not have done for the poorest Chinese
water traffic. What could a powerless and helpless stage director
do but stand in the wings, wringing his hands and hoping that
no overt breakdown would occur.

Singers brought their own costumes. No one would notice
whether or not they were appropriate until the first performance, simply because there was no earlier chance to view them.
Stage rehearsals were reserved exclusively for operas revived
after lengthy absences, while the opening *Tristan* of the 1937
season went on without Bodanzky's having laid eyes on the ill-
starred pair of lovers. Weigert journeyed to Flagstad's and
Melchior's hotels, where he made sure that they knew the cuts
and remembered their roles, which with Flagstad meant a perfect and Melchior an approximate resemblance to the composer's wishes. While the chief conductor had to get along with
these kinds of preliminaries, the stage director was a mere relic
and, if he took himself seriously, a person of ridicule.

Sachse had already been with the Met for a few seasons and
had suffered as much as any man could. He had a profound
knowledge of theatrical history and opera in particular and was
a great gentleman with whom it was a privilege to spend time
and talk. In the pre-Hitler days of Germany he was an *Intendant* — the top official who administers opera houses, without
necessarily being a stage person. He was as grateful as most
refugees for the chance to make a decent living within his own
professional sphere, although his acute unhappiness over the
dismal conditions came out at even the slightest opportunity.

He would sit down at the start of act one of *Rosenkavalier*
and spend a long time on the most delicate minutiae in the
overtones and nuances between the Feldmarschallin and Octa-
vian, though he had the two finest and experienced actresses
alive in Lotte Lehmann and Risë Stevens. In the meantime the

host of small roles for the lever would assemble and wait for their turn. By eleven-thirty an assistant stage manager would point to the waiting humanity along the walls of the room, as if to say that this was the urgent task and should be considered. The lever is indeed a most complicated and tricky scene, usually enhanced by the untimely misbehavior of the small dogs offered to the Feldmarschallin by the Animal Vendor. Sachse, resenting the reminder, would blow up and explain to all and sundry that he was in the midst of the most significant scene, the relation of the lovers, compared to which the lever was easy. This prompted a murmured "easy like hell" from several veterans of *Rosenkavalier*.

I, with memories of Wymetal, made a quick diagnosis that Sachse was quite comfortable with the leading roles, to whom searching explanations in depth meant something, while his lack of technique in blocking and arranging the mechanics of the lever inhibited him with the large crowd of small-role singers and choristers, whose primary concern is the luncheon break. Sachse was in the wrong pew. But after his easy blow-ups, which were soon followed by good humor, he was a source of amusing stories and valuable, pertinent information.

But having in my first week tasted the blood of my real profession, conducting, all the hours of pounding *Rosenkavalier* on a piano seemed a waste of time. I was then a young man in a hurry.

More to my liking was my second conducting assignment. *Elektra* was being rehearsed for once with the full cast of singers on stage. After a runthrough of the first scene, a most difficult bit even by the difficult standards of Richard Strauss, Bodanzky wanted me to repeat it, partly for the benefit of the young ladies who were Maids and the Overseer and partly to observe me in the real auditorium of the Met. It is one thing to do an orchestra reading in a small room, undistracted by singers and their stage movements, and a totally different task to conduct in the theater with the stage forces. For an opera conductor the first shock is invariably the difficulty of hearing the singers through the sound of the orchestra's instruments, which are so much closer to his ear. The next problem is the distance from the singers, with a resultant small time lag in their reflexes that can lead, if not tightly controlled by the conductor, to a constant lack of synchronization, with the orchestra ahead of the voices — a not infrequent experience even in otherwise reputable performances.

I must have passed that test as well as the first, because a few weeks later I was asked to conduct an *Elektra* performance — without any further orchestra rehearsal for me.

When I was not actively busy, I went to watch Abravanel at work. After sitting in on a few of his rehearsals I thought I understood his difficulties at the Met. He was a fine musician and a good conductor — which after all has been proved by his long career in the symphonic world of the United States. There his basically unclear beat is not the liability that defeated him in theater work. The tightness of rehearsal time also made life for him more difficult, depriving him of the chances to get his way across to orchestra and singers.

It was early in December when Bodanzky announced to me officially that my debut performance as conductor had been scheduled for January 21, 1938, a Thursday, in a regular subscription evening, with *Die Walküre*. The cast, except for the tenor, was one which the books about Golden Ages extol: Elisabeth Rethberg, Flagstad, Karin Branzell, Ludwig Hoffmann, and Emanuel List. Even the missing Melchior would be replaced by Paul Althouse, who was far better than any of his first-line successors for thirty years after. For me it was a distinct advantage not to have Lauritz Melchior in the cast of my debut, as he was erratic and a trial for conductors more experienced than myself. Hoffmann in the role of Wotan pleased me, too, because of the tension I had felt between Schorr and myself since our days in Salzburg seventeen months earlier.

The weeks between the announcement and January 21 went by in a fog. I sat with the score, which I had already studied meticulously and of which I knew even the smallest note, still going over it with a fine-toothed comb. But no reading can quite replace those rehearsals of acts two and three for which I had not done any actual conducting. Only the ignoramus I was then would have the fool-courage to accept an assignment of this kind. To make matters even more difficult, I was not willing to conduct as an understudy is expected to, keeping the tempi and all interpretive ideas of the chief who is being replaced for an evening. To me the concept of merely doing what Bodanzky had set up was unacceptable, and I planned to follow my own ideas as much as the improvisatory nature of the occasion would allow.

There were some piano runthroughs with individual singers, who were mostly very agreeable, except that it was almost impossible to get hold of Flagstad, who was in and out of New York for her many concerts, scheduled in sandwichlike tightness between her opera appearances.

At a young age, without experience with the long sessions of Wagner's works, hardly abridged, I worried much more about my stamina than I did thirty-five years later when that question never bothered me. I was frightfully nervous and thought foolishly that there were concrete ways of behaving to make sure that I did not get fatigued before nightfall. Fortunately I had an unplanned luncheon invitation under slightly bizarre circumstances, which now, so many years later, makes the hour after twelve-thirty better remembered than the stretch between eight and midnight.

Every great city has a few blocks where the center of the music world is located. Fifty-seventh Street from Seventh to Sixth avenues is the nearest New York equivalent to the *galleria* in Milan. There were no outdoor cafés, but next to Carnegie Hall there is still today a famous gathering place for all kinds of musicians and ballet people, the Russian Tea Room.

One of its daily customers was the basso Emanuel List, whom I had known well since my first summer in Salzburg. Not only was he the Commendatore in that now far distant *Don Giovanni,* he had engaged me many times to play for him privately while he studied concert repertoire, mainly the glorious lieder of Franz Schubert. We had the kind of excellent relationship that is based on mutual advantage; I greatly appreciated the chance of getting to know the later volumes of Schubert's songs, and he was glad to have a good pianist for very little money.

Having emerged from extreme poverty he held on to every copper piece with such tenacity that his tightness became proverbial. The only expenditure of any size appeared to be for his wardrobe. And, as I had occasion to note during the few weeks since my arrival in New York, the daily luncheon in a place not exactly on the cheap side. He had, as soon as we met in November, briefed me with the important intelligence that "a young man of talent like you can eat for free in this town, because there are oodles of good families who would be honored to have you regularly as a guest." It spoke well for the generosity and hospitality of New York, so agreeably different from the formality of Europe, but I never felt that this was my way of saving money or making new friends. My pay was, to my relative calculations, royal, and my expenses very small. I had one hundred dollars a week for the entire Met season, which consisted of sixteen weeks on Broadway plus the two weeks of preliminary rehearsals, and management held an option on my services for the spring tour, which meant a potential addition of four more weeks. The Met also had paid my big expense, the ocean voyage, and it is a fact that in percentage ratio of income to outlay I never again saved as much as I did during my first season. A great luncheon in a very good Italian restaurant was sixty-five cents.

On January 21, 1938, I decided to take a little walk, not too strenuous lest I tire myself for the evening, but just enough to get the extra oxygen for an afternoon nap. I searched more than I walked. Why would I have landed on Fifty-seventh Street? It seemed strange to me that everything in New York was exactly like the day before, with nobody bothering about my red-letter date. So I hoped that in the music block some people would be huddled together and comment in great awe that this was the new man who would conduct that evening. But there was nobody who huddled, nobody gave a darn, and I ambled along, anonymous and deflated. At that moment the formidable countenance of List came toward me from the opposite direction. We chatted for a few moments, and then, miracle of miracles, he took pity on me and in most cordial tones asked me to lunch with him, as his guest, at the Russian Tea Room. It was a kindness that I have rarely encountered again, or so it seems. I had been wandering like a lost sheep, too nervous to go into a restaurant for my lunch, and here was the most unlikely of candidates inviting me, which meant first and foremost company and a chance to talk for an hour.

My debut passed and it was immediately apparent that I had come up to expectations. Again Bodanzky helped enormously by not being in the theater for my great Thursday evening, which proved to me his complete confidence in my ability to handle the situation, and I appreciated that very much. Things then happened very quickly. I had a lot of questions to answer, as the press got hold of me and wanted to know how at twenty-five years and eleven months I was able to bring off such a stint. I did not know enough English then to pun that to me it was more like a stunt. The Met asked me to do *Elektra* and another *Walküre*, and a few days later I received a letter announcing that the option for the spring tour had been exercised and I would conduct the two operas that had been Abravanel's, *Lohengrin* and *Tannhäuser*. Best of all, within six weeks of my debut performance, I had a new, two-year contract from the Met as conductor.

The word assistant was missing, though it was clearly understood between us that I would, in addition to conducting a few
works assigned to me, spell my ailing chief when necessary.
This I gladly agreed to do, with the proviso that I would not be
asked to do single acts, as had been Bodanzky's habit when
Riedel was his main helper. Then Bodanzky would sit out a
second act and go back to his post for the third. In my protest
action against such a shoddy system I found Mr. Ziegler most
helpful and actually glad that somebody took the bull by the
horns and objected to something he himself had disliked and
resented.

I had no time for anything but digesting my own happenings and I felt that such a story was quite unique — I suppose
this is a well-known reflex to sudden spectacular success —
when darker realities fairly exploded from one moment to the
next. On the thirteenth of March Austria was finished as an
independent country and my return was made impossible. At
least I had seen enough of my German colleagues after 1933 not
to wish any firsthand experiences with the Hitler Reich. My
immediate concern was my permit to remain in the United
States.

When I had received the original first engagement from the
Metropolitan I found out that the visas permitting entry for
permanent stay in the States were all gone for several years
ahead. Austria, a small nation of 6 million, rated 1400 immigrants annually by the quota system of a law passed in 1922.
In order not to miss this great opportunity of getting to America I had asked for the alternative, a temporary visitors' visa,
good for six months. These six months would be over on the
eighth of May, but by the middle of March I had no idea what
I would do with my spring and summer, since Salzburg was out
for me and even returning to Vienna looked like an unnecessary
risk.

Being the proud possessor of a brand-new two-year contract that proved — I thought — my indispensability until the end of the spring tour in 1940, I submitted this document with my application for an extension of my stay for another half year. This I did confidently without benefit of legal advice. Knowing only part of the immigration laws, I thought that the one concern of the United States government was the ability of the foreigner to support himself and this I could triumphantly prove by that splendid document, my new contract. Then I literally forgot the whole thing and went on the spring tour with the opera company.

Touring has been and has remained my favorite way of life. I took to it like a duck to water. The Met went to Baltimore, Boston, and Cleveland in those years, in special trains of all-Pullman cars, with the atmosphere of a glamorous circus and with invitations to a never-ending sequence of parties. I, now announced as conductor for the two early Wagner works, was on every guest list, as the hostesses of the three cities would not want to miss the "new boy" at their grand-opera suppers or cocktail affairs. Everybody, except a professional freeloader, gets tired of these grotesque social functions very quickly, and yet few artists have the courage to say "No thank you." The theory that it is necessary for one's "career" to go to these affairs is a total bluff. It is we performers who are necessary to give society hostesses an additional pretext for inviting their friends and knocking out their eyes with the "names" they assemble. It is only "names" that interest them in any case, though they mispronounce or forget them frequently.

Such parties were amusing as long as I spent the time with my colleagues, but to be buttonholed by some drunken husband, who had no idea of what the whole fuss was about, who confused composers, singers, and titles while pretending to ask for enlightenment, was too much. For me the worst parts were the after-concert suppers where food was delayed while everybody drank and drank hard liquor. I never ate before conducting and wanted a meal afterward. The parties seemed at first to promise that, especially since restaurants open at those late hours are the exception in New York and do not exist at all in the provinces. It took me many years to do away with party-going, but by then I had had enough forever.

After returning from the three-week trip we had another turn in New York. It was traditional to play a few performances during Holy Week, which was highlighted by two *Parsifals*, one on Wednesday evening, the other a matinee on Good Friday. Prior to the tour the work had been rehearsed a bit more than the general repertoire, since two annual performances did not suffice to revive it without extensive preparation. By another clairvoyance of Bodanzky's I had conducted the second runthrough of the Flower Maiden scene, by far the most difficult in any *Parsifal* rendition.

Having toted up nine performances of four operas that I had not conducted before 1938, I was prepared to coast for the last week of the season, or just sit on my laurels, when on Tuesday in the late afternoon a violinist friend of mine named Werner rang me with an alarming story. He shared a general physician with the Bodanzky family and, I did not know how, found out that this doctor had advised Bodanzky not to conduct the long and tiring *Parsifal* on Wednesday evening. That was the end of my laurel sitting; I took the score down from the shelf and dug into it. For some reason the management did not know or did not wish to decide earlier than absolutely necessary whether to replace Bodanzky and waited until eleven Wednesday morning to ask me to conduct. I felt that this showed a singular lack of consideration, since I might have gone out and knocked myself silly drinking and been groggy the day after. Thanks to my friend Werner I had been warned.

That evening went magnificently, as I have, even among Wagner's work, a special affinity for his last opus. By Good Friday Bodanzky was able to conduct, for which I was very glad. Each performance during that first season took much too much out of me, and I knew then that nobody could tolerate this kind of strain for long. As the Met season drew to its close that week, I was called by Charles and Alice from their home in Virginia, inviting me to spend as much time as I wanted as their houseguest.

It must have been April 17 or 18 when I made the four-hour journey to Washington, D.C., during which time I was able to pass in review the five and a half months of so many momentous developments. What had bothered me most was my good friend Constance Hope, nominally my agent, whose main labor, publicity, was brought into play on my behalf. Up to this day I have not accepted the idea that facts must be altered to create an image that differs from the personality of an artist as he really is. I had fought with Constance — amiably enough — about every story she distributed. Soon after my debut she brought me to a big manager, Arthur Judson, who wanted me to quit opera and go right then into the symphonic circuit as guest conductor to exploit as soon as possible my initial impact and success. This I refused to do, and while it cost me forever the support of the most powerful agent, I knew that I was not ready. For me it was always essential to feel myself master of the material I had to handle. The special gift of faking, which I did so well on the piano, was never my best suit in conducting. The horror of standing in front of a group of instrumentalists and knowing less than they prevented me from getting into such shallow waters. My musical career was slowed up considerably by staying at the opera too long, but my nervous and physical health benefited.

Looking back from three and a half decades I cannot fault my decisions in 1938. I had skipped too much of the conventional circuit already; I had strained my faculties to the limit, and I needed time to consolidate my musical position. I had ahead of me over four months without professional commitments.

At Union Station in Washington I found Charles and Alice awaiting me, and we drove without delay across the Potomac and into the hill country of Virginia.


## LBJ

After an hour and a half we arrived at Longlea, a large farm, dominated by a magnificent house, which had been built for Alice and her children. By then a son, Michael, had joined the little girl, Diana. Charles had chosen a spot close enough to the nation's capital since he dabbled in politics behind the scenes and had to be near a major airport for frequent trips to Texas, where he owned and operated a number of newspapers. From his tales I gathered, after stripping them of the many baroque ornaments, that he had found Alice, about twenty-five years his junior, as a secretary to a state senator in Austin. Her father had gone bankrupt in the crash and she was forced to work. Charles persuaded her to quit her job, the state capital, and Texas, and since his way of persuading people was quite compelling, he succeeded and they took up life together, unable for the time being to marry.

In Virginia they ran a great house with eighteen servants, over whom a German butler and his wife, a superlative cook, held sway. There was a constant stream of guests, to me an entirely new crowd of real Americans, mostly Texans and Southerners, who were such a contrast to the Europeanized Met-Americans that I hardly understood the conversation. The accents were new, the lavish and easy life with martinis served at eleven in the morning was new, my room with its elegant antique furnishings was new, the heat in April was new, the

eighteen black servants were new — I just sat goggle-eyed.
Then Alice, concerned lest I get bored, invited friends of mine
to join us, among them Zadel Skolovsky, who regaled us with
a classic quote: A few days prior to his arrival Alice suddenly
realized that her household was unprepared for the young man's
kosher diet. She wired for suggestions and received this reassur-
ing and modest message: "Can eat everything, except meat,
fowl, and shellfish. Love Zadel." Rudolf, the butler, later confided with a devilish satisfaction that the breakfast eggs of Mr.
Skolovsky had been prepared together with the general bacon,
lifted out of the pan, and served as if specially heated in a separate dish uncontaminated by the forbidden food. This first
guest appearance of Zadel did not foreshadow for any of us that
in the future he would be — for a short period — husband to
Alice.

The days — a continuous feast — passed quickly. I had no
immediate worries about my mother and aunt in Vienna, who
wrote reassuringly about themselves, until on a Saturday afternoon, April 30, I remembered with a terrific shock that I had
received no reply to my application for an extension visa. I
spoke at once to Charles, who decided that on Sunday morning,
May 1, we would drive to Washington, where he could enlist
the help of a young congressman from Texas in whose third
district Charles owned some newspapers that had supported the
man's candidacy in 1936.

We motored to the capital and checked into the Mayflower
Hotel, where a little while later a lanky young man appeared.
He treated Charles with the informal courtesy behooving a
youngster toward an older man to whom he is in debt. That
young fellow was Lyndon Johnson.

After listening impassively to Charles tell my story, with a
little added drama about the victims of Nazi persecution, the
congressman left and we drove back to Longlea. Johnson later
told with great gusto what happened in Washington after we

adjourned. By Monday morning the research had been done to clear the desks for the phone calls. The Immigration Department had rejected my application, but by a fortunate delay this reply had not yet been posted. Johnson knew that a government agency could not reverse itself, but he also had studied the reply forms used and exerted his pressure to have the customary phrase "you have seven days to leave the United States" changed to "you have six months . . . ," which meant to us precisely the same as if the application had been granted in the first place.

While this offered a welcome breathing space, Johnson's office tackled at once the larger problem of getting my status changed to that of "immigrant" and permanent resident. This change could only be accomplished by my going abroad. To forestall my being perchance locked out Johnson called Havana and got the consul general on the phone. It was established that there were plenty of available quota numbers in the consul's jurisdiction.

By a strange quirk of history, Roosevelt's speedy recognition of the *Anschluss* between Germany and Austria made these quota numbers available. In 1937, I was an Austrian who would have had to wait until God knows when to obtain one of the 1400 visas allotted to that small country. In May 1938 the total of the German and Austrian quotas was 26,400, and many entries were available.

I left by boat for Havana, in my pocket, aside from various papers and documents, a masterpiece of a letter composed by Johnson's chief assistant but signed by the congressman. In it the consul was advised by the young statesman that the United States had a holy mission to provide a peaceful haven for musical geniuses nervously exhausted from persecution and radical bias. This moving piece we read prior to my departure on the terrace of Alice's home, drinking our fourth martini before a superb dinner, harassed, if at all, by an occasional mosquito.

It all went like clockwork; the permanent visa was issued

without hitch and I returned to New York and on to Virginia, where in the little town of Alexandria I took out my "first papers," which expressed my "intention to become a citizen." I cannot pinpoint the exact day, but it was less than four weeks after I had first laid eyes on the young Lyndon Johnson.

Now I was in a position to send affidavits to my mother and aunt, whom I urged in letters to prepare their own voyage to New York. Then I went to Europe for a variety of visits, guessing quite correctly that this might be the last possible time before other barriers to free travel appeared.

I kept in touch with Lyndon Johnson for thirty years. When he ran for a vacant Senate seat I sent him a contribution. When he became a senator I found him on the far side of the aisle — according to my ideas where he should not have been — and I wrote him of my disagreement. His reply — invariably prompt and always courteous — was a classic: "Your letter makes me proud that I could have a hand in making a new citizen, who would so well use his citizenship." That was about the only real content of the letter, which said nothing but was disarmingly and charmingly personal.

By the coincidental timings of our careers, Lyndon Johnson was vice president when I went as music director to Boston in 1962. Prior to my first tour, which included concerts in Washington, Mrs. Johnson rang me in Boston to propose an after-concert party at their residence, which was Pearl Mesta's house in Georgetown. It was a grand affair, and among the invitees were a few people whom I specially wanted to meet face to face. There was a photographer who shot dozens of frames, and several people asked me for the story of my first meeting with the vice president, when, how, and about what. After telling the whole 1938 visa and immigration saga, one more picture of the vice president and myself was demanded. We sat down on a sofa, and Lyndon, putting his long arm around my shoulder, asked me, "Erich, when we tell that story of the consul again, what place should we make it instead of Havana?" I have cherished this particular remark of Lyndon's because it shows a side few people ever saw, the sophisticated man whose image remained that of a cornball.

After he became President, Johnson asked me not only to many a White House dinner, he appointed me to two official positions, Trustee of the Kennedy Center and Director of the Public Broadcast Corporation. He attended one of the regular Boston Symphony concerts at Constitution Hall and spent the entire intermission in the green room, where I introduced him to a number of orchestra members.

I tried in every way to be of some service to Lyndon as President, but in the end I am afraid that LBJ did not make any real use of me. The Johnsons did not feel at ease with anyone but professional politicians, and I realized that for him the old friend Leinsdorf was a windfall as a direct link with the musical, artistic, and cultural world of the United States. One of his aides said as much to me. But once a man is in this unimaginably complex office of President, time and place for talking is cut down to near zero, which I regretted no end.

My final visit with Lyndon Johnson was at a time when he faced the worst crisis of his life and career and when I was in deep gloom. Of that more in its proper place.

# PART II

# Lehrjahre

## American Apprenticeship

# San Francisco

In the early months of 1938, a short time after my New York debut, the San Francisco Opera invited me to be with them during their fall season that year. The San Francisco Opera meant literally Maestro Gaetano Merola, a Mediterranean of the more colorful variety, a conductor and impresario, a man who had the vision to start regular opera on the West Coast in 1922 with his own money. By 1938 his company had grown into the second most important on the American continent. Although a sometime conductor himself, Merola at heart was an entrepreneur who really thought that conductors were created only to accompany singers, that orchestras of more than fifty pieces were a devilish invention of German origin, and that two stars, soprano and tenor, with garnishment, were all that was necessary for a glamorous evening. By the mid-thirties he had made his peace, though grudgingly, with the "fancy" notion that works by Wagner and Strauss had to be included and that a number of nuisances, such as arrogant conductors who asked for rehearsals galore and string sections of ruinous cost, might be necessities.

Meeting Merola in New York, where he stopped en route to Milan, was a great treat, and he remains, in my memory, an unforgettable character. To convey his English in phonetic writing would require some brand-new symbols for the sounds that were his own invention: "Eja, Lainzadorfa, these maestri are doinga everyting possible to get de Teatro Lirico broka."

He switched forth and back between his native tongue "anda de Kingsa English" whether his partner understood him or not.

Of uncertain middle age, a natty dresser, with a birdlike face of parchment-dry skin topped by two eyes that stared at a very wide angle in opposite directions, Merola was a great charmer and no mean philosopher. I was won over by a quality dear to me: he never said "art" when he meant "money."

When I left our first meeting I knew what my task in San Francisco would be. Fritz Reiner needed an assistant for the preparation of *Die Meistersinger* and *Elektra,* for which he had been engaged as conductor, and, to make the trip worth my while, Merola also wanted me to conduct a new production of Debussy's *Pelléas et Mélisande,* never before presented in California. *Pelléas* was scheduled for three performances, the last in Los Angeles, where the company repeated over a one-week period the entire repertoire of the previous six weeks in San Francisco.

*Pelléas* was the prize I coveted, and it raised me to such a state of elation that I never bothered to think through our most peculiar arrangement. This double role of assistant conductor and conductor of certain performances had come about because of my duties at the Met resulting from Bodanzky's overwork and uncertain health.

With all my high opinion of self I still had enough cool objectivity left to realize that Merola could have found a more obvious choice to direct *Pelléas* and a number of earnest, eager, and willing assistants for Reiner.

It took me several months, until I was in San Francisco, to understand what a fine game had been played.

I was still quite new, and my own briefing had been insufficient. Fritz Reiner was known and valued as a first-rate conductor who demanded lots of rehearsals and in general a perfectionist attitude from the organizations he dealt with. He had a year earlier done a season of opera in Philadelphia (where he had taught at the Curtis Institute since 1931), which was spoken of very highly yet failed to continue.

From Merola's own disjointed narrative and the stray comments of third parties who knew the "score," I could gradually piece together a bit of background against which to evaluate my own engagement.

In 1936 he had ventured into the most ambitious project of all, producing the entire *Ring* cycle in one short fall season. It was, of course, with the new star Kirsten Flagstad, partnered by Lauritz Melchior, and conducted by Bodanzky. The latter, not used to a theater where Wagner was new and not merely the twenty-fifth repetition it was in New York, had to spend many hours rehearsing a green orchestra. He also demanded the Wagner tuben, bothersome special instruments that had to be imported from the East together with their players, causing the hard-pressed impresario undreamed-of expense. When I met Merola eighteen months after these events he still sputtered about the numerous nuisances caused by *questa benedetta tetralogia*. His maximum indignation was reserved for the extravagance of bringing four musicians from New York. It turned out they played as much off pitch as any local brass player would have done at no extra cost.

Yet the Rubicon had been crossed, San Francisco had tasted the blood of the giant, and Wagner became indispensable for succeeding seasons. The collaboration with Bodanzky remained a one-time affair, but no matter how bothersome and costly it was to present *opere tedesche*, Merola was pragmatist enough to know that a first-line opera company had to do it. He was not an anti-Wagnerite out of political or artistic resentment, as Bing proved to be, he merely had to overcome his own background, which had not prepared him to put up with demanding conductors, exacting stage directors, and myriad complications, such as having to produce steam, fire, rainbows, riding amazons, crashing edifices populated by gods, giants, dwarfs, and, occasionally, even human beings.

"How different the *Traviata*s and *Butterfly*s without extra brass, produced, directed, designed by Armando Agnini, my nephew and man of all stage trades who does everything but sing, never bothers the stars with newfangled ideas of Stanislavsky, and yet causes unalloyed pleasure to all but the boring intelligentsia, who contribute only trouble." Such was the soliloquy that gave me my first insight into an original man, one whom I learned to like and appreciate. Merola was a master at rolling with the punches, and, having made a truce, if not real peace, with the fact that the German repertoire had come to stay, he dared to hire the noted Fritz Reiner, a conductor far more demanding and exacting than Bodanzky. Reiner was well known for his perfectionism and his thoroughly disagreeable manner toward one and all.

I arrived in San Francisco after a memorable cross-country train journey in luxury unknown to me before and reported immediately to Merola's office. His first question was oddly similar to Bodanzky's a year earlier: Was I fully prepared for *Elektra* and *Meistersinger* because "it is entirely conceivable that this Maestro Reiner might find so much wrong that he would walk out and in that case, my dear Leinsdorf, you must conduct all three operas."

Here was the reason for my engagement and the peculiar combination of having a contract as "conductor and assistant conductor." I was the insurance policy. With his shrewdness Merola had found a weapon with which — or with whom — he would fight back if Reiner became too hard to handle. His bait, offering me *Pelléas*, had been perfect. He was sufficiently cynical of artistic criteria to calculate that the Debussy work, unknown as it was in California, would cause him no trouble even if the "new boy" did it badly. For *Elektra*, which I had already conducted at the Metropolitan, and *Meistersinger* I was more security than Lloyds of London.

Now I understood the entire scheme but did not mind one bit. I had my own performances, a wondrous score, a brand-new production, and, in comparison with my recent past, lots of rehearsal time.

I have often thought how difficult it must be to prepare an audience for understudies. How Merola secured me, an oven-fresh New York success, to backstop the risky Reiner was a masterstroke. No established conductor would have gone to a nine-week engagement for a total of three performances guaranteed.

The fall was altogether enchanting. I have never lost my delight in San Francisco's beauty, including the spectacular fog as it streams in from the Golden Gate Bridge. The company was a most congenial group, most of whom were staying at the no-longer-existing Hotel Empire, a short walk from the opera house. Domestically inclined singers had housekeeping apartments which led to much visiting back and forth, more eating and drinking in jolly company, and the generally easy relationships we imagine a traveling circus troupe to have. Blum's, the famous confectioner, was our favorite meeting spot for refreshments after late-evening rehearsals, but best of all were the lavish parties given for the whole company by enthusiastic opera patrons. There was a gusto and naive joy surrounding these events that made them most attractive.

Artists denounce all receptions as heavy bores, which they usually are, with the notable exception of the shindigs in San Francisco. I remember a buffet supper for which our hostess had thoughtfully prepared operatic references, which were stuck with tags into the divers goodies on the laden table. A huge turkey carried a sign reading: "I am Elsa, a goose, because I asked the forbidden questions." Once an opening-night party was given in honor of the *Figaro* cast, and as we arrived the door was flung open by our highly excited, ecstatically fluttering hostess with the sounds: "Oh, how I love Mozart — Tirilirili . . . Ti . . . Ti . . . ," which were her lyrics to an essay in coloratura vocalism.

The doyenne of all the grandes dames was surely Mrs. Siegmund Stern, sister of Eugene Meyer, the famous publisher of the Washington *Post*. She had, among other large contributions, donated a park to the city. In a particularly beautiful spot, named Stern Grove in her honor, free concerts were given Sunday afternoons, one of which I attended as soon as I was free. The visit gave me fair samples of Mrs. Stern's hospitality and of Merola's versatility. The picnic provided by the lady's retainers would have satisfied the most demanding gourmet, but the music performed by members of the local orchestra might not have had the same effect. Merola's way with the baton was graphically described by some musicians, always acid critics of conductors, as consisting of only two basic beats — clockwise and counterclockwise. Yet he was generally liked because his conducting was not merely an outlet for a mean personal power drive. When he conducted one or two operas during his season, he did it in a paternalistic rather than domineering manner, beaming with at least one eye at the singers, highly pleased with everything that was going on and probably counting the money he was saving by doing the job himself. He knew his limitations and never attempted the sophisticated scores of *Otello* or *Gianni Schicchi*, remaining quite happy with a *Traviata* or a *Cavalleria*.

His forebodings about trouble with Reiner proved correct. There was a new wrinkle to the way in which the conductor's complaints and demands were presented. Reiner completely by-passed Merola, for whom he showed open contempt, and made direct contact with Robert Watt Miller, the board president. Miller was a rich socialite, much smarter than he appeared at first glance. He listened patiently to the indignant Reiner — or to other incensed guest directors — calmed the troubled visitor, and later consulted his general manager to solve the problem. It was Reiner's sport to discredit Merola in toto, an effort that failed. He also tried to steal rehearsal time

allotted to *Pelléas*. I caught him hands down when he asked
Merola to give him time "*Pelléas* does not need." At this
moment I simply yelled until everything was back to normal.
Reiner, though an outstanding conductor, caused similar situations with all his managers and is, a few years after passing
on, not at all recognized for the superlative musician he was.
Merola, not as easily discredited as Reiner thought, continued
and finished his days shortly after the thirty-first opera season
of the company he had founded.

From the moment I knew about my *Pelléas* assignment I
became deeply involved with the work. I not only studied text
and music, I started once more to go through Debussy's entire
lifework. While my Viennese musical education had been very
fine in many respects, it was not all-encompassing. The prevailing attitude, which was to brainwash students with the absolute superiority of the German-Austrian main line of composers, implied that all else was inferior and hardly worth a
second look. My gratitude for this opportunity to immerse
myself in one of the greatest non-German works was matched
by my awareness that I was on the spot and must do it better
than a native Frenchman. The previous winter had already
shown me that the general view of American cognoscenti was
the opposite of mine. It was commonly thought that a German
background disqualified a conductor for superior interpretation
of French or Italian music and vice versa.

I had spent part of my summer vacation in Brittany in order
to absorb the atmosphere that was such an ideal setting for
Maeterlinck's tragedy. Listening all day to the language and
looking out on this stark landscape guided me to what I still
believe was a deeper penetration of a mysterious work than a
simple reading and playing would have given me.

As soon as I began rehearsals in San Francisco I noticed that
the orchestra (identical with the Symphony) showed an easy
familiarity with the French style, a tribute to Pierre Monteux,

music director since 1935. The thinness of the strings, a great
drawback in German or Russian music, is so common to French
orchestras that it was calculated in Debussy's scoring and did
not detract from the general excellence of the instrumental
performance, particularly the woodwinds. These all-important
parts were played wonderfully, with perhaps one reservation.
The excessive zeal of the first bassoonist produced attacks that
sounded to me like the creaking of an unoiled door hinge. This
opinion was not shared by one Leopold Stokowski, who, after
hearing our Los Angeles performance, sent me a message of
praise with a special query about the "marvelous bassoon effects" I had obtained. This was an important lesson for me.
If a Stokowski, with his extraordinary ear for sonorities, considered those creaking noises a novel effect it meant that certain
rough sounds could be heard only at closest quarters.

Indeed, a conductor hears many things that cannot be detected even in the first row. I became convinced of this when
comparing my impressions of famous violinists while standing
next to them on stage with what I heard sitting in the audience.
What are scratchy attacks at a distance of three feet become
merely vigorous sonorities of great clarity after they float across
the footlights.

Our *Pelléas* turned into a rare success. Besides the excellent
orchestra we had a most imaginative production and, as was to
be expected from Merola, superb artists — Janine Micheau and
Georges Cathelat — for the leads. All this showed me most explicitly what makes a great impresario: shrewd guesswork, a bit
of risk-taking, plus that infinitely important factor — luck.
Merola had that with me. He had no right to assume that a
twenty-six-year-old novice, about whom he knew nothing,
could do justice to that complex score.

What made San Francisco so valuable to me over the next
three years was Merola's broad-mindedness. He let me conduct
works the Met would not assign to me. I was already labeled a
Wagnerian specialist, just as my mentor Bodanzky had been

pigeonholed before me. I had not foreseen the result of my early publicity, which was such that thirty-seven years later, when I appear as guest conductor, a symphony orchestra will still ask for some Wagner!

Not that I don't admire Wagner as the greatest nineteenth-century genius, but I hate to be confined to a limited repertoire, no matter how grand. The tendency to neatly delimit this pianist as a Chopin player and that conductor as a Mozart specialist is a symptom of a scientific age excelling through specialization. Music, as I never tire of repeating, is an encyclopedic art. I have found, indeed, that the self-styled Bach and Berg experts often prove in the end not to be so very hot in their demarcated precincts.

To my immense joy I was asked right after *Pelléas* to conduct *Fidelio* in San Francisco the following year. Even after forty years I still consider it a privilege to prepare and perform some of these milestones of our culture. A dream cast with Flagstad, Melchior, and Kipnis would be singing, Herbert Graf was the stage director, and a magnificent set was already on the drawing board. Other details around that season were less pleasant for me. Merola asked me at the time of issuing the written contract to yield one of my *Walküre* performances to Edwin McArthur, Flagstad's piano accompanist. The great soprano had made it a precondition of her coming to San Francisco that he be engaged to conduct all *Tristan* performances and one *Walküre* repeat. This reduced my own activities to a total of five evenings in six weeks, a ridiculous schedule for a young man. It seemed strange that a manager could be told by a singer, no matter how distinguished, who should conduct which opera and when. Subsequent history tells us that not only Merola but Johnson and Bing bowed to similar demands. My own definition of a twentieth-century prima donna is "a singer who dictates the choice of her conductor and his choice of the tempi of her music."

After my fourth consecutive visit I did not return to the West Coast opera season until 1948, when things were no longer as gay as before, perhaps myself included. The war had something to do with it: intercompany relations were less cordial, union rules stricter, and pay scales higher. Merola was getting on in years and showing the strain.

One particular story from my days with Gaetano Merola and the San Francisco Opera would be fitting material for a film. I found him in the chorus room at the piano while a squat young man sang very loudly the well-known melodies of Canio. Merola waved me to sit down while the coaching lesson continued. He tried to guide the tenor to more cultured sonorities, explaining how he might better control the unruly stentorian noises of his naturally good voice. After another ten minutes he had had enough and bade the man farewell with the admonition "Bisogna studiare, caro, sempre studiare."

When we were alone he unfolded the saga of a young motorcycle policeman named George Stinson. A year before, this fellow had sung a few Irish ballads at a stag gathering in the Bohemian Grove, a socially exclusive country club to which not only Merola but many of his directors and supporters belonged. Several of these well-lubricated men thought so much of the voice that the vision of a latter-day Irish-American Caruso seemed only too logical. With spontaneous generosity, money was pledged to stake the fellow to a leave of absence, a six-month study period in Milan and the wherewithal for his large brood to keep going during the interim, until the great opera houses of the world overwhelmed him with lucrative engagements. Merola, of course, was asked to see to all necessary technicalities. "And whaddayou know, de fellow away from ome goes to de bordello instead of de lessons, he drink vino rosso and eat pasta, he gain dirty pounds and come back knows nodding and I hava scheduled his debut as Canio. Now it isa up to me to teacha de fello de role." Dress rehearsal was three weeks away from the moment we had this little talk!

When the moment came it was quite apparent that one general runthrough with orchestra — the customary preparation for anything as familiar as *Pagliacci* — would not do, and, for the first and probably last time in the history of that company, a second full-dress rehearsal was set for the next evening. And then the great night! Every member of the company had secured an invitation to some director's box, or any kind of standing room admission, to see the circus troupe's little cart appear from the wings with Stinson standing atop beating his drum.

Was it nervousness in a man of great strength or too much tension? When the cart stopped stage center, Canio gave the drum a hit and the drumstick with fist and forearm went right through one drumhead, shattered the second, and reappeared on the far side. The owner was helplessly stuck, not knowing how to get back to first base. I can't tell what happened next. I left Miller's box as fast as I could and headed for the bar. When I asked about Stinson a few months later, he was back on his motorcycle.

Bob Miller, perennial president of the opera company, was among the Stinson sponsors. He looms as the strongest personality among the gallery of trustees and board members with whom I had to deal during my many years with musical organizations in America.

In Bob's make-up was a streak of the maverick that was most attractive, setting him apart from the textbook socialite. He matured late, having lived in enforced idleness until his father died and all sorts of chairmanships became vacant for him to occupy. After he turned fifty and became active his earlier drinking problem was solved for good.

His favorite haunt was backstage, and it was the rule rather than the exception that he got up during his wife's preopera dinner parties and left for the War Memorial, where he wandered among stagehands, choristers, and other participants, never taking off his Homburg, which irritated the superstitious theater people, who frown on hats as a jinx.

After Merola's death he kept Kurt Herbert Adler — who had been first a superlative chorus master and later an indispensable opera administrator during Merola's decline — but refused him the appointment as successor to the general directorship until he promised not to double as conductor. Miller had been appalled by the clockwise-counterclockwise exhibitions of Merola and, expecting nothing better from his successor, insisted on a pledge of abstention. This was duly made; Adler was confirmed and did not conduct until after the mourning period of Miller's death.

While there was not a single trait Miller and I had in common, I count him among the very small band of my real friends. He had that rare quality of saying what he thought in words that would have been rude in a poor man but in a wealthy one were considered charming frankness. I like it in all brackets.

My favorite among Bob's innumerable abrasive comments came in 1963 when I visited San Francisco with the Boston Symphony on a transcontinental tour. The symphony manager of the San Francisco Orchestra, our hosts, was fussing over the sad delay in the construction of a new acoustical shell, designed to improve the sound from the stage of the War Memorial. He apologized to us, having hoped that it might be baptized during our concert.

I thought during the Third Brahms that everything on stage was perfectly satisfactory and had my opinion confirmed when Bob Miller, whom I hadn't seen in several years, walked into my dressing room, Homburg and all, not even saying hello but merely exclaiming exuberantly: "I knew it! I knew it! We don't need a new shell, we need a new orchestra."

In 1971, I was in San Francisco to start a tour with an English orchestra and got interviewed on the radio for a program eulogizing Miller. I caught myself at the last minute, realizing that I was about to tell that story — which would not have set well with the local musicians.

After 1948, when I was involved as permanent conductor of

a symphony orchestra in Rochester, my visits to the San Francisco Opera became more difficult to schedule and the intervals precluded any continuity. Three more visits, in 1951, 1955, and 1957, were part of my quest for change of pace, for enlargement of my repertoire, but then I stopped accepting the engagement, especially because Adler — notwithstanding our continued personally cordial relations — is not a man for whom I chose to work. Thus the delightful Bay City and its attractive opera season have remained incidental, while New York's Met has become the nearest thing to my second home, musically speaking.

I guess that the initial welcome I received in New York, the chance for a refugee to make a loudly echoing debut two months after arrival, implanted a feeling of gratitude and of belonging that still lives in me — three and a half decades and five managements later.

## The Met

Returning to New York from my San Francisco debut in 1938 I looked forward to the pleasant prospect of rehearsing *Tannhäuser* and *Lohengrin*. Having taken on these two operas unchanged for the previous spring tour, I now decided to open up as much of the formerly deleted music as I possibly could. *Lohengrin* had suffered the most, with eleven portions of the score omitted, some quite substantial, others short and left out only to spare a moment of special difficulty by making a detour around it. My indignation about this kind of violation of a masterpiece has never abated. Either do a great work as it is or leave it alone.

Three sources are responsible for the generally accepted system of cutting. Singers may demand the omission of tiring portions in their roles, always explaining that they are non-essential. Stage directors, primarily convinced that the action is all that matters, tend to abbreviate ensemble pieces that are static and boring to them. Finally, there are managers all over the world who suggest shortening for reasons of economy. More music means more rehearsal time means more money. Or more music means longer performances may mean over-time means more money. It looked to me as if not one but all three of these influences had left their marks on poor *Lohengrin*.

There was no formal music director at the Met, and there-fore nobody ever checked on what I was doing. The chorus master was ecstatic at having more music for the chorus to sing, the librarian opened up the pages taped together in the orches-tra material, and the coaches prepared the understudies as I had bidden them. The stars never came to rehearsal and found out what was up only a day prior to the performance, when they had their runthrough of a role. So it happened that manage-ment got the first inkling that something was different only when the second intermission in my first performance came considerably later than the timing book showed. A friend told me after a few days how at eleven twenty-three, the moment when the final curtain used to come down, the three managers assembled in Johnson's office to sit and stare at the moving minute hand of the wall clock, morbidly fascinated by the ghastly puzzle of what to do if the show ran beyond midnight and into the worst fate, overtime payment to several hundred people, orchestra, chorus, stagehands, ushers, and sundry others. When at eleven fifty-one a messenger from backstage an-nounced that the final chord was around the corner, the father-land was saved for the moment.

Several of the leading singers protested the opened cuts, which made their roles longer and more strenuous, but, after realizing that artistic integrity in this case did not mean higher expense, the management backed me up.

Yet, unbeknownst to me, a campaign by several of the stars to unseat me did begin at that time. A quick history of opera in America may be useful to appreciate my mounting difficulties.

Grand opera had been an imported European luxury and developed in the United States not as an indigenous form of entertainment but strictly as a series of guest stints. In the 1920s it was still the rule for an entire group of German singers to travel on the same boat across the Atlantic, do their six or eight weeks, and return, again en masse, to Europe. The original languages in performance did their bit to keep everything distant and so the principal foci of interest were the great voices. Even Toscanini had to swallow this bitter pill, and I believe that it was responsible for his violent resentment of the whole Met. Why would he have said repeatedly that the Met must burn down before opera can flourish in America? Of course the Met was only a symbol. The main problem was — and still is — that opera is a sporadic enterprise in the United States, and a permanent institution is the first essential opera needs to be an ensemble art. It was quite clear to me even at age twenty-six that Bodanzky had attempted to give battle at some early time in his tenure but had thrown in the towel long ago.

I went along the road of my own convictions, with the added awareness that my admired Maestro was watching. Not that I pioneered any novel philosophy, I simply went about preparing an opera as European companies did.

Cuts were by no means the only blot I tried to wash out.

At the Easter *Parsifal* during the previous spring I had noticed that Melchior, in the protagonist's role, left the stage during the grail's unveiling in act one. He stationed himself so cleverly on the side that at some point, with the help of a kind electrician's dimmer, he slipped out, resting for a good half-hour in his room before returning on stage in the nick of time before being addressed by Gurnemanz. Since the latter's query to the "innocent youth" means "Do you know what you have witnessed?" and quite obviously Parsifal–Melchior had witnessed nothing while being in his dressing room, the end of the

act — and all that followed — became senseless. For the bulky
tenor the only criterion was that standing still in a short tunic
tired his feet and was hazardous for his health. After every
performance the press howled in protest, but the management,
while very unhappy, did not have the guts to take Melchior out
of the cast, although René Maison, the alternate, was a much
finer artist for that role, albeit not with a voice like Melchior's.

I never had a functioning DEW (distant early warning)
built in my system. At some point in my second year, Mr.
Ziegler, for whom I had the greatest affectionate respect, said
in his very mild, low-keyed tone, "We in America do not go for
slow tempi." I was fully aware that my pacing was not as fast
as Bodanzky's, in whose conducting I detected more impatience
and hurry than breadth of Wagner. Yet I would never have
qualified for the adjective "heavy-handed," which is the ear-
mark of the proverbial Teutonic Wagner style. By the standards of that period my whole approach was never slow. (Standards of pacing do change almost as if it were a matter of
fashion. For instance, the thirties were faster than the sixties
in musical pacing.) I took Ziegler's remark as a harmless philosophical comment and never caught the implicit message that
trouble was brewing, with some great singing stars pouring the
fuel on the fire. I paid no attention and never for a moment
contemplated speeding up to please Ziegler's American penchant
for faster tempi. The season seemed to go by without incidents
or accidents, and at its close I felt that I had consolidated my
position, my debut had not been a fluke, and I could look into
the future with confidence.

In the summer of 1939 I got married, and after a Canadian
holiday, followed by my second San Francisco Opera season, we
returned to New York to find Bodanzky quite ill. The Met
asked me to kindly rehearse his operas in addition to my own,
which meant for the first two weeks a daily schedule of six hours
conducting, involving perhaps seven or eight operas, a formidable task of mental juggling. The schedule was tight enough to

make even Thanksgiving morning a workday. At intermission Ziegler, tears streaming down his face, came to my room and announced that Bodanzky had passed away that morning.

For the economically hard-pressed management it was the easy thing to do nothing and let me carry on both repertoires, which I, with the bold and silly courage of youth, did. The season opened and, flushed with the feeling of being indispensable and made of iron, I conducted everything from soup to nuts.

One afternoon, a few hours before the first seasonal *Götterdämmerung,* which was also my first public essay of this awesome score, the doorbell rang. I was told a journalist outside wanted to get my reaction to statements made by Melchior in an interview printed that afternoon. New York then still boasted nine dailies, and I forget which one had carried the tenor's brain child. I sent word that I had seen and read nothing, which meant that I had nothing to say. Almost at once the phone rang, and it never stopped. It was first the Met, then Constance Hope and again Constance Hope and the Met until evening when we had to leave for the opera house.

The Met was worried lest I say something to make the situation, still not clear to me, even worse. Constance Hope was more than embarrassed, as she was Melchior's press agent as well as mine. From the several calls one could deduct that Melchior had stated with much fanfare how I, my talent notwithstanding, was too young to take charge of the entire German repertoire and a more experienced conductor — Reiner was mentioned — should be brought in to replace Bodanzky. The original interviewer, in the good tradition of American fair play, had gone to Edward Johnson for a comment before printing Melchior's. The Met's general manager, a man of temperament and spirit, blew his top and lost control of his vocabulary, saying that Melchior was typical of "old boats" objecting to a young man of unorthodox attainments — and more in my defense. The afternoon's highlight came when my wife announced that Lauritz was on the phone, asking to speak with me. I refused, having nothing to say to him and not wishing to upset myself a few hours before a performance. It was no use — my wife got rattled and nervous, and I had to say something to Melchior, who would not hang up without having talked to me. So I went and said, "Hello, Lauritz," which was echoed with "Hello, Erich." Silence. I waited, he waited. I was sure that he expected a flood of abusive language, and when it did not come he finally spoke: "Isn't this terrible?" "What is terrible?" I wanted to know. "What Johnson said about me." Me being him, Melchior, the old boat. I then wanted to know what he thought of his own statement, to which he said: "Lies, nothing but lies by people who wish to tear us apart." Us being him and me. We had sat together at parties and on tour but there was no trace of close intimate friendship. I felt that this phone conversation was becoming useless, as he was obviously trying to get out of a corner and was instead involving himself more deeply with foul excuses, so I said something conventional and civil to him, conveying that I would not shoot him from the rostrum during *Götterdämmerung*.

American sportsmanship turned that evening into one of my greatest personal triumphs, and the nationwide publicity that followed made my name better known than ten consecutive seasons of uneventful good work could have.

One of my friends in the Met orchestra informed me by phone that the musicians would organize an extra fervent demonstration to back me, and, indeed, each time I appeared for the next act, I received the biggest acclaim from everybody, public and orchestra vying with each other for length and decibels of clapping and shouting.

The upshot of these noisy approvals was that each intermission became unduly extended and the show ran into a few minutes of overtime, which the management refused to pay, claiming that the musicians themselves had helped to prolong the evening. It was quite obviously a manifestation buttressing management's position, and yet when it came to paying a few hundred dollars, they tried to wiggle out of it. The dramatist Johann Nestroy once said that some people consider three pennies a game too much and prefer to play for the honor rather than loose a few small coins.

Another kind of problem, more delicate and fortunately not fit for publicity, came up in the wake of Bodanzky's death. On the season's list of operas was *Fidelio,* under normal circumstances a special treat for me and particularly so after having done it with splendid results in San Francisco. And yet there was a peculiar catch about the Met's version. It had always been performed with composed recitatives replacing the spoken dialogue. The substitution of music for the original was one of the proverbial vandalisms for which the Metropolitan had been notorious in Europe. Worse, the composer of these recitatives was none other than Bodanzky. I was caught between the devil and the deep blue sea. To do them was inconceivable for me, to omit them would show me as callous, ungrateful, and cruel to the memory of the beloved elder; in short, it would be a bad public-relations job.

Ziegler helped by replacing *Fidelio* with extra performances of Flagstad's other operas. I was out scot-free.

For over a year I had lobbied with Johnson to let me conduct *Pelléas* whenever it came back to the Met. Now, with a cruel overload of assignments, the Debussy work was due for revival, and what had been intended as my third opera was, because of Bodanzky's death, my tenth score in this hectic season. I was confident of repeating my West Coast success but received instead a thorough drubbing by the New York press. Aside from a totally miscast Mélisande — a grave fault to be sure — I felt that the score was performed in the same style as in San Francisco. My "style" seemed to be the issue. It was said to concentrate too much on "design" instead of on the "color" of the scoring. These terms are imprecise and quite arbitrary, but they do denote two approaches to music in general. This blow was quite severe, because I did not wish to be a "German conductor," out of his depth in a French masterpiece.

Later, when I did more symphonic work, I found again that I was not only at home with the French "impressionists" but that I had a special affinity for their music.

If life permits one a long enough wait, many puzzles get answered. In 1971 Pierre Boulez prepared and conducted *Pelléas* at Covent Garden, and most critical descriptions of his rendition used terms quite like those applied to mine in 1939, with the small difference that the adjectives were this time part and parcel of an enthusiastic approval. I think that the lapse of thirty-two years and the novel ideas prevailing on interpretation accounted for the change in taste. It is not a flippant comment to say that musical performance is as much subject to fashion as clothing. Today this is more easily detected than in times before records existed.

My way with *Pelléas* was obviously a few years too early, but it taught me another lesson, that there are two criteria in music, one for live and another for recorded performance. In theater and concert hall, projection and dynamism are the basic elements that communicate with the antennae of listeners.

By contrast all microphone-directed music demands the most careful intimate approach, as there is obviously only a very short distance from performer to the nearest mike, which in turn projects into a machine that plays in a home rather than a large auditorium.

*Pelléas* is by any standards an intimate work, and perhaps my way with it was too alien to the large Met horseshoe.

I have never dwelt long on reverses, which in that season would have been fatal to my ability to carry on with the load. As it was, my health suffered a setback as a result of conducting seventy performances in twenty-one weeks. As soon as the spring tour was over I began to have all kinds of strange symptoms, and in my search for relief I ran into quacks, who pumped me full of useless injections until after much floundering a

Viennese nose and throat man found that my tonsils had to be removed, not a pleasant adventure at twenty-eight. The after-effects were more disagreeable still until a lengthy dental treatment cleared me up for good.

After the diverse excitements of my first three seasons, debut, full conductor, public controversy, and overwork, the fourth round in 1940–1941 was distinctly dull and anticlimactic. There was no element of novelty or of artistic improvement noticeable anywhere. One of the worst features of the Met's system, yet an essential one, consists of planned cast changes, often to an extent where no two performances are sung by the same people. The small print on the ticket stubs gives the customer notice that money will be refunded only if another opera is substituted for the announced work. But if an understudy steps in at the last moment to fill the gap because a Flagstad or a Callas reports unwell, the ticket holder is out of luck. Met casting means always to plan for doubles who are attractive artists in their own right, and that in turn means guaranteeing them appearances in the role they will be "covering." During my six years with the Met there was indeed a plethora of fine alternates, but the mere change of one artist to another brings an element of insecurity into any show and our Met performances were never overrehearsed to begin with. In my efforts to improve opera performance I was invariably frustrated and had to be content if they did not actually deteriorate. In one of my seasons I had to put up with ten different casts for ten *Tannhäuser* performances. I began to wake up to the reasons why the Met was not exactly a conductor's dream castle. But however trying the conductor's problem, there was another person who had worse to bear, the stage director.

For my first four seasons Leopold Sachse was the responsible stage director, although it was clear to nearly everyone in the know that there were no stage rehearsals and that singers ignored the calls for any blocking or dramatic rehearsals Sachse might schedule. He could play around with third understudies, who had to obey, but I doubt that Sachse ever saw Melchior except ten minutes before a performance.

Then came Lothar Wallerstein, who in Vienna was not only principal stage director but the real power in shaping all artistic policies at the opera. What he said went, and what he wanted he got — in Vienna. Now that same man saw his name on posters credited with the histrionic and visual portion of performances for which there had been not even the shadow of adequate preparation. Unlike Sachse, who from time to time had tantrums that relieved him somewhat, Wallerstein ate himself up in quiet frustration. He felt his comedown with bitterness, yet he still had to hold on to this hack job to keep body and mind together.

One of his least enviable tasks was to train the new Wagnerian heroine, Helen Traubel. In one short period, following the United States entry into the war, the Met lost both Flagstad and Marjorie Lawrence. The former went back to Norway to be with her husband; the latter, at the very moment when she would have become the leading Wagnerian soprano, was stricken by polio. The strange deity of the theater then sent us a big, handsome woman of German-American parentage out of St. Louis. Helen Traubel had a beautiful voice that soared easily over any kind of orchestral surge yet could be full of sweetness and lyricism. Here the gift of Providence stopped. Helen Traubel brought only those biological attributes with her; otherwise she had no talent and not even ambition. Her favorite posture was sitting and her favorite activity eating. She was a good soul, full of laughter, and could be a delightful companion until serious concentration on learning roles was asked of her. She became the most important person to the Met management, who hoped to keep the lucrative Wagner music dramas in the repertoire; that was possible only as long as somebody was at hand to do the great female roles.

It took four people to administer her coaching sessions: Wallerstein to explain what to do and to show her how to do it, a pianist to play the music, a prompter to give her the words, which she could not remember even with the most professional help, and me to supervise her so she did not make musical errors and forget her part while learning how to move around. As if this were not enough, she demanded from the management, probably at the urging of her husband, who was even lazier than she, that her rehearsals take place in her own suite, as she was afraid of catching cold if she took a taxi from her hotel to the opera house. There was nobody in the offices at 39th Street who had the simple guts to say "No," such were the anxieties about this lady's potential to uphold the flag of Brünnhilde and Isolde.

And so the four of us, stage director, pianist, prompter, and conductor, journeyed to the Essex House and did our best to teach her the Irish princess and the daughter of Wotan.

I recall one rehearsal when Helen stood, like the Statue of Liberty, telling an imaginary Brangäne of the time she found herself in front of Tantris with the sword in her hand to avenge the death of her betrothed — at which moment Helen stopped dead in her tracks without moving from her Statue of Liberty stance, slightly turned her head toward Wallerstein, pointed with her left hand at her high outstretched arm, and asked: "Doctor Wallerstein, tell me, what do I do with *this?*" — this being her own outstretched arm. The laughter that greeted the inquiry was a mixture of amusement and despair. She herself howled in merriment, and one could not be angry with her, for it all was too absurd and too far removed from any serious artistic endeavor. We were there to pilot by all available means a gorgeous voice through a number of great roles.

With success and greater personal security Helen developed less amiable traits. She was so bent on not getting tired that nothing could induce her to sing a portion of Isolde's role in act three that is often omitted. I hate this particular cut with a passion and pleaded with her to sing the scene in its entirety, but no words budged her. Forgetting all the formerly professed gratitude for our time and effort in coaching her, disregarding the arguments for artistic integrity and the appeals for her cooperation, she stubbornly clung to her idea of singing as little of a role as she could get away with. Crumbling like some termite-eaten structure were my lengthy efforts to present the great music dramas more completely. Of course Traubel secured and got the willing and able assistance of Melchior, whose meal ticket was again safe with an Isolde and Brünnhilde around, while I began to realize that my stay at the Met had to come to an end or I would become sooner or later a cynical routineer, complaining in private and compromising in public whatever I believed in.

## *The Green Wagon*

Traveling with large companies is both exhilarating and irritating. I am still very fond of touring and prefer any time a peripatetic engagement to a stationary one. In prewar days all was new and exciting to me; the special all-Pullman train, the hotels, the parties, and, best of all, the chance to become better acquainted with colleagues. At home base nearly everybody has some routine that he suspends on the road, allowing time and leisure for person-to-person contact that can be most stimulating.

By 1942 I had made four spring tours with the Met and one to the Northwest with San Francisco. There, after a performance in Portland, Lauritz appeared at the official supper with a pencil-thin mustache, which had us in stitches. None of the local people had seen him off stage and noticed only our merriment. When, with coffee, Lauritz took his napkin and eliminated his mustache with one swipe our hilarity was explained, but the whole joke was obviously much resented.

A year earlier, some Met members had put on a similar show. We had a long and boring train ride from Dallas to New Orleans. After a short night's sleep we were spending the daylight hours in the club cars when a bright lad got the idea of arriving in New Orleans in disguise.

A beard in 1940 was still the exception rather than the rule. For several hours while the Special sped along, our wig-maker, a fellow named Senz — without any first name known to man — looked through his precious collection of hair to find fitting adornments for the tenors and conductors. Why baritones and stage directors were not outfitted remains a mystery.

At the New Orleans terminal the company was met by the local committee, reporters and many photographers, and the usual fans and gapers. I alighted with a Landru beard, my colleague Pietro Cimara was an early edition of Ho Chi Minh, and tenor Erich Witte had been transformed into a young Brahms. Except for the camera buffs, who had a field day, our joke went down very poorly and the Met was not invited back for several years. This was not all due to the beards. Management had misjudged the musical bent of the city. They had figured on making the strongest showing with French operas, playing up the background of Louisiana. This was a mistake. The Met's French wing was always the weakest and the performances did not impress.

From the comedies of beards and mustaches I learned to be extremely careful with witty ideas when playing the provinces, where the people are sensitive and look sternly on any attempt to consider them less sophisticated than New Yorkers. The political inferiority complex about the Eastern establishment goes deeper than just politics — it is all-pervasive.

Later, when I toured with symphony orchestras, I made sure that no jokes were played in the hinterlands, and extra efforts were made to show how seriously we took our visits.

On a run-out (a term meaning that the company returns from a trip the night of the performance) from San Francisco to Sacramento with *Walküre,* the young soprano who was Ortlinde became suddenly afflicted by laryngitis and was unable to produce her battle cry, "Ho-yo-to-ho." She stood on top of the rock waving her spear while a helpful colleague backstage sang her few battle yells in a powerful soprano voice. That colleague was Kirsten Flagstad.

The largest and most monstrous house is surely Public Hall in Cleveland, which seats ten thousand. From the rear of the hall the stage setting looks as small as one of those crowded picture postcards people send from vacation with "Wish you were here" on them. I wish I had never conducted "there" it was so absurd. The voices got electronic amplification, the orchestra none. Any balance of sound was purely accidental. Yet the week of the Met in Cleveland was and still is the highlight of the local music season. Judging by personal experience it must be (things continue more or less the same) a banner period for the producers of whiskey, gin, and vodka. It is not documented by any scientific poll but only by my personal observation that at the Met evenings in Cleveland the sight of a sober male patron is as rare as a three-dollar bill.

The Met and the San Francisco companies wade into such places with all kinds of operas and perform them without any rehearsals. Sometimes the sets are totally unusable and are replaced by makeshift scenery. The Lyric in Baltimore has such a small stage (reachable only via a semicircular staircase) that for a *Walküre* in 1940 the Met had to unearth some long-discarded, junky old sets. To make a rocklike mountain, our stage crew used wooden steps and stairways from the Baltimore carpenters' shop, putting the Met's old painted canvas pieces in front. Alas, the stairways and platforms were a little too low, allowing the singers' heads to appear above the rocks like in the fun postcards made at country fairs. Schorr and Flagstad covered by landscape with only part of their torsos sticking out is quite different from what Wagner wanted. Worse happened during the last five minutes of the work. The Lyric was the proud possessor of a steam mechanism that is all-important for a great illusion during the Magic Fire Music. Unfortunately, the steam was louder than the orchestration, and added to it was a chemical that irritated mucous membranes. Every stage in the world has air drafts, and the prevailing ones in Baltimore are such that the steam moved toward the orchestra, whose members began a symphony of coughs, then toward the audience, which chimed in so prominently that the glorious final pages might have been renamed Wagner's Magic Cough Music. Undeterred by such involuntary humor, a fine Southern gentleman ran a splendid party afterward, treating us to a jeroboam of vintage champagne, to a marvelous dinner of seafood and game, and to speeches extolling the great Metropolitan Opera. There was one man who actually believed them, and that was Edward Johnson, our general manager.

The following morning we were leaving Baltimore in our special train for Boston and I was sitting with Ziegler in a compartment when Johnson appeared full of glee and swelled with pride. "Ned," he said to Ziegler, "they want *Götterdämmerung* next year." "Eddie," was Ziegler's instant reply, "this won't be possible." Crestfallen, Johnson wanted to know the reason. (Ziegler had been as appalled as I by the goings-on, a Wagnerian parody.) "How can you get the horse on stage with that semicircular stairway?" Ziegler asked. Need I confirm that we did not bring *Götterdämmerung* to Baltimore. Many years later I played a concert on that stage with the Boston Symphony and found that it barely held all the players for Mahler's Fifth Symphony, yet we had performed *Walküre* on the same boards.

If I needed a special push to make me leave the operatic fun and games it was the 1942 engagement in Boston. When the

United States entered the war in December 1941, nobody knew how show business would fare. The Boston committee sponsoring the annual Met visit was fearful of poor attendance and proposed to switch from the limited capacity of the beautiful opera house on Huntington Avenue to the vast auditorium of the Metropolitan Movie Palace downtown. It seemed more democratic and better business to offer five thousand seats at lower prices.

The tour pattern in those years was always to begin a three-night stand in Baltimore Monday and travel Thursday to the Back Bay Station, arriving in the afternoon, performing at eight that night. Sets and costumes were shipped earlier, of course.

It was the end of March, cold, windy, rainy, and the train from Baltimore was quite late. I had been free to go to Boston a day earlier and now, an hour before curtain, I walked to the theater where the unloading of trunks and instrument cases was still in full progress. Through the open shaft a lot of icy air was coming into the dressing rooms; this was later balanced by a solicitous house manager who turned the heat up. What nobody knew was that this kind act also raised the temperature in a crowded, already overheated auditorium to intolerable levels. When I went out for the prelude I felt as if the mercury had already hit ninety-six degrees Fahrenheit. Then, in chronological order: one of King Henry's pages fainted with a loud thud, Ortrud (Kerstin Thorborg) got a violent nose bleed in her scene with Elsa (Astrid Varnay), and Elsa lost her voice completely in act two and had to whisper her words, without any attempt at singing, for the rest of the act. Disaster of disasters, we discovered during intermission that there was no understudy around. Maxine Stellman, resting in her hotel for the next day's *Zauberflöte* under Bruno Walter, was awakened, came to the theater, and was persuaded to help us with act three; from her recent studies at the Juilliard School she knew only part of it but bravely agreed to sing as much as she remembered; her lines in the final scene, which she had never learned, were presented in an aleatoric and enthusiastic rescue effort by the two-dozen chorus ladies, who had assisted many an Elsa over a quarter century. It was perhaps lucky on that evening that the German text was not universally understood; Elsa's last line is *"Mein Gatte, mein Gatte"* ("my husband, my husband"), which, sung by twenty-four ladies, would indicate that Lohengrin was perhaps a polygamist.

Any claim that this was a great opera company seemed utterly preposterous to me. In later years such a story made people laugh and I myself found the odd humor in it. However, it is one thing to tell it in five minutes and another to preside over the original five-hour happening. If there was one redeeming feature of this great Boston disaster it was my firm determination to end this torturous affiliation with the Metropolitan Opera.

By pure coincidence I witnessed another semicaricature of an opening opera performance in the same theater nineteen years later. The bill was Puccini's *Turandot,* the stars were Birgit Nilsson and Franco Corelli, the conductor Stokowski, and I sat next to Bing in the audience. Toward the close of *"In questa reggia"* in act two Nilsson held the high C longer than the tenor. Furious over this, Corelli stalked off the stage without completing the lines of his role. Bing rushed back to find Corelli throwing a tantrum, cursing Nilsson and refusing to continue. But what is a *Turandot* performance without the aria *"Nessun dorma,"* which opens act three. Bing persuaded the tenor to continue and to consider taking his revenge by biting Turandot in the ear during the first kiss at the great dénouement. This appealed to Corelli, and all proceeded as suggested until at the final curtain Nilsson called for the general manager, loudly crying: "Mr. Bing, get me a veterinarian, I have the rabies."

Bing told me later that the conductor had not noticed anything at all.

*Plus ça change, plus c'est la même chose.* Opera under the
auspices of private financing, without the most lavish subsidies,
cannot be sent on the road without becoming a shambles.

## Between the Devil
## and the Deep Blue Sea

My motivation in chosing my profession was the desire to
make music on a level of excellence, such as my own abilities
would permit. Or, to put it another way: monetary considerations or thoughts of material security were not uppermost in
my mind. Yet here I was, age thirty, in a "secure" post I could
have kept for life, with my musical progress halted at that
most dreadful of way stations — routine.

I had refused to admit that repertory does compel one every
so often to play routineer. There is a difference between the
"sometimes" and the "always." I blamed myself for having
concentrated entirely on opera, for not having followed Judson's advice, and for continuing to put up with the prevailing
conditions. I saw my situation with some alarm, because in the
five seasons since coming to America I had conducted very few
concerts, perhaps a dozen, and those in summer seasons, which
lacked the distinction of a regular symphony series. Against
such an inconspicuous record my log of operatic activity
amounted to some 200 performances of seventeen different
operas. No wonder I had been tagged and put in a pigeon-
hole marked "Opera–German–Wagner." Quite suddenly it had
dawned on me that I was in a corner, and I was aware that it
would be fiendishly difficult to get out.

I had noticed that in the United States the role of conducting
symphony concerts was apparently incompatible with operatic

activity. This has changed over the decades of my own career, but still I am often asked what the difference between the two branches is. In the forties, when I was chafing to get out of the Met and had no name as a concert conductor, I blithely said that there was no difference, and deep down I still defend that answer. Music is music and conducting music is indivisible. Yet there are subtle differences.

In Central Europe there was no barrier between opera and symphony. Conductors who were exclusively symphonic were the exception. The only prominent one I can think of is Willem Mengelberg, but then there was no opera in the Netherlands.

The exclusively operatic conductor is mainly an Italian specialty, but there again the symphonic activity in the peninsula is very sparse compared to the ubiquitous *stagione lirica.*

The musical scene in the United States was — at least up to 1950 — almost completely dominated by the symphony orchestra, and the few concurrent opera seasons, spanning approximately six months, made "doubling in brass" very difficult for reasons of schedule. (I found this out when I tried to continue my guest stints in San Francisco after I became conductor of the Rochester Philharmonic.)

Musically and psychologically the principal difference and difficulty for many conductors is the presence of the human voice in opera. Oratorio singing is traditionally a quite different vocalism, performed usually by smaller voices, better musicians, and in a stationary position. The opera singer has a larger voice to control, is often innocent of musical culture, and must move around on stage. There is the further difference that the oratorio singer has the score, and on stage one sings of course from memory.

While the human voice, in the highly taxing opera parts, needs more consideration than any other instrument, the conductor ought to have no essentially changed approach or attitude. I have found that the symphony specialists who eschew opera (for a variety of alleged reasons) are also mighty rigid with their symphonies and overtures and have frequent problems when they are paired with instrumental soloists. There is a false concept abroad that an orchestra can be conducted with less flexibility than an opera.

It has been true that a number of very successful concert conductors have gone through many performances without mishap, while these same men could not possibly have arrived at the end of act one in any opera without a total breakdown. This discrepancy in ability has been apparent every time I had a group of conducting students for training and teaching. No problems show as long as they go at a Brahms symphony, but as soon as I propose the great Tamino and Speaker recitative from *Zauberflöte*, they break down.

The first important difference is acoustical. On the concert platform the conductor hears every instrument from a firm distance that never varies. In the opera house the principal musical instrument, the human voice, is here and there and everywhere. Sometimes it may not be audible at all to the conductor, which does not always mean that the orchestra is too loud. There are various reasons, some caused by a stage set that does funny things to the sound. Then a system of lip reading is the only way for the conductor to synchronize stage and orchestra. In Bayreuth I found the second act *Tannhäuser* so hopelessly poor in vocal sound that after a general rehearsal Wagner's grandson, head of the festival, ordered a ceiling from the warehouse to prevent the voices of the chorus and soloists from fleeing through the open flies. The stage designer was at fault.

The second big difference is the beat. Opera demands a large and clear manner of giving the time, while anything vaguely resembling conducting will do for a symphony orchestra. Among the symphony lions who ventured into the opera pit was Stokowski, who insisted on his style of batonless, beautiful air molding. The first verdict of the Metropolitan Opera's insiders was that the chorus sang on Chicago time while the orchestra kept Eastern Standard. The many people moving on stage cannot keep their eyes glued to the conductor. When they glance at his beat, it must be crystal clear where he is, and that constitutes a world of difference from the fixed musical forces on the stage of Carnegie Hall.

The most essential difference is the conductor's attitude toward his musical partners. The meeting of minds between musical director and singer is essential, and this may be the problem for directors who are limited to concert. They have perhaps never conceived of the principal oboist as an equal. But if he is good, he should be treated as an equal and not as a laborer on whom the boss's concept is imposed. If a conductor always makes music in partnership rather than as a dictating baton wielder, there is no difference between opera and symphony conducting.

That there are many operatic practitioners who do not know how to do a Brahms Second Symphony only means that their personalities are equally uninteresting when they conduct *Butterfly*. But then who ever really bothers to notice the quality of conducting in *Butterfly?*

Fortunately, this enforced fencing-in of conductors has changed, at first gradually, as the European émigrés arrived and showed that it was not only possible but very attractive and musically rewarding to have one man appear at the Philharmonic and at the Met in the same season.

One single factor, continuity, was much better served then; there were no guest conductors at the opera but merely five or six regulars. But in the 1973–1974 season the Met used seventeen different conductors. It is true that the number of opera performances had more than doubled, but the constant change of leadership confuses orchestra and chorus to a high degree, and this is regrettable.

## *Cleveland*

In 1942 I was in a cul-de-sac. Normally I would have placed the problem in the hands of an able agent. At some point between my first visit in 1938 and 1942 I did sign a management contract with Arthur Judson, but his vanity and arrogance never forgot nor forgave my walking out on him after our initial meeting. I certainly was no favorite of his, and as it is logical that no agent can take care of more than a small number of artists, I was among those who were mere names on a printed list. This is another fact of life that I began to comprehend early and that I have had to explain over the years to dozens of young, ambitious, and discontented artists: essentially, there are no agents or managers, only brokers.

Ever since I came to the United States the federal government has made valid attempts to break up the monopolies in music management. Whatever the Justice Department has tried, nothing has been accomplished, for the simple reason that the vast territory of the North American continent is musically totally and completely dependent upon New York City and its "establishments." Thus, in the end the fault for the provinces' slavish obedience to New York brokers must be charged to the lack of independent judgment by the music committees in the many hundreds of smaller communities. Only the universities have their own — independently thinking and selecting — managers.

In late 1942 the music director of the Cleveland Symphony Orchestra, Artur Rodzinski, announced he was leaving that post to become conductor of the New York Philharmonic. My friend Charles Marsh, whose labors in my behalf had resulted by November 1942 in my becoming Citizen Leinsdorf, felt that something ought to be done to help me and that perhaps he himself could do it. Now he entered — to my ultimate regret — the field of management and promotion.

Without bothering me with any details he enplaned for Cleveland, returning a few days later with the amazing news that he had found there a "long-lost acquaintance," a Czech immigrant named Thomas Sidlo, who, by merest coincidence, was now president of both the symphony's board and the Met's local board. Charles gave me a thumbnail sketch of this important man; a successful corporation lawyer who made his personal fortune in real-estate operations of Van Sveringen, he had recently, at a very early age, retired from active participation in business to devote himself "to the service of God" — as he put it. By invoking the Lord he meant the better things of life, which included music. But he still maintained an office with a secretary to keep an eye on Mammon, without which his services to the higher Deity might not have been possible.

According to Charles he lost no time in preliminaries and his road was not at all rough, since Sidlo, knowing me from five Met visits, had formed a most favorable opinion. He was pleasantly surprised that I would want to be a candidate for the symphony post, since to him — and this was confirmed a hundred times later on — the opera was glamour and excitement and color and evening clothes and fun, while the more puritanical instrumental affairs at Severance Hall were undoubtedly noble and necessary but not nearly as interesting and stimulating. He had also been hard put in his dealings with Rodzinski, whom he called neurotic. If Sidlo were alone, I would be appointed at once, but, like all good parliamentarians, he had a board of willful, independent people to manage and had to reconcile their differences.

As the 1942–1943 season progressed — it is astonishing to me, as I think back, how late decisions were made then — a complicated but not at all unusual picture emerged from the banks of the Cuyahoga. All organizations in the United States that deal in "culture" have a nonprofit status, permitting their wealthy patrons and supporters to donate substantially toward maintenance and continuation on a tax-deductible basis. Hence, the generous tycoons, heirs, or any other variant of the original Maecenas are the sine qua non for the existence of the great orchestras, the museums, the opera companies, and any other arty manifestations not paid for by the government.

Cleveland is "a rich city," which translates "a community where enough wealthy people can be induced to make large donations."

The boards of most, if not all, orchestras are basically made up of people who either give plenty or who have a mastery of making the "fat cats" give plenty. To the latter category belonged a Mrs. Adella Prentiss Hughes. She acted as if she *were* the Cleveland Orchestra. There were some who not only disliked Mrs. Hughes with great passion but who would almost automatically vote against anything and anyone she promoted. She was, like many domineering women, truly formidable, full of vitality, peremptorily decisive, musically knowledgeable — which made her part of a small board minority — and so direct as to be considered by softer and less-outspoken people rather tactless. At first it was considered a boon, then a drawback, that she became leader of the Leinsdorf faction. There were two other groups on the board, one for George Szell under Percy Brown and one for Vladimir Golschmann, whose candidacy was supported by the richest and most generous donors, the Dudley Blossoms.

All told it was a very mixed bag of directors who would vote and a difficult parliament, in which Tom Sidlo sat on the woolsack. This was totally different from the New York scene, which was dominated by old families and old money, with a proportional representation of "Our Crowd" members. The Cleveland board was mostly made up of immigrants who had made within their lifetimes huge fortunes they now wished to share in a way peculiarly and solely American: by supporting something worthy, of which they knew little or nothing but which had always loomed as the "Good Life" and by paying back the opportunities and windfalls of their own business careers.

Several of them were on my side, and when, after much juggling by Sidlo, the votes were counted, there was a three-way result: nobody had an absolute majority, but I had the largest percentage and the appointment as music director for three years.

There was nothing wrong with this; it was as legitimate a way to become a permanent conductor as it is for a politician to win office with a margin of 40-30-30.

I might have been in Cleveland a good long time had it not pleased the armed forces to desire my expertise in strategy, tactics, and logistics just when I began my new situation in the fall of 1943.

My elation over having made the "difficult" jump from opera to symphony was very short-lived, as various complications appeared almost instantly on the horizon. As the 1942–1943 season drew to a close in early spring, I received repeated notice of musicians leaving the orchestra for the navy band. A most enticing deal was offered to instrumentalists by the naval command, which saw an opportunity of forming a splendid musical group in the capital for the duration of the war. Instead of taking the chance of landing in the infantry or being a mail clerk in the service forces, any musician could enlist for three years. Many young and splendid players did, for the best reason imaginable: staying out of combat. To me this meant the headache of making replacements from a vastly reduced pool of musicians. If this were not enough, Rodzinski had asked two key men, the principal violist, Lincer, and the first cellist, Leonard Rose, to accompany him to New York. On the other hand, he left me most generously a concertmaster who was an unmitigated nuisance.

Tossy Spivakovsky was a case. Later on, when he could, he left orchestral playing and made a solo career. As "leader" he was badly miscast. Having a totally unorthodox way of holding the bow and favoring fingerings that suited his peculiar hands, he still insisted on imposing his ways upon the other strings, causing resentment and negative feelings, some of which naturally rubbed off on me.

All these problems notwithstanding, my first season started very well. (This I found documented much later when a journalist researched files and old clippings while preparing a festschrift for the orchestra's fiftieth birthday in 1967.)

Concerts were in pairs, Thursday and Saturday nights. It was good not to have the traditional Friday matinees, the bane of all American symphony orchestras, attended as they are by a sellout crowd of gloved elderly ladies, whose preconcert chatter has more strength than their applause. My first program was purely orchestral, but for the second we had the collaboration of Rudolf Serkin. That was Thursday, October 14, 1943. On the fifteenth the morning mail delivered a letter bringing me "Greetings from the President." This time it was the President of the United States, and it meant my reclassification from a deferred status to I–A.

All my life I have had a curvature in the lower spine, a weak back, and not very excellent feet — the classic case of a body that is generally not considered ideal for marching or crawling or firing from the prone position, the curricula of basic military training. It was also a fact that several of my younger colleagues had been rejected by the draft for such arcane reasons as maladjustment, all of which made it appear logical that my reclassification was not going to be followed up by an actual induction into military service. That was a grave miscalculation. All my rejected colleagues had presented themselves to a New York draft board, while I was now a well-known person in a provincial town where attention is paid to many details for which the metropolitan bustle of New York has no time.

I suspected then and had it confirmed later that it was publicity and only publicity that put me into uniform. One of the principal calamities was that Mrs. Hughes lost her nerve and began to chatter all over town that there was "nothing to worry about" since she knew that my orthopedic problems precluded an actual draft. In a time of stress, when men were taken away from their jobs and their families, such idle talk must have smelled of a fix. The clincher came when the senior music critic of the Cleveland *Plain Dealer,* Herbert Elwell, not exactly my most ardent booster to start with, mentioned in the closing paragraph of his concert review that there was no cause to worry about the uninterrupted continuation of the season's musical direction, since "it is known that the medical board of the Selective Service will reject Mr. Leinsdorf." By some ingenious timing this gratuitous comment appeared on the Friday morning I was making my way downtown to answer a notice from the medical board.

During the lengthy procedure preceding my medical discharge from the army I got acquainted with a colonel from the Disposition Board, who confirmed that a people's army had the same need for an "image" as any politician or other public figure and that inducting prominent men was a test of a democracy's incorruptibility. Anything in print, even less obvious and explicit than Elwell's prophecies, made it a certainty that the candidate would be accepted, as long as he had to the lay eye two arms and two legs. "They don't examine them, they only count them!" the colonel said.

I have never been given to paranoid fantasies, but I still have a feeling that there was some funny business going on in the weeks between my reclassification and my examination. One day the *Plain Dealer* printed a letter from a woman who took issue with a gossip column in which it had been murmured that my back and feet were not in order. Her husband was drafted in spite of having "worse troubles," she wrote. I wondered about the attitude of the paper in printing this. Only a few months earlier a number of important local citizens had expressed their negative vote, and just as Mrs. Hughes could talk a lot, so might others.

At the end of December I left Cleveland for Columbus, from where I was assigned for my entire military career to Camp Lee, Virginia. Of the army I have only good things to say. As soon as the public-relations concerns were taken care of, every effort was made to avoid any damage to my health, and I was even excluded from exercises I would have gladly taken.

The whole thing was a total waste. I lost a post, and the government spent a lot of money and man-hours in my behalf without much visible return. In the long run I got over it, but in 1944 it left me with an empty feeling of uselessness. If there had been any reason to think I was doing anything at all for the war effort I would have felt better. As it was I had literally nothing to do for at least nine months. That was the time it took for the legal machine to grind slowly toward my medical discharge. But I had, for once, a lot of time and leisure to think. Camp Lee was called a country club; it *was* a relatively comfortable place and I, after six weeks of basic — which in my case was basic no-training — had permission to live off the post. The whole period was Time Suspended. Even one week before my discharge I could not be sure when — or if — it would take place. In at least one respect such enforced idleness is salutary. It shows even the vainest how things go on, apparently none the worse for one's absence, and the deflating effects on the ego are immensely healthy. It was a chance to get wise at a relatively young age.

Shortly after my induction I turned thirty-two. There was one son, born in July 1942. Another child arrived in July 1944 while I was at Lee, from where I traveled on a short furlough in military style to Long Island to see the new offspring. Otherwise it was easily the longest summer I have ever spent. According to optimistic expectations I should have been discharged within two months of induction, especially since the army had abolished "Limited Service" as useless, yet I had been kept in a state of unlimited nonservice.

In Cleveland the management had been hard put to complete the season on a hand-to-mouth basis. Up to my actual passing the medical exam the manager, Carl Vosburgh, could not engage guest conductors because I might not leave. When the decision was in, the time was very late, and first-line conductors were not sitting around awaiting the chance to fill in for draftees. Now, in the middle of 1944, I saw the Cleveland organization's whole problem clearly and did not like one bit what I recognized as the alternatives. This time a whole season and maybe more had to be filled with conductors, and I had no illusions whatever that anybody would make great efforts to "hold" my post. Mine was not the job of a salesman or a secretary, which one could manage with temporary help. This was a first-line symphony orchestra, and what with all the wartime replacements of musicians in service, it was an odd lot badly in need of a good, steady, permanent conducting hand.

By midsummer I had turned fatalist, amusing myself by volunteering to give political orientation lectures to the troupes, who at Lee were mostly postal clerks and cooks, whose interest in the political ramifications and worldwide implications of the war was, to put it mildly, marginal.

Musically the high point of my service period came one fine day when another enlisted man, Victor Babin, and I were asked by our detachment commander to arrange the potted palms as an embellishment to the auditorium.

We did have a band training unit at Lee, headed by two captains who were high school music teachers. They treated me beautifully and most kindly but saw to it that my activities were never too close to their assignment of training bandsmen. As in civilian life, they were apprehensive lest I take their jobs away. That this was the last thought on my mind they could not have possibly guessed.

One of the nicer changes occurred when we got a new company commander, George Huddleston. He was a church organist in civilian life and as antimilitarist in attitude as one can be. He made the remaining months of my sojourn at Lee ever more agreeable, and after we all got back to our other lives he and I remained good friends.

When, after many interviews and examinations and x rays and bureaucratic delays and exhausted indifference in my heart, discharge came, it was so sudden that not a soul among my family, friends, and acquaintances was prepared. When I drove out of Camp Lee for the last time my immediate goal was a post office to wire the Cleveland Orchestra.

It was only a short time before the 1944–1945 season was scheduled to open. Of course it had been set, down to the smallest detail, yet I hoped that at least some of my colleagues would show generosity and withdraw. That there were various laws guaranteeing to returning servicemen their positions, with all emoluments and seniorities, did not interest me in the least. Ours is a world of a different spirit, and if one is not wanted, it is only demeaning and embarrassing to insist on the letter of a contract. That was my attitude, and since nobody made a move I had nothing on my calendar for the season ahead.

Arthur Judson, who was agent for every one of the guest conductors, might have raised a finger to do something in my behalf, but he did not. My old friend and first American manager, Constance Hope, attempted to help by writing Sidlo that in her opinion I was not only entitled to an immediate resumption of my duties as conductor but that it was against the existing laws to keep the arrangements for 1944–1945 as they had been made. From her well-meant and brave effort I have learned how a blunt, common-sense approach can misfire when it is directed at smart legal minds. Not only was her letter of no effect, it led to a request from Sidlo to her, demanding the formal written withdrawal of her letter or the Cleveland organization would not negotiate the details of my "third" season,

1945–1946. The original contract was for three years. What was there to negotiate?

That showed me where I stood. It was obvious, at least to me, that my absence had given the board members who had voted "nay" more than enough time and substance to insist on their candidates. When we finally got around to the detailed arrangements for 1945–1946, it was quite clear how the dice had fallen. One third of the concerts for Szell, one third for Golschmann, and one third for me. I had no choice but to agree, as we were all "represented" by the same man, who would take the same commission (or a larger one?) from the other two conductors as well. Where was his incentive to fight, for me or for anyone else, to come from if his final take was sure in either case?

I balked only when Vosburgh presented me with a similar division of assignments for the contracted recordings. The orchestra had a firm commitment from Columbia for three releases — still the 78 r.p.m.s in those days — and when I learned of the plan to three-divide these too, I declared to Vosburgh that I would rather resign altogether at that very moment; my ultimatum was to have all recordings, or the title and post of music director would be at their disposal at once, without any third season.

Since I got, after a short wait, exactly what I insisted on, the assumption is that an equally insistent agent could have done a lot after my discharge in 1944.

As it was, the Met needed me for a number of performances during the winter of 1944–1945, and in April I traveled to Cleveland for the final pair of concerts that had been left open in the expectation that I might conduct them, even on furlough if still in the army. As it was, the constellation of all my Cleveland enterprises seemed poor. I rehearsed my program, with Bruckner's Fourth Symphony as the pièce de résistance, and, as usual, was resting between the Thursday-morning rehearsal and the evening's concert when Sidlo rang me with the information that President Roosevelt had just died. It was April 12, 1945.

The concert, after a cordial welcome for me, was a subdued affair. Aside from the news of the day, Bruckner in 1945 was not exactly the most popular of composers with the subscribers of the Cleveland Orchestra.

During my short visit I met with Vosburgh to make detailed arrangements for that one third of a season to which I had agreed in lieu of what was called my third season. I had decided by then not to bring my family to Cleveland, not to establish a household, and not to wrestle with an obviously split board over a post that had been put into jeopardy by the curious happenings of the past two years.

Here I am sure that many of my colleagues would have acted differently, taking up the fight on the diplomatic front with every possible weapon at their disposal. One of these is Presence in the Community with Family. This leads to an active social life and the same continuous campaigning we read about in the political columns. The doorbell ringing and the handshaking of the electioneering candidate are in our world the cocktails, suppers, and, first and foremost, the luncheons, at which short speeches from the dais show to the citizens that the musician is "just another good guy."

I do not look down on such methods for anyone who considers a position and what it entails important enough. I simply do not.

It is in the overall concept where people differ. I have my own kind of admiration for those who act in ways contrary to my personal code. And my code is not one I try to impose on others. It is, I am fully aware, a code of personal inertia, of personal independence, and of insisting that music and social life be separate. I decided to live alone in a sublet, do my concerts, and let the chips fall.

From the opening concert on I felt free and easy and gave some of my best performances. When I arrived for the second

of my installments, Sidlo informed me that they had decided to
hire George Szell. When many years later I read Barbara Tuch-
man's *Stilwell and the American Experience in China,* I found
the appropriate quotation for my first excursion into the major
symphony realm: "We took a hell of a beating."

## *A Cleveland Postscript*

The rise and artistic growth of the Cleveland Orchestra
during Szell's twenty-four-year tenure is now musical history.
From my own brief involvement I know enough to appreciate
that Szell was perhaps the only man known in the music world
who could have made that always very good orchestra into one
of the three or four greatest in the West.

More than musical qualifications are necessary to produce
such results. Rodzinski in the decade of his leadership always
wanted more string players, begging, arguing, threatening, bargaining — to no avail. Szell got it without delay. From the day
Severance Hall was first opened nobody thought much of its
acoustical properties. Szell got the stage rebuilt with somewhat
improved results. Under Rodzinski the orchestra played in New
York once every few seasons. Szell established annual cycles of
five programs that became the most successful orchestral concerts of the New York winter. In 1962, when Lincoln Center
inaugurated Philharmonic Hall, the Philadelphia and Boston
orchestras switched from their regular Carnegie Hall visit to
the new auditorium against the better musical judgment of
their two music directors (Ormandy and myself). But this decision was pressed by forces beyond us music experts, the inter-
locking directorates in the realm of high finance. Yet Szell
never followed suit and remained in Carnegie Hall. He stated
after playing one of the four opening evenings at the new hall
that his best advice would be to tear it down right away. This

made him not very popular but highly respected. And in 1976 the hall will be torn down and rebuilt.

Szell had the knack of speaking not only the language of the musician but that of the banker and academic as fluently and as well. The rarity was that a man of great erudition and intellectual interests should have the patience to deal with symphony board members, not an entertaining lot as a rule. To deal effectively with that part of the Establishment is a special ability, and my own appreciation of it is the stronger for never having excelled at it myself.

It took Szell twenty-three years and the strong urging of a mutual friend to invite me back as guest conductor for the 1970–1971 season, and then for the total of one pair of concerts. But in the summer of 1970 he died, and we never got a chance to go over past history together.

With all my awareness of his singular merits, no great affection marked our relationship. Our paths had crossed on several occasions, we had discussed music as one would among colleagues, and there the matter ended. Yet what happened right after his death affected me considerably. The orchestra, in a dispute over salaries, went on a strike that lasted six weeks and delayed the season's opening. If this was intended as a memorial for the departed who brought world fame to the orchestra, I did not think much of it. While his widow packed up the household she could read in the papers such statements as: "The orchestra must have a voice in the appointment of the next music director, not to run again into such authoritarian rule as with Szell."

My first return to the Cleveland Orchestra since 1946 was, by some strange force, arranged like an extra special event. It was at Carnegie Hall in a program that — a year earlier — Szell had made for himself but which suited me for peculiar reasons. The first half was all-Mozart, for which I need no persuader, and after intermission it was Bruckner's Fourth, the same work with which I had made my inauspicious reentry on the day of Roosevelt's death. Now, in February 1971, it was as happy and gratifying an evening as I can recall.

One month later, in March 1971, I finally walked into Severance Hall, almost to the day twenty-five years after my exit. Since then a warm relationship with the orchestra and frequent guest-conducting appearances have been established, culminating in 1973 with my participation in the orchestra's tour to Oceania.

I look forward to each visit with that wondrously fine group of musicians. I don't gild the lily when I claim that in the long run I perhaps got the better deal. No matter how absorbed I might be in my work, to live in a city such as Cleveland seemed very trying to me in 1943 and still fills me with misgivings. Even now we have problems finding accommodations to our liking. The downtown area is often deserted after business hours and the streets are not as attractive as they once were. Whenever two weeks at Lake Erie are on my calendar we make sure of getting into some semiprivate apartment in a pleasant neighborhood. In any case, I always take pleasure in good friends and the prospect of first-class music-making.

## *Postwar Europe*

As soon as Sidlo had told me the news officially I began to work on other possibilities. The old homily about mounting a horse right after falling off seemed to apply here too. I certainly did not wish to return once more to the Met or to any other opera company.

It was helpful that Arthur Judson came to life. Now that he had his satisfaction of being proved right — one of his most cherished sports — he felt perhaps an obligation or, less probable, some remorse, but, whatever his thoughts and motives, he acted and acted effectively.

Soon after my return from the second Cleveland installment he mentioned the possibility of a five-week guest stint with the Rochester Philharmonic and commented that this might be followed up by a permanent engagement. The last music director of that orchestra, José Iturbi, had resigned in 1945, and, of the crop of guests appearing since then, none had pleased them enough to be offered the post.

Fall was a long way off, and I dreaded another involuntary sabbatical. The one at Camp Lee two years earlier had done me well enough for at least another decade. Luckily, a few invitations from Europe arrived, and by the time I finished in Cleveland I had only a handful of days in New York (we had moved to the suburbs at the end of the war) before taking the plane for London.

It was, of course, my first trip across the Atlantic since 1938, but I felt as if the span of time had been much, much longer. Not only had my life been on the eventful and hectic side, the war itself had made the Atlantic seem much broader and more impassable than a mere eight years of normal open seas would have. To me the boarding of the plane was like the start of an excursion into the unknown. First, I had not flown the Atlantic before, and that alone was a great adventure. Less than thirty years later it sounds improbable that one flight was on a Constellation and the return on a DC–4.

London was new to me anyhow. While I had no yardstick to compare it with its prewar condition, there was no doubt about the bomb craters all over town, the long queues for shopping and transport, the rationed meals, with even the elegant restaurants limiting a customer to three courses at a *prix fixe*. I actually received from home a few small parcels with food and had enormous success in giving away chocolate bars.

The musical side was also quite seamy. The best place to perform, Queen's Hall, had been bombed, and the mammoth Albert Hall, with a capacity of six thousand, was by no means ideal for symphony concerts. The London Philharmonic, which had engaged me for a large number of concerts, played in the town halls of outlying communities, such as Walthamstow, Watford, Wembley, and Croydon, while in the center of the city we performed at the Stoll Theatre on Kingsway. It was the nicest place of the lot but has been torn down since. The town halls have proved so superb acoustically that in some of them the record companies hold all their sessions for opera, oratorio, and symphony. In 1946 I felt that our concerts for the people of those outlying parts of Greater London were better as a social service than as memorable music-making in honor of Beethoven and Brahms. The orchestra was, understandably enough, in poor shape, and not improved by a lack of rehearsal facilities. It is quite shocking that it should have taken nearly thirty years for the London Philharmonic and the London Symphony to raise the funds to acquire a fixed rehearsal hall of their own.

At that time there were, aside from the BBC Symphony, just these two orchestras. They were self-governing, with a board of directors made up of players who elected from their midst a chairman. The directors also engage the manager, whose task it is to get lucrative dates for the orchestra. Concerts in England are no different from those in other places, which means that ticket sales are not nearly enough to defray costs. Essentially all the London orchestras (two have been added since my 1946 visit) depend on recordings for their income. The Arts Council does provide some subsidy for the public concerts, but fundamentally the musicians have no guaranteed income. It is only their own sense of loyalty and team spirit that allows any kind of continuity. In 1946 I thought that what I observed was a makeshift arrangement to keep music alive over an interim postwar period, but when later on I went regularly to London to record and to do concerts, I realized that this was the way it was all the time. Neither on the Continent nor in the United States would musicians stand for it.

I also considered the setup temporary because of the personalities of the Philharmonic's manager and co-manager, both of whom were registered members of the Communist Party. In certain respects I was correct, because they were ousted and a trumpet player became a most efficient managing director. I can't say that I took to the group, and it is only fair to assume the mutuality of such feeling. (Much later, under quite different auspices, the orchestra and I made memorable trips, and some of my best musician friends are in that band.)

Part of my engagement was a tour that led us through the Midlands, into Scotland and then over to Belfast and, finally, Dublin. Here was a kind of paradise, without rationing and without any scars. The Shelbourne Hotel was filled with hungry Londoners who took their small allowance for export and dashed over the Irish Sea to fill their stomachs.

Another somewhat tragic part of that engagement was a recording for Decca of the Immolation Scene from *Götterdämmerung* with Marjorie Lawrence singing the part of Brünnhilde from her wheelchair. She had made a most courageous comeback, and one of my first concerts in that particular series was with her as soloist. She was wildly applauded, and while she had never been a faultless vocalist, I thought that it all came off remarkably well. The microphone, however, is a merciless thing, without the critical faculty of the human ear. We can edit out what may be unpleasant and disturbing; we take the whole personality rather than the imperfect detail, but not so the mechanical pickup.

The sessions were quite a sad story. For several days we tried to get something usable, but in the end the engineers, the producer, and I (and perhaps a lot more people with whom we did not exchange views) realized that nothing of these efforts could be utilized in a commercial recording and nothing was ever published.

On balance my first visit to England did in no way prepare me for later years, when London would be one of my favorite cities, where my best records originated and where the public is among the liveliest and most enthusiastic.

Continuing on to the Continent, first to Paris and later to Holland, I had to conclude that the peoples who, for one reason or another, folded before the Nazis made a much quicker recovery than those who had been braver and resisted. Melancholy. In a devastated spot in the Netherlands I met with Viennese friends who couldn't tell enough of how much further ahead Belgium was. Evidently the reward for giving up. Paris was jumping.

Musically it was more or less the same everywhere. In times of great stress and general need, music serves elementary demands; it takes the place with the common essentials of life. Standards are low, because the tremendous amount of discipline required for the highest quality cannot be mustered easily. During those weeks in Holland the country was still recovering, not only from the enemy but from the liberators as well. The Steinway representative in The Hague told me how he had been offered 1400 cigarettes for a grand piano. From his story it was not explicit whether he had refused or accepted.

The first orchestra of the Dutch Radio, the Philharmonic, was in 1946 a very promising ensemble, and I returned during the following years several times, always hoping for a development that seemed potentially there yet never came. In 1961, after doing Beethoven's Ninth Symphony with them in public at the beautiful Concertgebouw in Amsterdam I gave up. The sad truth is that radio prevents any normal tensions from developing, and without such high voltage the collective performance style remains flat. One or two hundred people invited to sit in a studio can never replace a genuine audience, which pays admission and makes a special excursion for an event. The case history of radio musicians everywhere is the best proof that material values cannot replace human contact. Neither the ample budgets, nor the resulting economic security of the individuals, nor the most splendiferous studio buildings with their canteens and lounges can make up for the vital element of constant attendance and the attention of a live public. There is no earthly way for a radio performer to know if his "house" is crowded or half empty. There is no way of waiting until the expectant hush has settled over the auditorium.

The German radio companies — nine networks in all — have found it necessary to expose their orchestras regularly to a public that is treated not like invited studio guests but like any audience anywhere in the world; tickets are for sale, subscription can be obtained after a seasonal program is announced, the concerts take place in regular halls seating no less than one thousand and the studios are relegated to rehearsal room.

All such efforts notwithstanding I have noted with considerable regret how many of these radio-sponsored ensembles fail to grow and in some cases even decline.

There are several causes, the principal one being the unmanageable amount of music to be absorbed. New works are programmed all the time, and neither they, nor the traditional repertoire, is played more than once. Being conscious of this does not help much. Ratios of rehearsal to concert in an American symphony orchestra are one to one, while in a European radio they can be as much as five to one. The end result is that the musicians knowingly and consciously learn and forget in a never-ending sequence.

In addition to these well-known problems comes the bureaucratic strictness of network administrators who spend — in Europe — public funds and won't let down on the quantity of the schedule. It is a sad situation because of the enormous potential represented by the talent in many of these groups.

I can imagine that some futuristic man, conceived by artificial insemination, raised in chemically processed oxygen, and fed with scientifically developed pills, will be emotionally satisfied to perform for microphones only.

We who breathe polluted air, who eat pork and drink whiskey, must have contact with people who have bought tickets to scream and yell and clap and boo and hiss and ask for autographs and cough maddeningly in the soft passages and leave after the third movement so as not to miss the commuter train.

Back in New York, much buoyed up by the whole experience of traveling and seeing the Old World again, I went to Judson to get briefed on my forthcoming guest appearance with the Rochester Philharmonic. According to his digest and my personal impressions, the Civic Music Association, which sponsored the orchestra, was firmly controlled by the manager, Arthur See, a man in his late fifties then, very able and fully aware that the size of the city and its leading brains allowed only for limited goals. He never tried to reach beyond the not very high ceiling of a conservative Upstate New York community. He was sound and healthy, without neurotic hang-ups, and this in spite of a polio condition that had left him crippled. He showed magnificently what man can do in overcoming a bad handicap. He propelled himself with the help of two braces and a cane, his car was equipped with manual throttle and brake, he enjoyed food and drink, and was a sociable and well-educated man happily married to a most brilliant Frenchwoman, Geneviève.

Back in the late twenties, he had had a great idea that provided him with a lifetime job and his city with a symphony orchestra far better than that of any town of similar population, at least in the United Sstates.

He was financial secretary of the Eastman School of Music, one of the important American conservatories. It is part of Rochester University, an immensely rich school. The three-thousand-seat Eastman Theatre — all these places and institutions had been founded and endowed by the camera wizard George Eastman — had shown films and for musical accompaniment had had an orchestra of some forty-five players. With the arrival of sound movies, these musicians became superfluous overnight, but Arthur See decided not to allow the group to be disbanded.

He formed the Civic Music Association to support, in the classic nonprofit, tax-deductible pattern, the newly named Civic Orchestra. With its four dozen members only light popular fare could be performed. This was successful but not quite enough to justify an elaborate nonprofit corporation.

The Eastman School had so many gifted and highly capable instrumentalists that it was a logical and simple idea to form around the core of the Civic a second ring of musicians to bring the orchestra up to symphonic strength. It also meant that for each season of symphony concerts only the necessary number of players was added, thus avoiding the waste of many orchestras who carry on their permanent roster instrumentalists needed only every third week. In Rochester a second harp would come in when a work required two harps but not otherwise. The disadvantage of frequent changes in personnel, what with graduates leaving town, was more than made up for by the enthusiasm and spirit of the young Eastman students.

The five weeks of my guest concerts were successful, and by the time I returned to New York I had been offered the position of music director, and with Arthur Judson's blessing a contract for several years was signed and sealed. I was enough of a pragmatist to know that it was a good break for me, and around Christmas I left once more for Europe, knowing that a post was awaiting me, come fall 1947.


## *Vienna*

Lothar Wallerstein, having had enough of his Met chores after a few seasons, returned to Europe as soon as postwar conditions permitted. Vienna welcomed him back, and he began immediately to plan for new productions, at first in Vienna's second opera house, because the building on the Ring had been bombed out, and only the shell remained standing. When casting about for conductors Wallerstein found that most of the better people were still under a cloud and not permitted to appear in public, pending their denazification. The richly diversified music life of Vienna was at that moment a virtual monopoly of Josef Krips, whose partially Jewish family tree had forced him to sit out the war years and scrape together his living as a private coach and as a laborer in a food-processing plant. Now, during the suspended condition of so many colleagues, he did everything. Wallerstein thought it would be good to get somebody else to help and made the authorities in charge cable me an invitation. After getting assurances of quarters in an American army hotel, I accepted.

The circumstances of my arrival were appalling. As the train approached the line where the Russian zone began, we stopped while soldiers went through the cars, waking passengers and looking at our papers. I was short a "gray card," and a soldier wanted to take me off the train. A man sharing the compartment with me got much more nervous than I and, fortunately for me, rang for the porter, who, in turn, helped by suggesting that I grease the palm of the worthy Russian, which I did while explaining my mission with conducting gestures and attempts to sing some operatic strains. After some extended greasing the soldier sighed about *Kultura* and how we both would be in chains if our irregularity were discovered, but he left me in the car and I continued the journey. By that time I had already decided that the East system would have to forgo my visits after this one.

By coincidence my "American hotel" was one short block from the apartment where I had lived for the first twenty-four years of my life. It was a very comfortable, simple inn, where the food was still most excellent, due to the splendid combina-

tion of U.S. supplies and Viennese cooking. The place was oc-
cupied by officers and, judging from the daily breakfast scene
downstairs, by a bevy of more or less attractive Viennese ladies
who shared the comforts of a warm room and ample meals with
their protectors.

The production was Jaromir Weinberger's *Schwanda the
Bagpiper,* a work more brilliant than profound but a good show-
piece for all hands, including the conductor. Rehearsals went
well but very slowly because of the municipality's restrictions,
which allowed the flow of cooking gas only three times a day at
fixed hours. This meant the most unwelcome interruptions of
stage and orchestra sessions, with everybody rushing home for
a warm meal. On the other hand, nobody minded that the
theater was shut to the public when we needed an extra evening
to rehearse or that the première was put back until we were
ready — something impossible in more normal setups.

The contrast between the world of make-believe and the real
one of postwar Vienna was staggering. We had new stage sets,
costumes of good materials made with fine craftsmanship, any
number of rehearsals, a good cast of singers, a splendid chorus,
and a first-class orchestra. Going through the exit door one was
met by rubble in the streets, not yet removed eighteen months
after the end of hostilities, long lines at the food stores, cold
flats due to a total lack of heating fuel, scarcity of public transport, and armed guards between the zones of the city. Inside
the Volksoper it might have been 1907, but outside it was every
bit 1947.

At the premiere of *Schwanda* I had a new experience. Never
having paid much attention to announcements and their word-
ing, I was not aware what the papers had printed. As I entered
the darkened house, not the low pit that makes the conductor
invisible to the stalls, I walked to my rostrum in total silence.
Not a hand moved, not a noise was heard; it might have been
a memorial service in a church with the priest entering for a

solemn requiem instead of a comic opera about to commence. It was a stillness of hostility.

The overture is a boisterous piece, an irresistible combination of popular tunes and running, busy fugal passages, wrapped in a glittering orchestration modeled quite deliberately after that other Czech folk opera, *The Bartered Bride.* It is always good for a big hand, yet on that evening it brought forth an ovation as excessively prolonged and loud as the silence nine minutes earlier had been ghastly. The whole show was a huge success, and I was invited to conduct *Fidelio* at the Theater an der Wien, a smaller house serving temporarily but one with a historic patina that gave me more than passing emotions. *Fidelio* had its première in that same house in 1805, and here I was conducting it 142 years later. These are moments that should remain golden memories, yet my native city was never one to permit untroubled enjoyment of its great values, as shown by the situation outside the musical world.

Suddenly I was engaged for concerts with two of the noted organizations, the Philharmonic and the Symphony, in addition to both opera houses, but I never lost my awareness that this was not due solely to my beautiful eyes. They pounced on me because of the shortage of available conductors. Much later I found my theory corroborated in a book entitled *Das Grosse Orchester,* a kind of festschrift by a critic, Heinrich Kralik. I looked at the index and, finding my name listed for page 221, read: "The second postwar season was marked by the increasing visits of conductors from abroad — Volkmar Andreae, Paul Paray, Charles Munch, Eric [sic] Leinsdorf. However, in that same year a turn of events took place and there 'surfaced' [yes, exactly that term is used, *"tauchten wieder auf"*] the familiar and celebrated names of artists who have been for many years intimately tied to the Vienna Philharmonic, who belong to it as it belongs to them: Hans Knappertsbusch, Clemens Krauss, Wilhelm Furtwängler. The temporary separation of the or-

chestra from its indigenous conductors followed in connection
with all those measures that were to give an opportunity to the
responsible authorities — of the occupying powers as well as of
the homeland — to gain clarity in an exceedingly complicated
and difficult situation. The totalitarian regime and the war
upset the soul and the conscience of humanity deeply. How
should all this become balanced and orderly again? As always,
all-healing Time proved the best, most benevolent helper. Two
years sufficed to create an open road to reconciliation, to reason,
perhaps also to silencing personal rancor . . ." (My translation.)

During my sojourn I was well aware that in more official
circles no great joy was manifested over the splendid reception
I received, but then I was always keenly alert to any slightly
paranoid interpretations and dismissed my misgivings as the
proverbial suspicions of an overly sensitized system. But when
I read later Herr Kralik's florid phrases, it did occur to me that
perhaps the "surfacing" of prohibited performers during that
same year was speeded up by some fears that the Viennese, as
fickle a public as any, might — *horribile dictu* — accept those
nonindigenous foreigners who invaded the Imperial City under
the flag of the occupation.

What could I make of Herr Dr. Gamsjäger, managing director of the Friends of Music, for whom I conducted a pair of
concerts, including Walter Piston's "The Incredible Flutist,"
when he phoned me after the first of the concerts and waxed
most indignant that I should have "desecrated" — *"entweiht"*
— the holy Musikvereinsaal with such music. (Piston's suite is a
mildly modern, pleasant score of light caliber, no milestone but
an appropriate way to present one side of 1940s American music,
my very purpose in selecting it.) I was dumfounded by Gamsjäger's violent outburst and still regret that I did not then come
up with the retort that a hall where Herr Hitler had been guest
of honor in the official box could not be desecrated and surely
not by a thoroughly harmless piece of music.

I could observe for myself, in a most entertaining case, just how useless the entire idea of denazifying musical and theatrical performers was. Engaged by the concert-society of the opera chorus to do a Bach program, I was also asked to agree to a soprano who, it seemed to me, had been under some political cloud. This I checked with my friend Henry Pleasants, intelligence officer of the U.S. Army and fully on to the finest tricks of anybody in Vienna. He advised me not to be utilized as a cover for a politically most questionable individual. The panel for the denazification of artists was made up of a group of four officers from the four occupying powers who needed unanimity to ban anyone. However, the lady was clever enough to share her leisure time with a U.S. general, which meant that the American panel member could not vote to prohibit her from appearing in public. Personally he was most anxious to do so and as soon as his general was recalled from Vienna he had the case reopened. But in the elapsed time span the soprano had been successful in conquering a Russian general, and now the panel expert of the Soviets suddenly had no objection to her continuing to sing. I refused the entire engagement rather than provoke some future brouhaha.

My stay in Vienna was barely two months but appeared to me considerably longer, and when my train crossed the border into Switzerland I felt like a latter-day refugee, escaped from odd and grisly conditions.

In 1958 and 1959 I recorded in Vienna under the auspices of RCA, but as far as the local music administrations were concerned I might not have existed. It is not my way to solicit, and I decided to wait until such time when the residues of the past had been fully absorbed. Once again I found that the only important thing is to survive, since it took twenty-six years for me to make my next public appearance in my native city, which came off in such style that it was worth waiting for.

## Interval

My visits to postwar Europe convinced me, as if it had ever been necessary to do so, that armed conflict neither settles nor changes anything. At least not the modern type, which is decided less by bravery than by industry. If I desregard for an instant all humane and moral considerations, I can be made to appreciate that in past wars the victor got spoils not obtainable without violence. This may be robbery, but it makes logical sense on its own premises. Now in 1947 it was the victor who paid the vanquished for the damage done to keep him obediently in line lest he embrace the other wartime ally. It was mad and senseless.

My return trip was made by train and boat. I was already slowing down for a six-month hiatus, which I welcomed for much-needed contemplation.

I had spent my thirty-fifth birthday in Vienna and felt in my bones that I qualified no longer for that "young man" label on which my early reputation was based. Yet no symptoms of middle age made their presence known to me. The decade from thirty-five to forty-five would be the crucial one, as I knew from having read psychologists and directly observing many artists.

With all my good schooling I had moved along on a combination of talent, drive, instinct, and enthusiasm; there had been so much approval and success that I had floated some distance on the proverbial cloud nine, but I was suddenly startled now by discovering how much I had done on sheer intuition and how much I did not know consciously. Since then I have become convinced that this waking-up process is so often the missing link when a *Wunderkind* reaches manhood, having lost the *Wunder* together with the *Kind*.

In more normal progress this metamorphosis from youthful

and brilliant guesswork to fully conscious awareness takes place too, but only twenty years after physical puberty. Those who emerge from that decade with their instincts unimpaired but now fully buttressed, knowing how "it is done," grow and mature, while others get submerged by that aging process and reappear in their middle years disillusioned and forever fatigued.

In my own case I realized that I had missed the years of apprenticeship in small opera houses. Instead I had performed for most of the past decade in the brightest spotlight, paired with veteran stars, subject to constant pressure without the relief of any time off to take a deep breath.

What beckoned now in a more provincial setup was a bit of shadow. Any wise performer prefers to play a great classic piece for his first time in Wichita rather than in Chicago. In that spirit I welcomed the prospect of Rochester, confident that this was what the imaginary doctor had ordered for me. It should have come fifteen years earlier, but if that was not to be then, better now than never. I did feel the need for a little time away from the center, where the proverbial "action" is.

I had not calculated the vast difference between the provinces in Europe and in America. In Europe cities such as Ulm, Aachen, and Osnabrück are still the steppingstones to Berlin, Munich, or Vienna, while the smaller towns in the United States are completely unmarked dead ends. This proved Rochester's one and only serious drawback. I was by no means the only one to get nearly stuck, and Rochester is not the only city that should have a No Exit sign over the concert auditorium. If a conductor's career in America is seen as a stepladder to the so-called Big Five (Boston, Chicago, Cleveland, New York, and Philadelphia), the last fifty years have witnessed only three instances when any of the "five" took their new music director from an American provincial organization. For a time Minneapolis had the reputation of a steppingstone, because Ormandy went to Philadelphia and Mitropoulos to the Philharmonic from there, but then the spell was broken.

This began to bother me after a few years in Rochester, because musical standards were high and the orchestra improved so much that we got a splendid recording contract from Columbia, yet none of this seemed to bring any scouts or make any dent in our provincial limitations on touring.

My impression is not merely an egotistic reflection. Fifteen years after I left Rochester a new journalist came to New York to interview me in relation to the then current problems of the Rochester Civic Music Association. He began by saying that the era of my incumbency was called the "Golden Age."

There again the centralization of music in America worked against us. With Arthur See's tight budget we got to New York only once in nine years, for a matinee at Carnegie Hall, which was partly messed up by a late baggage car. Since we had no instrument cases, we started late. The hall had to be vacated by 5:00 P.M. to prepare for that evening's booking, so one of my three selections went by the board. Worse than the reduced program and the resulting frustration of a waiting public was the poor taste left by such a mishap. Public and press need not and should not be made privy to the prosaic backstage complications. If an orchestra that visits New York ten times a season has one mishap in a span of a few years it does not much matter. But to have a cut-down program, start late, and have to make spoken explanations and apologies from the stage at a one-shot affair is the clearest definition of dark hinterland. Too bad, because our music was not.

Why some setups remain condemned became clear in the way the recordings were handled. Normally an orchestra such as Rochester's does not make records. We got that break because Columbia's big Philadelphians had a standby clause necessitating the payment of all 106 members, even if only half of them performed on records. That meant that recording much of the classical repertoire was a great waste of money, since no more than seventy or seventy-five players are necessary until mid-nineteenth-century scores are played. Columbia decided to have Rochester play Mozart, Haydn, Schubert, and some Beethoven. No standby money had to be paid, and they got very well-received performances. Until . . .

Until one day the stopwatch of the producer, David Oppenheim, failed to function properly and we slid into overtime by three or four minutes. Alert to the varied pressures of our professional lives and anxious to nurture the advantages of this recording relation, I called the players' committee of the orchestra together to explain what had happened. I knew without being told that Mr. Oppenheim would never let on to his superiors in New York that overtime had been caused by his own defective watch. It would be "the slowness of the orchestra" and "necessary repeated takes." This, I suggested to our committee, could be avoided by closing an eye and forgetting that a trifling three or four minutes of overtime had occurred. After I had made what I thought a lucid and sophisticated explanation, the chairman got up and said, "But we went into overtime, didn't we?" I knew then that smartness was not going to prevail. I adjourned the meeting, nothing was done, overtime was charged and collected, and within a year the whole recording activity had ended.

Other musical projects bore fruit and led to better things. In my first season at Rochester we had a tour date at Rutgers University in New Brunswick, New Jersey.

Arthur See had asked me some months earlier if I would mind doing one number with the university's glee club, their suggestion being Randall Thompson's "Testament of Freedom," with words by Thomas Jefferson. Glee club is associated in my mind with beer and pretzels, but I was assured that this was a most serious group, which had performed with Koussevitzky. I had to concede that such an endorsement was sufficient assurance and accepted. The glee club was splendid indeed, and this experience became the start of a long association with the choir's

director, Austin Walter, and the head of music, Howard Mc-
Kinney, who was the proverbial "prince of a man." We planned
to perform another number for the following season (1948–
1949), but after that we knew the repertoire for male choir
and orchestra was virtually exhausted, unless we dug into the
dead-letter library.

I mentioned to the Rutgers people that 1950 was Bach's two-
hundredth birthday and how about one of the great choral
works? McKinney and Walter got wildly excited but had to
reserve judgment until there was a chance to do some fence-
mending between the men's college and Douglass, the women's
college, which had its own choir and music department. As so
often happens in small setups, the conflicts were worthy of
bigger places. It finally came to pass, however, after someone
suggested that the delicate problem between the two chorus
masters would be solved if I rehearsed the mixed chorus. Otherwise it would never go well, as the women's glee club would not
wish to be trained by Walter or the men by the other choir
master, whose name has escaped me forever. For one entire
winter I drove twice a month to New Brunswick, rehearsing
until all hours, even spending the night when icy weather made
the roads hazardous. I gladly did this in the service of Johann
Sebastian, and we had a quite splendid three-day Bach festival
in Rochester, where the whole college choir visited us for the
general rehearsals and performances. Later, at Easter, we all
came to Rutgers to repeat the three Bach programs, and since
then the mixed choir has been a going concern and appears
regularly with the orchestras of Philadelphia and New York.
In 1966 I picked up the collaboration once more, this time as
conductor of the Boston Symphony, on the occasion of the
university's tricentennial, for which they had commissioned a
difficult, very modern work, "Et in occidentam illustra," by
their composer-in-residence, Robert Moevs.

My own very personal reward came in 1952 when, on suggestion from McKinney, the university presented me with an

The Leinsdorf clan in Vienna. Erich appears second left, next to his mother.
His aunt is second from the right.

The young Leinsdorf, approximately
age 19. *(Max Schneider)*

On the stage of the Musikverein in Vienna, 1935. Leinsdorf is at the piano. Maestro Toscanini commands the podium.

Leinsdorf in 1938, as he appeared on the stage of the Metropolitan Opera. *(Wide World Studio)*

A curtain call in San Francisco, 1939, after *Die Walküre* with Armando Agnini, Kirsten Flagstad, Leinsdorf, Herbert Graf, and Julius Huehn.

Leinsdorf conferring with singers, instrumentalist, and composer to discuss appearances with the Rochester Philharmonic Orchestra, 1948. From left to right, singers Rosalind Nadel and Anne McKnight, violinist Isaac Stern, and composer Alec Wilder. *(Hope Associates Corporation)*

Leinsdorf rehearses the Rochester
Philharmonic Orchestra in the Eastman Theatre in Rochester, New York,
1949–1950. *(Loulen Studio)*

Kurt List, Vienna-born composer and
critic, with whom Erich Leinsdorf
recorded all the Mozart symphonies,
1955. *(Metropolitan Opera Archives)*

On tour with the Metropolitan Opera Company. From left to right, standing, John Gutman, assistant manager; Etienne Barone, backstage call boy; Rudolf Bing, director; Mrs. Gutman; Francis Robinson, assistant manager in charge of the press; Paul Jaretzki, assistant artistic administrator; sitting, Leinsdorf; Robert Herman, assistant manager in charge of artist administration. *(Metropolitan Opera Archives)*

A typical recording session with the BSO in the early sixties. Leinsdorf is on the phone to the control booth.

Discussing a score with BSO concertmaster Joseph Silverstein.

Leinsdorf conducts the Mozart Requiem at a Holy Mass for John F. Kennedy at the Cathedral of the Holy Cross in Boston, January 1964. Kneeling at the communion rail (l. to r.) are Joan Kennedy, Rose Kennedy, Jacqueline Kennedy, and Ted Kennedy. *(Lenscraft Photos, Inc.)*

Leinsdorf, Cardinal Cushing, and Jacqueline Kennedy.

Rehearsing Rosalind Elias, Leontyne Price, and Philip Maero for *Madama Butterfly,* 1962.

Leinsdorf compliments Leontyne Price, on *Così Fan Tutte,* 1967.

Listening to the playback of the recording of *Un Ballo in Maschera* in Rome, 1966. Leinsdorf is at the center of the console, soloists Shirley Verrett and Leontyne Price in the foreground, Carlo Bergonzi on the far left.

Leinsdorf recording a Prokofiev piano concerto with John Browning as soloist.

Leinsdorf with Peter Ustinov discussing over champagne the introduction of a new group, the Boston Chamber Players, 1965.

Chatting with students at the Berkshire Music Center at Tanglewood, in Lenox, Massachusetts. Colleague Richard Burgin is in white shirt sleeves.
*(Whitestone Photo)*

Three generations of Boston Symphony Orchestra conductors — Leinsdorf, Pierre Monteux, and Charles Munch. *(Whitestone Photo)*

Henry Cabot, President of the Board of Trustees of the BSO, addresses a few words to the orchestra — Leinsdorf listens. *(Whitestone Photo)*

Hungarian composer Zoltán Kodály with his wife, talking with Erich Leinsdorf and students at the Berkshire Music Center. *(Whitestone Photo)*

Leinsdorf discusses the score of the Carter Piano Concerto with Jacob Lateiner. *(Whitestone Photo)*

Miss Iva Dee Hiatt, of Smith College, rehearses with Erich Leinsdorf and students at the Berkshire Music Center. *(Whitestone Photo)*

Leinsdorf shares a bow with soprano Beverly Sills, Tanglewood, 1969. *(Whitestone Photo)*

A moment backstage at Tanglewood with Joan and Ted Kennedy. *(Whitestone Photo)*

Leinsdorf with LBJ in the Oval Office at the White House, 1968. Douglass Cater is in the background. *(Okamoto)*

A big kiss from Birgit Nilsson for Leinsdorf, after the first performance of Wagner's *Siegfried* at the new Met, 1972.

Rehearsing. *(Whitestone Photo)*

honorary doctor's degree, the only one of my four I feel was deserved.

The story of a college glee club being developed into a major musical organization was a credit to the enthusiasm and enterprise of two men, McKinney and Walter. It is an outstanding example of what can happen if two people with spirit and imagination are present when an idea is launched. If Rochester had had two men with only half the initiative and receptivity of these two professors — a pejorative term in the mouth of an American businessman — we could have made the potentially first-rate orchestra into a major musical organization, of which there cannot be too many.

But, alas, it was not to be.

The leading citizens of this upstate and upstanding community lived in such a closely knit social situation and there was such consciousness of rank that no action could be taken on any issue or idea until Kodak's deputy, followed by the bank's ambassador and the representative of Bausch & Lomb, had made their corporation's policies known. Since Kodak, the undisputed leader, was invariably on the supercautious side, which, in translation reads "no" to most questions, nothing ever came of any impulse. All the lesser fry kept mum or voted obediently with the great camera firm. This was not entirely contrary to Arthur See's wishes. He wanted first of all to run things his own way, since any propelling move for action from others would diminish his prerogative, and he had worked diligently and smartly to create a rubber-stamp board, which is not difficult in music, as most American businessmen know nothing about it.

The other power in town, the university, was represented in all Civic Music matters by the composer Howard Hanson, who had been selected when still in his twenties by George Eastman as the school's director. Hanson wanted to be more than an educator and tried to have virtually all phases of music-making either in his own hands or in those of trusted Eastman graduates. He was most capable as the school's director and as supersalesman for Howard Hanson. For some reason he and See were at loggerheads. I always suspected that for Arthur fighting Howard was like a sports activity, because he did it with such open gusto. In the end the pond was too small for more than one big fish, and when I fully understood this I began to feel claustrophobic, since I was unable to leave and quit.

Suddenly I knew why a number of my predecessors had lasted only a short time. Albert Coates, Eugene Goossens, and José Iturbi came and went, because the encroachments by the Eastman School made their existence unpleasant. To put it most simply, Hanson wanted the orchestra as well as the school, but See would have none of it, saying that Hanson could not expect to appear one night as conductor of the school's senior symphony with free admission and the next as conductor of the Philharmonic at regular ticket prices. See was right in principle, but he should have given Hanson at least one subscription program each year to keep him less dissatisfied. But Arthur would not budge and stubbornly refused to offer any token of peace.

Soon after he died in March 1953 I realized fully how much this poor, crippled man had fought the good fight and how sorely we would miss him. I was then in my sixth season as permanent conductor and nervous at being stuck. Except for 1948 and 1951, when I had wrestled successfully with Arthur for a schedule that would permit me to play San Francisco before we opened in Rochester, I had hardly any chances of getting out. Perhaps I would have been less fidgety if he had been more liberal and let me have my guest appearances elsewhere.

The Rochester season was spread out over many months, with intervals here and there, because a small town can't support weekly symphony concerts. Because of this situation I never could decide whether to reside there or maintain the family home in Larchmont in southeastern New York. With children of school age and a newly arrived infant it was an insoluble problem and not a situation made for permanence.

After Arthur's death the organization nearly went to seed. Nobody knew anything. It had been accepted practice for the board members to rotate every year. With nobody in the same spot for more than twelve months, Arthur had been able to get his way every time by the simple demonstration that he knew best. The good citizens were content with this system, their presence on the committee being only one of several time-consuming honorific activities forced on them by their coveted status as city fathers.

In March 1953 it dawned on one and all that the Rochester Civic Music Association had been run as the most radical one-man show anyone could imagine. Tom Iannaccone, the young assistant manager, was a good boy, without the foggiest. Raymond Albright, then president, was willing and eager but also totally green and in the dark about everything, as well as being short of time. The best I could do was hold as many briefing sessions for the directors as time allowed.

After our final get-together when the season ended, Ray Albright assured me that his first task was to hire a new manager. He appeared to understand that our very special problem was coexistence and cooperation with the Eastman School and its director. Most of my tutoring had been aimed at explaining that we were not, like other orchestras, entirely autonomous, that Arthur's double job as financial secretary of Eastman and manager of the orchestra could not be duplicated in the future, and that the next man therefore could not have the same trump cards in dealing with Hanson.

Judging from the results, either my coaching was not effective or the pupils were not very apt. Just then my mind was on my forthcoming first trip to Israel, and when it was over and I returned to New York, my family and I moved for the summer to the mountains, a holiday made more interesting by our next-door neighbor, Vladimir Horowitz, who then had embarked on his long withdrawal from the concert stage. We spent many evenings together, and of all the fascinating topics we discussed I was most astonished at his remark that he could no longer face audiences, which he detested. He was as deeply as ever involved in his musical and pianistic work, making discoveries and forming new ideas, but referred to the public only with contempt. He also had broken with RCA after a long association because of the record company's insistence on a repertoire he despised. I was not yet affiliated with that great corporation and could only marvel from the sidelines at their immense stupidity, letting a Horowitz go and join the competition. Later on, after knowing the executives of RCA better, it no longer amazed me.

While we enjoyed the mountain air and the good company of the great pianist a small bombshell arrived in the form of a letter from Albright with a clipping from the Rochester morning paper. The letter and clipping informed me that a new manager, Joel Kimball, had been hired. The new man's background was distinguished by a total absence of orchestral experience: he had been traveling salesman on the West Coast for Columbia Artists Management, the biggest booking agency. A few mails later a breezy note came from the new man, full of cheer yet filling me with some skepticism and foreboding.

Immediately after Labor Day, when I was back in Larchmont, I had an urgent call from Albright in Rochester, asking me to meet him the next day in New York for lunch. He was most preoccupied, and it took no prophet to guess after the first two sentences that something was wrong with the new management. Kimball had put his foot into a mud puddle by making a major financial commitment to which he had no right and for which there were no funds available. The Civic Orchestra members, tired of playing pop programs in black jackets and striped trousers, found a sympathetic ear in Kimball. Wouldn't it be so much better and more successful to order some zippy outfits to make them look like a frolicking band? Then and there, between a few musicians and Kimball, it was agreed to go to one of the big clothiers in Rochester and order for every man and

Miss Malone, the harpist, a new uniform, to be charged to the Civic Music Association. As if this were not enough, Albright confided that he and his associates on the board were shocked that the new manager, coming from a $7000-a-year job, drove — imagine the effrontery — a Cadillac. He, Albright, president of Distillation Products, drove a Chevvy; Tom Hawks, the banker, drove a Ford; Arthur See had driven a Plymouth. I did my best to cluck my tongue in sympathy, having a hard time keeping a straight face. After seeing Kimball's picture in the paper, I had remembered his face and name from my visits to the West Coast. I had no proof or evidence, but my recollection was a pleasant person totally lacking in qualifications. I did have the restraint not to ask, "Why didn't you consult with me before hiring the man?" By Thanksgiving Day Kimball was paid off and had left Rochester.

Once more, Tom Iannaccone, the assistant manager, kept the season's routine going, but he could not stem the increasing skirmishes from the other side of the building, which houses the administration of the Eastman School of Music. Now the best string players would suddenly call in sick or were "just so busy with exams" that they had to be excused from rehearsals and even recording sessions. This absence showed itself very soon in the standard of the orchestra's playing. My seventh season was not a happy one, and when it had ended I could not wait to get by myself on a boat and make a European tour without fixed itinerary. When I returned, another manager had been found, but this time we were at least introduced before he was signed to a contract. His name was Jack Dailey, and I found him most likable.

In his work as manager a basic truculence came to the fore and brought Jack into fights and shouting matches with nearly everybody. By the time I left Rochester he and his wife were put through the disagreeable trials of frequent nightly phone calls without anyone speaking on the other end. He received threatening anonymous letters, and we began to have, for the first time in my memory of Rochester, union troubles. I had to quit, come what may. If I stayed on I could not avoid involvement in conflicts that were looming darker and darker on the narrow skyline of the small city. Every primer on good public relations and on the modern "science" of image building has it that in the announcement of a resignation the next stop and appointment must also be mentioned. Not having any genuine offer just then I was determined to find one.

## A Rochester Postscript

I do not consider myself angelic or free from human hostility, but I am not the type to wish "après moi le déluge." The board looked for my successor again without benefit of my advice. Their first choice used the negotiations to get himself a better deal where he was and where he wanted to stay. Finally they engaged someone of less than top caliber.

There have been constant comings and goings of conductors and managers; a long-drawn-out fight between the musicians and the board ended with the entire board quitting and a new group taking charge; an issue of personnel replacement brought the conductor and union before the National Labor Relations Board. While its decision vindicated management and conductor, it came so late that it was a Pyrrhic victory, the management having given up and the conductor having gone to greener pastures.

The new board brought a new manager who got them a new and very excellent conductor. A new leaf appeared to have been started until three years later manager and assistant manager left precipitously, quite obviously not exactly on cordial terms.

Too bad, because there lies the best of my nine-year efforts, and it would have been good to hear and witness the great potential I found there in 1946 come to fruition.

## *Thin Ice*

To backtrack a minute. One evening in early 1943 I was visited in my dressing room at the Met by Fiorello La Guardia. This was a pleasant and flattering event and very entertaining. It was wartime and the mayor found the city suddenly saddled with an old, ugly building, Mecca Temple on West 55th Street, after the owners were unable to come up with their taxes. Now "Hizzoner," as everybody called him, wanted to do something with the somewhat decrepit house, which had a theater with a 3000-seat capacity at its core. His plan was to perform opera at lower prices than the Met's, giving plays and musical comedies and ballets in between. Now he was looking for well-known artists in addition to the necessary fat cats for moral and publicity support, and his visit was an invitation to join the committee of founders, which I accepted as a matter of course.

From then on I was notified of annual meetings, some of which I attended, always cordially welcomed by the chairman of the board, a New York socialite politician, Newbold Morris, who had all the manner "that maketh it man," while the hard substance was concentrated in the head of the Finance Committee, a tax lawyer and enthusiastic amateur musician, Morton Baum, who ran the enterprise with great brilliance and singular ingenuity. His utterly simple method was to book reruns of the most successful musical comedies and apply the profits from such commercial theatricals to the perennially deficit-ridden opera seasons.

The first director of the opera company, known as the City Opera, was a conductor-impresario, László Halász, who added to Baum's skills a tremendous flair for discovering talented new singers and engaging them at incredibly low fees. New York's second opera company became immensely successful and drew a quite sophisticated audience, especially from the recently ar-

rived European refugees who loved opera but could not afford
the high admission to the Met. The company did a fine job of
performing the favorites, but much more important, there were
productions of operas not seen and heard before in New York.

For reasons still unclear to me, Halász and Baum fell out and
landed in a court of law, the former having sued the City Opera
for an unfulfilled term in his contract. While this went on, a
very good German conductor, Josef Rosenstock, was appointed
director. He did not have the same abilities as Halász. While a
superior musician, he lacked the qualities of his predecessor on
the nonmusical side. Whatever the ups and downs during his
incumbency, by 1955, five years after he had been hired, it was
known through the grapevine that the City Opera was again in
the market for a new director. I conveyed to Morris and Baum
that I might be available.

When after very little negotiating I was officially offered the
appointment, I went to Judson, who had been quite unable —
or unwilling — to help me out of the Rochester confinement,
to discuss this venture with him and to ask what he thought
of it. He made one of his best comments: "You will be on the
thinnest layer of ice and you may fall through if it breaks; but
if enough people have seen you skate, it may be worth while."
It proved to be exactly so.


## Israel 1953

As the Rochester years went by, I caught the eyes of the
man who, in 1948, had taken on the Philadelphia Orchestra's
summer concerts, an industrialist named Fredric Mann. He was
another wildly enthusiastic amateur musician, who exerted his
best efforts by presenting free concerts by that wonderful orchestra to his hometown. A most complicated mixture of the

best motivation and blatant self-seeking, Freddie Mann did not manage to become a great power in American music, which had been his aim. At one time he nearly bought the biggest talent agency, Columbia, and he was seen everywhere with great musicians. Yet some barrier prevented this dynamic and well-meaning man from being as constructive and broadly effective as he could have been with only a few minor repairs in his manner.

To me it was a joy to do a few concerts each summer with such a magnificent ensemble as the Philadelphians, and I kept my visits up until 1962. Nobody could work for Freddie very long unless he or she became involved with the Israel Philharmonic. By 1953 I had accepted an invitation for a series of concerts. Invitation in that case was to be taken literally. Somebody in the United States, perhaps Freddie himself, paid for the round trip, the guest artist was invited to live and eat in a house owned by the orchestra, and that was the full extent of remuneration. Since the orchestra was famous, having been conducted in 1937 by Toscanini and having made in 1951 a highly acclaimed tour of the United States under Koussevitzky, I looked forward to a great musical treat. I also had close relatives on my father's side living in a kibbutz near Haifa, for whom my mother gave me presents and greetings.

The flight, in prejet days, was long but very comfortable. The last leg, Athens to Tel Aviv, was made in the small hours of the night. Our aircraft, a DC–6, was filled with Americans on a guided tour. At some point one of the lot woke up from his nap and, seeing ahead of the plane some delicate pink on the far horizon, began in great excitement to cry, "Israel, Israel," which brought the whole mass of humanity to its feet. For the next few minutes the cabin was the nearest thing to a Holy Roller meeting, such was the ecstasy of the passengers. They had spotted the Promised Land.

The orchestra, called "Tismoreth" in modern Hebrew, owned

two prefabricated houses, which were located in a small plot just outside the city limits of Tel Aviv. Soloists stayed in the first, conductors in the second house. Both were served well and lovingly by Madame Shaoúl, a Bulgarian lady whose cooking should have brought her a three-star rating from Michelin. As it was, she managed to feed not only the orchestra's guest artists but a fairly numerous family, having the benefit of especially generous rations through her connections with the orchestra's management. From my childhood in Vienna I was used to and loved Balkan cooking, and that was what she served her guests. My enthusiasm pleased her, as she had been a bit subdued by the just-departed occupant of the soloist's house, Jascha Heifetz. The great violinist took it upon himself to break the prevailing ban on all music by Wagner and Richard Strauss and insisted, against better advice, on playing Strauss's sonata. After the end of that recital a wild man, awaiting him at the artists' door, insulted the violinist and hit him with a hard object on the arm. Heifetz packed his bags and left. It still has not been possible to lift this ban in the two decades following the incident. Musicians all swear that this type of chauvinism is not representative of anyone interested in music, that it is a residue from the trauma of the Third Reich days, but then some world-famous person, such as Artur Rubinstein, states publicly that Israel is right in not performing Strauss, because "he was an unimportant composer." I have always thought that musicians should do their talking in private, especially when they become so famous that their words carry too much weight.

The program and schedule of the orchestra were exceptionally taxing. The climate is not invigorating, and the hall, Ohel Shem, was small, which meant that each concert program had to be played seven times in Tel Aviv, twice in Haifa, and once in Jerusalem. The public is composed of the former residents of so many European cities that one could justly call it a select international audience.

I found the string section of the orchestra as fine as its reputation and the wind complement disappointing. True, no European parents encouraged their offspring to study the trombone or snare drum. It was always the piano or a stringed instrument, excepting the bass fiddle. That much was clear to me, but the American tour had been made by an orchestra that was uniformly excellent. What had happened to the winds? It took only a few discreet inquiries to ascertain that Koussevitzky, after his first few rehearsals prior to the tour, had simply insisted on calling a few French wind players as "ringers" to prop up the indifferent wood and brass sections. This weakness of wind players, a leftover from European Jewry, is balanced by the second generation of Israelis, as they go into many endeavors formerly barred to or by Jews.

During my visit, the occupant of the first house and my soloist was the pianist Shura Cherkassky. We took our meals together, and Madame Shaoúl served us lovingly, with many words of encouragement to eat more, words neither the pianist nor I needed. Cherkassky managed between mouthfuls to ask more questions than any sage could have answered. Everything interested him, who had bought what and with whose money. He was a one-man cross-examiner.

His pianism was flawless, his musicianship of the worst. He had absolutely no concept of any work he played, having mastered the finger portion to such an extent that he could and did change everything else from one performance to the next. What was loud today might be soft tomorrow, and what went presto on Tuesday might be taken slowly on Wednesday. If he had played Beethoven or Mozart I would have gone crazy, but fortunately he played only rhapsodic composers such as Liszt and Rachmaninoff, who should not be treated this way either, yet can stand such "interpretations" with less ultimate damage. Liszt himself was allegedly free and easy with the compositions he played.

My second visit to Israel took place just at the time I resigned from Rochester. I arrived at the very end of 1955 for a series of Mozart programs in commemoration of his bicentennial, January 27, 1956. My first evening was spent at Ohel Shem listening to a quite extraordinary enterprise by the Tismoreth and a local chorus, the Mozart Requiem, in modern Hebrew. Perhaps if Roncalli had already been Pope, he might have found ecumenical merit in such an experience. To be liberal is easy for me and difficult for culture policy-makers in a land like Israel, where the tensions of past suffering are more than matched by present dangers, yet I — born and raised a very conscious Jew — wish so fervently that this kind of utter nonsense did not take place in Israel. I believe more than ever that the work of art has its own laws and they should not be violated any more than the everyday ordinances of a municipality. It pained me to witness a distortion of a masterpiece.

January was much more agreeable climatically, and my round of concerts went well. It was too much to repeat each program so many times, but funds were rapidly accumulating and I was assured that on my next visit the orchestra would be in a new and splendiferous large auditorium.

Between this visit and the one in 1960 lies my short stint as opera director, which awaited me upon my return to New York. While finishing the symphony season with the Rochester Philharmonic, I began to prepare for the fall at the Mecca Temple.


## *The City Opera*

When General Westmoreland was promoted to chief of staff after a highly questionable tour of duty as commander in Vietnam, I, and many a like-minded person, was indignant that a bad job should be followed by a tremendous promotion. If anyone had closely followed my life and career, he could have told me to be less critical, since I myself got an enormous boost after a spectacular failure. It can be argued that I had some pretty tight alibis for portions of the City Opera fiasco, yet when all the returns were in, the most objective judge would still blame me for a botched-up assignment.

No wonder that I have become highly skeptical about recipes for success. In the end it is probably the public and only the public that decides who remains on stage and who retires to teaching posts in small colleges. In the short run the cards are sometimes stacked more or less favorably. The decade from 1947 to 1957 was certainly a case in point. Musical work with excellent results led to nothing more than a deteriorating situation in a provincial town, while a complete flop in New York brought me two splendid recording contracts and a return to the Metropolitan, not only as conductor but as a member of management.

As I began to formulate a repertoire for my first directorial season I felt that the City Opera needed a shot in the arm. This I thought to administer by planning a most unusual and ambitious repertoire for the six-week season. Featured were premières of Carl Orff's *Der Mond*, Frank Martin's *The Tempest*, and Carlisle Floyd's *Susannah*. I understood that such esoterica would not be quite as magnetic to the ticket buyers as *Porgy and Bess*, so as an opener I decided to do an Offenbach masterpiece, *Orpheus in Hell* — in English — to bring in the cash customers.

This was the second of two miscalculations. The first, naturally, involved money. The musical-comedy season in the summer of 1956 had not made a profit, which meant that the opera started without any reserves whatsoever. In such cases, it is customary to borrow from the box office. What there was in advance ticket orders did not amount to much. Now our hopes rested entirely on a smash for *Orpheus in Hell*. It was a flop and brought us neither honor nor greenbacks.

On the morrow of opening night, when we knew that our Offenbach revival had failed, the returns for the whole enterprise were in. A few days earlier Baum had told me that the spring 1957 season had to be abandoned due to lack of funds, and I pleaded with him to keep this secret in order not to discourage the company and the public. That too proved to be another mistake of a tactical nature, since later, when the cancellation was announced, it was debited to my bad season, and nobody believed that this decision had been made earlier independently of that fall's calamity.

I often felt that it was a bad idea to gamble a six-week season's fate on the success of one show, until many years later I learned that this was a most common practice. For example, Capitol records covered its errors for a long time with the huge profits made from the Beatles. One fine day, after the disbandment of that remarkable combo, Capitol's balance sheet went from a multimillion-dollar profit to a similarly large loss within one twelve-month period, only for lack of a success blanket. When I had digested that story I stopped feeling like a wild gambler in the *Orpheus* case.

More interesting are the reasons why *Orpheus* itself failed. This enchanting operetta pokes subtle and not-so-subtle fun at Offenbach's contemporaries, disguised in mythological garb. In the United States no schools teach Greek mythology, hence nobody knows much about Zeus's adventures or the gates of Hades. Styx is perhaps considered merely a bad spelling of the hinterlands.

My chief appointee was Leo Kerz, a scenic designer and stage director. He recommended that Eric Bentley adapt the libretto. Neither Bentley nor Kerz took into account our intentions or what the New York public wanted. Both men wished to prove the Brechtian dramaturgic concepts and went about it with a single-mindedness that brought them almost immediately into acid arguments with the cast. Norman Kelly, a good artist and a good Catholic, disliked some of Bentley's sacrilegious references, and several singers found the erotic language too clumsy and inelegant. The danger signals of a disaffected cast were all there before we started. I should have fired both men on the spot, but with time pressing on, I couldn't risk the possibility of losing the stage director and, worse, of having Bentley withdraw his adaptation, which he would have done. I am sure that fifteen years later his text would not have caused one raised eyebrow. It would have been just as heavy-handed, but compared to what gets by as theater now it was mild.

In my efforts to present so much of the offbeat — it was a mad idea to offer four novelties within six weeks — the bread-and-butter repertoire was shortchanged and failed to bring in the "other" public, the conservatives, who dwell on the déjà vu and déjà entendu.

Immediately after conducting the opening-night *Orpheus,* I was offered the chance to record for RCA Victor no fewer than three operas in the summer of 1957 in Rome. The man in charge of RCA's repertoire was George Marek, whom I had known since the days of Toscanini; we remained on more than cordial terms, until a combination of professional and personal problems led to a total estrangement. He was certainly the major factor in my getting engaged by RCA, for whom by 1971 I had recorded eighteen complete operas.

Not only I but the City Opera itself profited in the long run from that disastrous fall season of 1956. Some responsive and responsible foundation people recognized that unknown works could be produced only with an ironclad financial guarantee against the poor attendance that always remains a great probability for the untried.

The company rallied around a young and devoted musical secretary, who also had conducted some operas — Julius Rudel. Baum and Morris appointed him to the chair I had vacated, and the rest is history. My own contribution to that "lost season" was my salary, which I never got and never asked for.

Following the New York season we toured Michigan, and this gave me the leisure to do some thinking without pressure for the first time in several months.

I concluded that I should stay away from the managerial and impresario end of my profession, where there has to be an emotional and temperamental predisposition toward adjusting artistic ambition to fiscal realities. This, I submit, is antiperfectionist and incompatible with the standards a performer must uphold in his own right and for his own growth.

In Detroit I bade adieu to the members of the company and traveled to St. Louis for concerts I remember only vaguely. Fatigue overcame me, and I was quite content to look forward to a free holiday period and to more accustomed activity in early 1957, highlighted by a guest engagement with the great Concertgebouw Orkest of Amsterdam.

## *Back to the Met*

It was early December when my trials and tribulations were over and I was back in Larchmont. Soon after my return Rudolf Bing called and asked me to come see him as soon as it was convenient. For the six years he had been the Met's general manager there had been no contact or communication between us. I had been more or less disinterested in doing anything but symphonic work, and he had not shown any interest in his predecessors' artists. I had met him only once, in a tiny office in London when he was manager of the Glyndebourne Festival. That was in 1946, and we merely exchanged polite trivialities and let it go at that. Now, ten years later, he wished to see me quite urgently.

I was surprised, as I considered my stock low at that moment, but little did I understand that value in an individual depends also on demand and, as the ensuing visit proved, on being needed.

When I arrived at the old familiar house, I was shown in at once and welcomed most cordially. Bing came to the issue right away: Rudolf Kempe, his conductor for several operas, had cabled his cancellation due to a sudden attack of jaundice. Could I help out by taking over *Walküre,* which, as Bing put it, "is not an unknown work to you." We poured over the season's schedule, neatly arranged on one well-drawn sheet, and it showed at a glance that the dates of his performances conflicted with my concerts in Amsterdam. After glancing at more than the *Walküre* dates, I asked Bing if he had already made arrangements for an *Arabella* conductor. He was utterly astonished that I should be familiar with this Strauss work, so I told him that my intimate acquaintance with the score dated back to its Viennese première and how in 1936, for a *stagione* in Trieste, I had prepared and conducted it. That delighted him, and when I left his office an hour later we had concluded an agreement that was surely one of those rare documents pleasing to both sides. Much later, when we were working together every day, he told me once that before my visit he had given up on finding anyone to conduct *Arabella.* I did not tell him that I'd given up any chance of getting back to New York after my "disaster on 55th Street."

As I made my way from 39th to 45th Street, where my mother and aunt lived, to tell them the good news, I hoped again that I was perhaps through with the hinterland period; going on forty-five, I felt that the decade of adjustment should be over and the missing apprenticeship of my youth made up.

No doubt I had bitten off a great deal in that span after my arrival in America. I had brought my aging mother and aunt over from Vienna and settled them; I had married and was now father of five children. A musician does not have an eight-to-four existence, and he spends much more time at home than a regular professional man or businessman. I found the combination of a musical career with that of paterfamilias at times trying and often felt I was living in a house with a roof but no walls.

The happiest person to learn the news was my mother, who had never quite understood why anyone as well off as I should have left New York and the wonderful Metropolitan for such unknown locations as Cleveland and Rochester, which were to her still full of Indians. (She was unaware of the name of Cleveland's baseball team.)

She may not have been an expert on the finer points of reaching the stepladder to the top, but she had great common sense and was a moderate person, content when things went well. She was not greedy and was free of mad ambition. For her taste I had accomplished enough by being conductor at the Metropolitan Opera at twenty-six, and to her judgment all else was fancy and perhaps unnecessary.

Neither she nor my aunt ever learned the language, yet they became citizens. By going to evening classes in Manhattan they tried to learn by rote the answers to the questions that might be asked at the swearing-in ceremony; one time my aunt, eager to demonstrate her knowledge, was asked, "On what boat did you arrive?" She replied, "On the *Mayflower*." The class was recessed until the hilarity had stopped.

They were both inveterate readers and patronized the lending library. For the daily news they depended solely on the *Staats-zeitung-Herold,* the German-language paper in New York. I knew that during my years in "Indian" territory they did not usually find my name in that paper, which did not bother with such events as the musical doings at Eastman or at Severance. What is the use of having a famous son if you can't show anything to the kaffee klatsch at Eclair, the strudel and pastry emporium on West 72nd Street that was the reason for their daily pilgrimage. There they felt an atmosphere that, if not authentic, was the closest thing to the Viennese coffee house.

When, shortly after the holidays, I began to prepare for *Arabella,* I found some agreeable changes in the operation of the opera house. Rehearsals were plentiful, which meant calmer and less hectic work, with no need to look over my shoulder to check the clock. Time is important in a work that does not play itself. No opera really does, but there is a difference between a bad production of *Carmen,* which will always remain a work of genius, and a bad *Arabella.* The latter is a product of a tired pair of authors, an attempt, perhaps subconscious, perhaps calculated, to repeat the success of *Rosenkavalier.* Whatever the original motivations, the book is contrived and the music brilliantly orchestrated but uninventive. Like a vigorous youngster who thrives on any kind of food and wild activity, a masterpiece can take rough treatment, but a synthetic fabrication needs nursing and careful underlining of all that is strong and a concealing of all that is weak.

Bing, anxious to parlay *Arabella* into a success, was quite aware that it needed this kind of help and lavished every care on it, which made me happy. It was a great pleasure to work under good conditions in the house where I had labored so long on the proverbial shoestring budget. The performances were a triumph for production and cast and the work was treated according to each critics' predisposition. Some tolerated it, others dismissed it. Bing demonstrated his appreciation for the favor rendered him by asking me at once to return for a revival of *Figaro* in the 1957–1958 season. This would be no hardship, and I only hoped that the cast would be like the unforgettable one I had conducted in the winter after my army discharge, when the leading roles were taken by Rethberg, Sayao, Stevens, Pinza, and Brownlee.

While I had no wish to go back to opera after the 55th Street debacle, the Met projects were not full-time, and I felt that there was quite substantial symphonic activity on my calendar for the balance I sought so keenly.

Besides the three operas for which RCA had engaged me, I had also signed a five-year "exclusive" recording contract with Capitol, a California-based subsidiary of EMI, for just symphonic music. They were most generous in allowing me to record complete operas for RCA, with no formalities, just a simple notification from me to them. It did look as if I had now the best of both worlds, the instrumental and the operatic.

## *Recording*

My Cleveland recording sessions had been with the 78 r.p.m. system, which meant that four minutes, twenty seconds was the maximum length of each shellac disc on which the music was engraved. Then, in 1948, there came Microgroove and tape, which made everything much easier, as the engineers developed the skill of splicing. My Rochester recordings were already exclusively at 33 r.p.m. The engineers still didn't have much confidence in small inserts and splices, and we produced essentially continuous performances. When I started making recordings in London, where in the summers of 1955 and 1956 I conducted all Mozart's symphonies for Westminster-Paramount, the tendency to splice had not yet taken hold of the producer's fancy. In 1956 I did a little-known opera, Peter Cornelius' *Der Barbier von Bagdad,* for EMI in London, and there too basic policy was to record as much as possible in continuity, splicing only when absolutely necessary.

All this changed when we started making records in Rome. The schedule and the setup were in their way as attractively planned as my first visits to the San Francisco Opera. Everything was a mixture of fun, vacation, and parties, with a good deal of very tough work in between. Sessions were to start at 2:00 P.M. and we recorded *Butterfly* and *Tosca* on alternate days, to give the principal singers every other day for rest. We lived in Fregene, outside Rome, and I drove each day to the city, without traffic, without trouble parking, always in good time for an espresso at the corner and ready at the bell.

The casting was most illuminating. *Tosca* had three of the day's great singers for the principal roles, Zinka Milanov, Jussi Björling, and Leonard Warren. But for *Madama Butterfly*, George Marek had, for reasons still a bit vague to me, decided to make Cio-Cio-San and Pinkerton truly young lovers instead of middle-aged, overweight, vocal acrobats. He cast the roles with two young and attractive singers, Anna Moffo and Cesare Valletti, forgetting apparently that records are primarily to be listened to and not looked at. Anna's pretty face and Cesare's young countenance would not be as important to the record buyers and listeners as their delicate voices, which were too light for the roles. The album was in the end noncompetitive in comparison with issues of the same work on other labels. To make amends RCA recorded another *Madama Butterfly* in 1962, this time with the traditional vocal caliber of Leontyne Price and Richard Tucker.

Errors happen in the best of record companies, but the same basic boner was committed several times over by RCA's casting experts. George Marek was a man with an eye and he, with full support from his associates, bet that a few of their young singers might accomplish breakthroughs in the movies and become the equivalent of "classical Beatles." If it all sounds terribly unprofessional, this is exactly what it was, but still such wildly amateurish casting went on and marred several otherwise very good opera albums.

Our attractive young Lieutenant Pinkerton caused (involuntarily) a moment of considerable embarrassment. During a playback of the great love duet that concludes act one the producer, singers, and I sat in the control room listening intently. Suddenly there appeared next to me a very drunk Jussi, highly indignant at what he heard; he bent down and began to sing into my right ear how the tenor part *should* be sung. Of course, Björling singing into an ear carried better than other voices shouting at top strength, and there was no doubt that his synchronized effort and the comments he made while Butterfly sang and Pinkerton rested were not for public print or hearing. Yet everything that went on next to me was clearly perceived by everybody else in the small room. I began to perspire in perplexed embarrassment, trying in vain to silence Jussi, but he kept getting angrier, alternating critical comments with splendid demonstrations of the tenor's phrases. He made sure that we all knew what a mistake had been made in casting.

The playbacks were altogether a chapter at once hilarious and silly. Richard Mohr, the producer of nearly all RCA's operatic albums, warned me that some vocalists can never hear enough of their own voices and no matter how much their part is in the foreground, they will invariably scream that the orchestra is much too loud. With the recording system we had it was possible to make faked balances for the playbacks by vastly increasing the volume of the voice track, thereby pleasing the singers, who never suspected that later on, in the cutting room in New York, free from all egotists and their beefings, Mr. Mohr and his engineer would do exactly as they pleased.

Conducting the Rome orchestra was also something to remember and I remember it well enough to avoid similar situations whenever possible. The orchestra really knew the repertory operas and was proud of knowing them. Many members of the group did not even look at their parts and played away, in a trance, with great authority, but in ways that were probably an accumulation of traditional nuances that had trickled into performances over many years as singers took more and more liberties with the composers' music. My attempts to guide them back to a consideration of the basic solfège as printed in front of their faces was met by reluctance, resistance, and sometimes even chauvinistic side comments about the *"straniero chi pretende di saper meglio."*

Remembering the deportment of musicians in London, I could not believe the chaos caused in Rome each time we called an intermission. There are several breaks during any record session in order to give the principals the opportunity to listen and make their corrections next time around. The road to a good recording lies mostly in the artist's ability to improve from take to take, inspired and enlightened by the lessons of the playback. But the attractions of the buffet, the bar, and the smoking lounge were such that each recall of the orchestra took longer than the whole interval. In a London recording studio the members of the orchestra read a book, a paper, or a betting sheet, or do nothing at all, and when the call to continue comes they are ready within seconds. It proved so nerve-wracking to bring Rome's recalcitrant ensemble back to the floor that we tried to do with fewer playbacks, and eventually, after a studio was constructed outside the gates of Rome, RCA terminated all relations with the opera house and its musicians.

Among other difficulties was Leonard Warren, who had, against many odds, become unquestionably the greatest "Italian" baritone of his generation. His insecurity was the only factor greater than his singing, and it showed in many ways. During our sessions he would, whenever mucous or some vocal imperfection disturbed him, wave his arms to stop, or he would just walk away from the microphone. This was detrimental to the ensemble's already shoddy discipline, and I urged him to simply make a small sign to me and I would then interrupt the proceedings. This offended him, and for three days he sulked.

From the fourth day on all was forgotten and we worked together in harmony, which later, in New York, grew into a very warm, cordial relationship when we produced Verdi's *Macbeth,* first at the Met and then for records.

Not a single scene of any operatic recording could ever have been issued had it not become by that time a matter of course to splice the best portions of several essays into one so-called master. It soon came to a point of absurdity, where singers insisted on doing the end of an aria at the beginning to hit their high notes when they were fresh. That in most such pieces the climax is not only one of pitch but one of emotion and increased tension did not bother the golden-voiced stars. In 1959 I heard that another company with magicians for engineers recorded an orchestral track without the tenor even present, the plan being for the singer to fill in his part while listening on earphones to the already taped orchestral portion. I was mercifully spared this experience until my nineteenth full-length opera when the tenor (it is most of the time the tenor) was too indisposed during the regular sessions to sing his difficult passages.

Whatever frictions and fights were part and parcel of these recording days, all was washed down at a dinner, given for the casts of both operas by George Marek on the final night.

For me the summer led to a long and very mixed relation with RCA, with many ups and downs, with incidents and crises, most of which will appear here in chronological order.

By a coincidence almost mysterious in its perfect timing my newly established connections with the Met and with RCA would converge a few months later.

## Consultant

In late November 1957, soon after returning to New York from another — and final — engagement with the San Francisco Opera, Bing asked me once again to visit him as soon as it was convenient. I saw him on Thanksgiving morning, eighteen years to the day after Bodanzy's sudden death had changed my career. This time, too, a radical decision awaited me. Bing's story was that Max Rudolf, his artistic administrator, who actually ran the company, was moving to Cincinnati to become music director of the orchestra there with the start of the next season. Bob Herman, trained by Max to be his assistant, was slated as successor, which would leave the management of the Met without a musician of authority. Bing wanted me to fill this role. I would have no regular office hours or desk duties but would make my expertise and council in all musical questions available. I was invited to attend any of the continuously scheduled planning meetings but not compelled to do so. To make all this worth my while, Bing proposed a considerably larger conductorial activity, also starting from the 1958–1959 season. Finally I could count on a reasonable amount of leave for symphonic guest conducting. I was speechless.

This was not exactly what I had planned, but it sounded most attractive, and as there were no particularly strong alternatives awaiting my decision I accepted Bing's package, which included a fair financial deal. The only point on which we could not agree was my title. Bing rejected the obvious one, "musical adviser," with the comment that he would not wish anybody to assume that he needed musical advice. This was said, as so much else, with tongue in cheek but it had a serious undercurrent. It proved to be his Achilles' heel that he never conceded his essential unpreparedness in strictly musical matters.

After a few days we found in "musical consultant" a meaningless term that did not bother me and pleased Bing. For the next four and a half years I spoke my mind freely whenever I felt like it, and nobody knew if that was advising or counseling or consulting. In hindsight I am convinced that it was in 1958 that the slow decline of the Bing management began. Bob Herman was a most engaging and enormously able young man. In straight organization and administration he was more modern and efficient than Max. Yet nothing can make up for a lifelong intimate acquaintance with music in a person who runs a musical theater.

From my seat I watched the strange ways of the human drive for power. That most courteous young man began to take on ever more responsibilities and decisions until he had a voice in every department. With youthful vigor he waded into the highly explosive field of labor negotiations, which plunged the Met into three grave crises within eight years — their consequences still unresolved in 1975. Bob could not have prevailed had it not been for Bing's rapidly increasing fatigue. His dependance on his young helper became such that he was lost when he had meetings with important artists when Bob was absent from New York.

After I had been in Boston for a few years, surveying the scene at the Met from a distance, detached and only mildly concerned, I suggested to Bing a change in his staff. My Met successor, George Schick, had also left, to become director of a music school, and what Bing needed — as I told him — was nothing less than a music director. The best that he could reply at a time when he had already lived through two ghastly conflicts with orchestra and other unionized members was, "What do I need a music director for? I know myself who the best available Tosca is." As if that had been the problem.

Immediately after the interview on Thanksgiving 1957 I began to attend as many meetings as I could find time for. Max briefed me on all the issues that he knew of, and it was more pleasure than duty for me to sit in on the sessions, which were called "artistic planning." They could be as short as a half-hour or as long as four hours, and sometimes we even began at ten in the morning, took luncheon together across the street, and carried on until four in the afternoon. The two principal topics occupying the group, which consisted of Bing, Gutman, his personal assistant, Max — later Bob and his assistant, Paul Jaretzki — and myself, were immediate problems and long-range decisions. The week always started with a double check on even the smallest role for the seven performances commencing fourteen days later. The New York Sunday supplements listing repertoire and cast "go to bed" (into printing) Wednesday night. Therefore the Monday last-minute perusal to locate any possible mistake. Unforeseen troubles mostly concerned the health question of artists who could not rehearse that day or perform the next, and carefully laid plans were irritatingly dislocated. Health became an ever more delicate issue as plane transportation grew in speed. A future historian may find curious causal connections between technological advances and decreasing career expectancy, particularly among singers.

Long-range planning was concerned with new productions two seasons thence, and here another management member was needed. Herman Krawitz had to give us timetables for the preparation of sets and costumes after the producer and designer had been chosen and had delivered their sketches to his shops. Francis Robinson joined us when touring, repertoire, and casting were on the agenda, as he knew most about the folkways and tastes of Memphis, Dallas, or Atlanta.

Of all the topics the most time-consuming was casting, not of first choices for premières, but of cover artists, whom we never had in sufficient quality and quantity. In my early years at the Met I was already aware of the indispensability of good understudies, lest a performance had to be changed and money refunded, yet I never suspected how much time and effort went into locating and persuading and contracting covers number one, two, and often three.

To the theatergoer the word "understudy" is synonymous with disappointment. The Met management attempted to remove that feeling as much as possible and worked over the problem so much that for a while I thought "artistic planning" should be renamed "discover best cover." No European opera manager needs to worry about this, as he has numerous other companies at such close quarters that even an afternoon cancellation by a singer does not cause a crisis. The Met carries its own bench of reserves, there being no other companies on the American continent from which a *Frau ohne Schatten* or a *Parsifal* replacement can be supplied.

The most complex single item was the calendar. When I joined the meetings in December 1957 it had already been laid out for the 1959–1960 season. I was taken aback, when we discussed the first draft for 1960–1961, by the labyrinth of inter-

dependent factors. With seven performances a week each subscription series must be considered on its own terms; the one
on odd Tuesdays must not become a stepchild but receive a
catholic choice of repertoire and a fair allocation of headline
stars.

After Bob and Paul had checked and double-checked the
basic calendars the following types of questions would come up
at our next meeting: "Thursday B series has neither Tebaldi,
nor Stella, nor Milanov." Unacceptable. "For the nonsubscription night on February 28th, we have not even the shadow of
a cast for *Butterfly*." "The Friday A series has not had any
Wagner for two years." "Del Monaco has asked to have after
each *Otello* three complete days off, and here we schedule him
on a Saturday matinee, which is only two days after his last
*Otello* on Wednesday." "For March 19th we have no cover for
Lady Macbeth." Question: "Where is Mary? She has a contract
for the whole season." Answer: "Mary has a concert in Maine,
some important community affair. Mrs. Belmont asked if we
could allow her to go there."

Wherever a meeting began, it ended with the topic of understudy, double, cover, insurance.

While the cover or understudy had *always* been a vexing and
uniquely American situation, the sixties produced a brand-new
problem that reversed all standards of the past. The Met ceased
to be the financial magnet it had been from the first day artists
crossed the ocean. With European houses paying better and
sometimes passing a little extra cash — unbeknownst to the tax
collector — under the table to a valuable artist, New York
suddenly could not compete.

The ever-alert rank consciousness of artists asserted itself in
two different ways. Artistically the greatest lures for a singer
were a new production, the nationwide radio transmission on a
Saturday afternoon, and opening night of the season, in that
order of preference. Needing two sopranos for casts A and B
in a new production of Verdi's *Simon Boccanegra*, the balance

was established only after guaranteeing soprano B the broadcast and A the première. Each of these performances carried a maximum of publicity that could be translated into the most lucrative of all U.S. activities, a concert tour.

The more common symbol of stardom was the fee. Juggling and fencing became so difficult that Bing established a maximum that was inviolable . . . until somebody irreplaceable said, "I don't care, either you pay me more or I do not sing." Ingenuity found an honorable way out. The maximum fee was not exceeded, but a verbal promise was made that the number of guaranteed performances would be more than the number of performances sung.

Many singers come from primitive backgrounds, and several of the artists from abroad were never happy with the law-abiding ways of the Met, in particular the withholding tax. One day I sat with Max, when the tenor Flaviano Labo barged in, wildly waving his weekly check in front of Max's nose, accusing him of thievery. "What's wrong?" Max wanted to know. "This is the third week in a row that the sum on the face of the draft is sharply lower than that on my contract," Labo yelled. Neither a patient explanation of the law nor the probability of a later refund could convince the tenor that he had not been the victim of another Mafia, headed by the management, in having a percentage extorted from him. He tore up his agreement and left precipitously.

Other, less temperamental singers thought that it was possible to make income tax detours by hiring a smart accountant, who landed himself in jail and, mortifying to me as a bystander, some of the greatest singers in a law court, where they shamelessly lied to an incredulous judge. As a result the Met's books have to be as open to any questioning official as if the whole management had been indicted and, many years later, the catching-up process goes on implicating more topnotch artists. Many cancellations, made overtly because of illness, were from fear of the tax investigator.

My first meeting was enhanced by two stories with which Bing introduced me to the inner sanctum. When in a review of casting plans Max might read, "Rhadames — Mr. Eichenstam," at which calamity all present would groan and ask if such was necessary. Max could come back with the words "Wiener schnitzel," which were as final as a two-thirds vote of the Senate in a case of cloture. The reference was to the story of a man who entered a restaurant and was told by the waiter, "You will enjoy the Wiener schnitzel." To the guest's query, "How do you know I will order Wiener schnitzel?" the waiter came back with "That's all there is on the menu."

The other magic word shutting off discussion was *Schlangenmensch*. This is the story of a circus director who returns home, and his wife asks, "What have you found?" "A new contortionist, Schlangenmensch." "How is he?" "Don't know, have not seen him perform." "How can you do such a thing?" "I risk nothing. If he is good he can kiss his own — if he is bad he can kiss my — arse." When Bing returned from his annual summer jaunts in Europe and announced a new find, the conversation ended with *"Schlangenmensch"* if he had not heard the singer himself.

The benefits and what to suggest to their committees were a source of many long debates. Generally their members wanted not only all the best-known stars but had phobias that limited the choice of operas. The most difficult of these benefit committees was the one of the Mizrachi Women, under the leadership of Mrs. Wouk, the novelist's mother. They not only were most demanding but excluded as offensive to their creed any and all works where a church was part of the setting. This taboo eliminated with one stroke *Cavalleria Rusticana, Faust, Don Carlo, Meistersinger, Parsifal, Lohengrin, Suor Angelica, Trovatore, Simon Boccanegra, Boris Godunov, Tosca,* and, one year while I was present, a particularly annoying *Manon* by Massenet. The work was perfectly suited for management's overall plans, we had a topnotch cast and the right date, except that we were stuck with a perfectly certain veto on account of the third-act setting, the Church of St. Sulpice. Paul Jaretzki provided momentary relief by suggesting that we might, for that one evening only, announce that the third act took place in the "Synagogue of St. Sulpice." That time Bing was the only one who did not howl with laughter, though he usually had the keenest sense of humor. That wonderful quality seemed to desert him only when the Jewish question was on the agenda.

Any American or European manager in music or theater deals constantly with holidays of religious groups, among which the Jewish Day of Atonement is the stickiest. The opera played but no observing member would report for work. Hence no large chorus, no large orchestra could be planned.

That Bing hired black singing stars does not deserve much praise when such singers as Leontyne Price and Martina Arroyo were involved. He battled, however, for black chorus members. When the local opera committee of Atlanta suggested leaving the "Nigras" behind, Bing told them that he would rather cancel the forthcoming and all ensuing Met visits than yield to that suggestion. From then on this issue did not exist anymore and Atlanta as well as all other Confederate stages were enjoying a mixed chorus in both senses of the term.

With ex-Nazis he took diverse attitudes according to the artistic interests of the Met. Those whom the opera needed had not been tainted, and all those who were suspect the Met did not need.

He was single-minded about his task as general manager, accepting only what he felt was good and rejecting anything he didn't like. His interpretation of the Met's function was entirely in the traditions of the American bourgeoisie, with lavish productions and star-studded casts eschewing anything controversial. He was a master at getting attention and publicity, which is quite difficult for an administrative director who neither conducts nor directs. He did it by making himself purposely aloof, veddy veddy English, by making the most cutting comments to journalists who quoted them with elation, and by cultivating an image that made him well known, his name a household word, and, I am afraid, his personal life the handmaiden of the public persona.

Just as I began to get involved with the Met management they got involved with RCA. Up to that time the Met had made recordings for an organization called Record-of-the-Month, an offspring of the well-known Book-of-the-Month Club. The principal difficulty was that, absurdly enough, the Met could never cast any recording with its great name singers, because nearly all of them were under exclusive contracts to Decca or RCA. Then George Marek stepped in and concluded a tripartite agreement making all the stars available for recordings, since by special arrangement even the Decca artists could appear on these club issues. Everybody made a splendid deal, or so it seemed.

As this project, now called "Opera-of-the-Month," took wings with the collaboration of the formerly missing glamour singers, RCA, responsible for the technical production and manufacture of the albums, moved nearly all recording activities to Europe, where costs were much lower. The Met's indigenous forces, orchestra, chorus, and the second-line singers of smaller roles, were the losers. The name "Metropolitan Opera Recording" was prominently displayed on every album, more than implying that these were actually made by and at the Met. No wonder that the unions representing the betrayed members got furious and readied an attack, which came off for a disagreeable first round in the spring of 1959.

For that summer RCA had mapped out a big program with Reiner and myself as the conductors. Arriving in Toronto, the final stop on that year's Met tour, I found a wire from the American Federation of Musicians (the international union to which I had belonged since 1942) revoking an already granted permission to "record abroad." While it is not at all clear that a conductor can be compelled to abide by union discipline, neither I, nor any of my America-based colleagues, have ever tested this dimly lit area. My attorney in the 1950s was highly conscious of the "union" question and its political implications, and for a while his efforts were successful. When I made my first London recordings in 1955 (the Mozart symphonies) he sent a smooth, routine letter to the Federation and received a one-sentence answer that satisfied one and all as representing an inquiry for and a granting of permission to make records abroad. (American musicians feel that the lower rates in Europe have jeopardized their recording income and the fight to stop European recordings by American artists has never ceased.)

Now, for the first time, an already granted permission was canceled and that five days before I had to fly to Vienna. Considering the timing this looked like a determined challenge. I passed the problem on to the manager of RCA's "Red Seal Division," and between his labor-relations experts and the union a temporary peace, of which I never knew the terms, was declared. All I was interested in, and what I received, was the green light to travel to Vienna and begin recording two choice pieces, *Ariadne auf Naxos* and *Don Giovanni*.

But when in 1960 my lawyer addressed another smooth letter to the union, it was summarily rejected, and even the maneuvers of a friend, a general counsel for several labor unions who dickered with the top lawyer of the American Federation of Musicians, remained totally fruitless, and nothing could restore permission for me to record abroad that year. A personal message conveyed to me that the union was fighting RCA and not me, which was no comfort. RCA of course engaged a European-based conductor to replace me, which meant that in the end RCA was not inconvenienced or damaged but an American member of the Federation had been the loser.

While I recorded in Rome in 1959 — in addition to *Ariadne* and *Don Giovanni* a star-studded *Turandot* — negotiations between the three parties in New York, the Met, RCA, and the Federation, resulted in a truce, the price of which appeared to be two opera recordings made at Manhattan Center in New York under my direction with a full complement of the Met's orchestra and chorus. The works were *The Barber of Seville* and *Macbeth*.

A musicological oddity led to a new flare-up and disagreement between management and orchestra. The orchestration of *The Barber* requires one oboist. Only the Overture needs two players. Rossini had written that Overture for another work first, and he obviously did not rescore it when it served for the *Barber*. The orchestra was represented as demanding that the two oboists be engaged for all the scheduled sessions, and of course management objected. The outcome must be still in the payroll accounts, though it is no longer in my memory.

It was after my return from Europe in the summer of 1961 that I realized the truce had been less than peace. No sooner did I arrive in New York than I learned that the Met orchestra had made demands for increases amounting to a total of 137 percent of their former pay and Bing, after a board meeting, simply canceled the 1961–1962 season. This, in his view, would bring union and musicians to their senses. In my view, it was a fearful mistake to call off a whole season without considering the economic effects on several hundred people, most of whom did not even have any dispute with management. I am convinced that the summer of 1961 marked the beginning of a conflict that still smolders fourteen years later. Morale was very low, and in that atmosphere Risë Stevens telegraphed President Kennedy for help. He responded by inviting the high command of the Met and the union to the White House, where he fairly compelled them to submit to binding arbitration by his own Secretary of Labor, Arthur Goldberg.

In August, those hearings were held in New York, broadcast live by the municipal radio station. I listened to every minute in sheer fascination.

Bing counted on a compromise halfway between what management had offered and what the musicians demanded, but Arthur Goldberg, with whom I spoke a lot later on, dismissed that as an inadequate way of settling a dispute and, indeed, his award gave the musicians mere crumbs compared to what they had expected from an ex-general counsel of the steelworkers' union. It was not as stunning a victory for management as it was a defeat for the players, represented as they were now by privately hired lawyers, while their official union sat idly by. Unfortunately, Bing did not know then how to make peace. He was so totally taken up with everything on stage that he literally never lowered his eyes to glance at the people in the orchestra. This attitude was not lost on them. He considered the players an impolite, impertinent bunch who "refused to realize" that the public could not care less who played in the pit. Unfortunately this was not just said in private.

Goldberg arbitrated the economic issues but referred to a professional arbitrator the conflict over the dismissal of a horn player, Lester Salomon, who, according to the union, was penalized for being a shop steward. This case was heard in February 1962 by Theodore Kheel, and I had to appear as witness on the same day I would conduct in the evening my final Met performance before leaving — with pleasure — to take up my new duties with the Boston Symphony. The hour as witness was most revealing and quite depressing. I was treated by the union lawyer who represented Salomon with great courtesy; from the line of questioning I noted that the union's target was Bob Herman. The whole scene was worthy of an Ionesco play setting. At least forty of Salomon's colleagues had crowded into a conference room with a normal capacity of ten. I sat less than three feet from the poor protagonist, and the combination of insufficient oxygen with an oversupply of nicotine fumes made the place unbearable.

As always, after scenes of basically futile unpleasantness, I left in a melancholy mood and took it as a strange symbol of

my ever madder profession that my final day as member of the
Met should be divided between a labor arbitration and Mozart's
*Marriage of Figaro.*

During my years with the Boston Symphony I continued to
see Bing from time to time, usually having lunch with him
when we came to New York for our regular concerts. I did not
keep track of any details, but my interest was sufficiently alive
to notice that in 1964, the time of the next round of labor negotiations, the orchestra, after weeks of unproductive dickering,
agreed to carry on, without strike or lockout on the old terms,
with the proviso that any new benefits would be retroactive.

How and why this was accepted and allowed to simmer for
two full years we will never know, but in 1966, a few days before the opening of the new opera house in Lincoln Center, the
blow fell: the orchestra declared they would play the opening
night only and no more without a new contract. When I arrived at six-thirty to have dinner, before the inaugural performance, I saw Bing, who told me in quiet desperation that things
were in miserable shape. He was outside the new house to greet
Mrs. Lyndon Johnson and the Philippine President, but ninety
minutes later he stepped in front of the curtain and announced
that there was a new contract and that the new Met would not
be closed. His board president, Anthony Bliss, had negotiated
inside while he awaited the honored guests outside.

There was still no peace, and in 1969, at the next collective
bargaining episode, everything broke down. The Met did not
open for several months and when performances started after
Christmas one of their most valuable assets had disappeared.
For as long as I could remember there had been a legend that
nobody could get a good pair of seats on a subscription basis
until he inherited them, such was the queue for these choice
admissions.

During the long shutdown in 1969 many displeased New
Yorkers canceled their subscriptions. When the box office reopened, the legendary queue of two thousand awaiting impa-

tiently the passing of old ticket holders had mysteriously evaporated into thin air.

Between my first rehearsal for *Arabella* in 1957 and the performance of *Figaro* in February 1962 five years had passed, during which time I had had my fill of alternating marvelous musical experiences with those routine affairs that are, alas, inevitable if one spends too much time with opera. The former never failed to excite and elate me, while the latter were invariably melancholy evenings followed by short hours of depression.

When I concluded my Met affiliation in 1962 I had spent thirteen seasons of my twenty-five American years with that company. It may have been a love-hate relation, but it was always my second home.

# PART III

# The Boston Years

## The Boston Years

The invitation to conduct in Boston arrived three weeks after I had decided to leave the brokerage house of Arthur Judson. The fall of 1959 marked only my second full season as music consultant, but I already felt the glue hardening and myself getting stuck at the Met. To convey to Judson my concern I asked him, as a condition for extending our then renewable agreement, to guarantee me a certain annual sum from symphonic engagements. As expected he refused and I gave notice of not continuing with him.

My mother, to whom I brought the happy tidings that she would hear me at Carnegie Hall in thirteen months with a topflight orchestra, was already too ill to enjoy the news. In June of 1960 she passed away, followed seven months later by my aunt. The symbiotic relationship of the sisters was such that I knew neither of them could last long without the other, and as it was, my aunt went without any clearly diagnosed disease. After her burial in the winter of 1961 I proceeded to Boston for my debut there.

Part of the three-week schedule was the regular eastern tour, including a Carnegie Hall concert on Wednesday evening for which I invited Bing to sit in my box.

Early the following morning he called me at home to say that he had felt during the music a strong and unusual cohesive force between the players and myself, that there could be more to this than a dozen concerts, and could he be of any help.

I was surprised and touched, thanked him but discouraged any follow-up. I felt nothing could or should be done.

His sensitivity to the currents was keener than mine. Two months later I was asked to become music director without any interventions.

My debut on Friday afternoon, February 3, 1961, went very well, and while I was starting to dress for the repeat Saturday night, my forty-ninth birthday, a blizzard caused postponement of the concert. I stood at my hotel window looking down on the deserted Boston Common bemoaning my fate. If this was a bad omen — as I felt then — it only proves Freud's theory that there is no such thing as an omen.

On balance my years in Boston were the most fruitful of my life. When my stay ended I was not only more mature but have been ever since of a disposition that has made aging a joy rather than a sequence of anxieties. Whatever the difficulties, they contributed ultimately to an outlook on life's values that I consider positive and unshakable: All overt accomplishment is relatively unimportant if it does not allow for an inner balance.

My eighth concert was in New London, Connecticut. Afterward I had a snack with Leonard Burkat in the only open diner, which was already filled with members of the orchestra. Burkat was a music librarian who had become Munch's indispensable best helper. When I had finished, a most distinguished-looking gentleman rose at a nearby table, came over, and asked, *"Maître, êtes-vous content de vos ouvriers?"* To my affirmative reply he said, *"Et nous sommes content de nôtre patron,"* all in the vernacular of the factory. That was Louis Speyer, English horn player since a massive invasion of Boston by superb musicians from Paris in the 1920s. That short discourse was a pleasant confirmation of my own feelings that things had gone well.

After concert number thirteen I awaited in my hotel the moment to be off to the airport for my flight to Chicago when the BSO manager, Thomas Perry, rang. Making his compliments for the "glorious music!" he regretted that the following season was already so fully booked that the best he could offer was one solitary week of concerts. Would I do them for the sake of uninterrupted continuity after such an auspicious beginning? I accepted and left Boston on that happy note.

Boston was the first stop on the spring tour that I had to make with the Met in 1961. A few days earlier Perry phoned to ask me if I could arrive before the company and take lunch with him and the president of the board of trustees, Henry Cabot. This sounded pleasant enough because I had not met Cabot at all during my guest stint and looked forward to an agreeable hour. Little did I foresee that with the arrival of the main course Cabot would turn to me and say, "We would like you to come to Boston as Munch's successor as music director of the orchestra." He spoke plainly and openly of Munch's fatigue, that he would not continue beyond the summer of 1962 and that the trustees did not want the customary interim period of guest conductors, especially since they all were convinced that I was their best choice.

Cabot outlined the full extent of the position, and I listened carefully, without quite catching the shocking number of concerts to be done annually. He spoke mostly of his concern with the Berkshire Music Center, which had deteriorated since its inception. Koussevitzky, wanting to teach, had created around the outdoor concerts at Tanglewood a master class for young conductors, which led in turn to a student orchestra and gradually to other related and unrelated activities. After resigning in 1949 Koussevitzky still held on to the summer school until he died two years later, by which time Munch had seen enough of the task upon him to flatly refuse involvement with the Music Center. His title, director, was purely nominal by mutual agreement. Since 1951 there had been a vacuum in direction, and Cabot expected me to fill this and bring to it new thinking.

This was the only aspect of the vast and complex organization that he described negatively. He felt that the orchestra was in fine shape, an evaluation with which a year later I would have to disagree. The necessary and welcome period of seventeen months between appointment and incumbency gave me many chances of hearing the Carnegie Hall concerts under Munch, Burgin, Monteux, and Ansermet.

Now I had the finest appointment to be found and, best of all, was not involved in any intrigue. I could tell my children and, later, my grandchildren that I had once been a protagonist in a storybook happening, and had not always been involved in the proverbial backstage machinations. I had received a most important post only because my music-making found favor.

That April day marked the high point of my relations with Cabot. As man deteriorates from birth to death so did our feelings, and communications never again reached the easy cordiality and understanding of that day. Our agreement was for the customary three years but changed into a sine die contract after my second season.

I could see Cabot whenever I wished, as his time and availability for the orchestra's affairs were unlimited, his interest and devotion inexhaustible. His accessibility was unfortunately just as easy for the players, some of whom were in the habit of bringing their puniest complaints to him directly, by-passing Perry, a man of unfailingly pleasant and courteous demeanor. However, it soon became evident that the manager was often unable to face making decisions. He belonged to a species frequently encountered in the music world: he was neither a fully professional musician nor a trained businessman. He had taught English, which he had mastered to a high degree, and his letters could be full of the most felicitous phrases and sophisticated elliptical statements. He deferred in many matters to Cabot, whose affection for Perry was as sincere as the latter's admiration for Cabot. As soon as I had to make plans for my first season this state of affairs proved to be a bottleneck.

I asked Perry how much budget was earmarked for soloists, not an unimportant item in a season of twenty-four different programs. He gave me to understand that neither soloists nor guest conductors would figure large in the BSO season because the "glorious" orchestra itself with its regular musical leader was quite sufficient.

That was a wonderful way to feel. I knew that in his day Koussevitzky had conducted most programs himself and actually frowned on having soloists for two very simple reasons: he was not good in accompaniments and his concerts everywhere sold out to the doors.

My eyes, twelve years after Koussevitzky's retirement, had noticed an alarming number of empty seats in all the concert series, except for Friday afternoons, at Symphony Hall. I then thought that the trustees, who were mostly matinee patrons, and the manager were either unaware or did not care that the other concerts were less than fully attended. Saturday afternoons in New York looked terrible, and in Washington the Boston Symphony had abandoned its own subscription and gone into the local orchestra's series.

In my meetings with Perry I began to resemble George Bernard Shaw when he said to Sam Goldwyn: "Trouble is that you are concerned only with Art and I with Money." Here I was concerned with attendance, which I considered an indispensable factor in any performer's success.

I had to prepare for a total of 111 concerts, played in a dozen subscription series, and twenty-four programs for the summer festival at Tanglewood without any firm policy by the management on participating solo artists.

After this initial uphill battle, which was never decided, I got an agreeable surprise when I proposed to change the configuration of the regular five visits to New York. These trips were first established with railroad schedules in mind. In 1961 the final tour date was still a Saturday matinee at Carnegie Hall, for the now outdated reason that it was practical to make the 5:00 P.M. train from New York to Boston. After we had shuffled and reshuffled, our schedule in New York omitted matinees, avoided playing the Brooklyn Academy of Music on Friday nights which had been a perfect disaster in such a Jewish community, and pushed Washington from the sequence of New York dates, thus allowing the orchestra members four nights in the same hotel. All this was possible and welcome because we were in my first season starting a different pattern, moving the orchestra's New York appearances from Carnegie Hall to the new Lincoln Center, with the New York Philharmonic scheduled for the grand opening concert on September 23 and the BSO to follow on Monday, the twenty-fourth. Nobody knew at the time how the hall would be, for if anyone had, the high spirits with which I had mapped out the first season would have been somewhat dampened.

The next problem, at least for Perry, was typical of his general problem. He wished to have me go along with the Boston Symphony's endorsement of the Baldwin piano. For some reason it seemed difficult for him to explain to me that the Baldwin company was of great importance to the orchestra organization. Not only was there the matter of a substantial contribution, but more significantly, the Music Center at Tanglewood every year got over seventy pianos for practice and other school purposes, without charge. A tuner was assigned to the Berkshires for each year's sessions. I, as well as other conductors connected with the BSO, could get free loans of Baldwin pianos — there seemed no limit to the generosity of the firm and the overall value to the Boston Symphony. Yet it took Perry a presentation of some length to get to a point where I, now on to his aim, interrupted with the words, "And we should have as soloists some pianists who prefer the Baldwin." Even after my acknowledgment of the situation, he continued to explain the delicacies of selecting artists who were identified with the Baldwin endorsement. Thus, I did find it difficult to establish open and easy communication concerning the myriad problems, large and small, that go into the making of a long and complex program!

Fortunately there was always something easy and positive after each convoluted topic. As soon as the Baldwin matter had been settled, Perry informed me that Richard Burgin, associate conductor and concertmaster for decades, would retire with Munch, but only as concertmaster. This was doubly good news. While I rejoiced at being able to start by filling the most important place in an orchestra with a musician of my choice, I was equally happy to have an experienced veteran of the Boston Symphony as associate. Burgin was a first-rate musician, a good conductor whose work I had already observed, a mellow person with a fine sense of humor, and persona grata with his colleagues.

The appointment of the new first violinist was an uncomplicated matter. For an orchestra such as Boston's, the best talent is available for principal chairs, and even within the violin sections there were no less than ten players who auditioned for me, but when all was said and done the inside dope had been correct: a young man on the third stand, Joseph Silverstein, won hands down — a difficult stance for a violin player — to the displeasure of a few important musical figures in New York. He had won the Naumburg, a coveted award, and got with the prize a good start for a solo career. Being a wise young man, Silverstein preferred the life of the concertmaster and thereby disappointed his judges, who probably would not have elected him had his true intentions been manifest. The appointment was very helpful to me musically, as we had in most matters similar tastes, while in nonmusical problems I fought some unhappy battles where he was involved, although he did not deliberately contribute to my difficulties.

The other half of the Burgin incumbency, the position of associate conductor, turned out to have been handled in a less satisfactory manner. It is the rule in all symphony orchestras that the associate — or assistant — conductor, the standby or understudy or cover conductor, in a word the person who will direct should the principal chef get ill, is present at each rehearsal to learn the program and to witness all the details and nuances agreed on between conductor and players. When I started my regular turn in September 1962 I never saw Burgin at any rehearsal but thought nothing of it, assuming that for a man who knew as much as he, the constant presence at rehearsals might be annoying and unnecessary. In the past he had sat at the first desk, filling both his tasks, and I was confident that he had no need to witness the practice sessions for another Eroica or Prokofiev symphony.

After my opening concerts we journeyed to New York for the special affair at Lincoln Center, and he was there with us. The next time I saw him was five or six weeks later, when we made our first regular Eastern trip. Back in Boston I finally asked Perry about Burgin's erratic appearances and what I should make of them. With some of his usual hesitancy he unfolded the arrangements that had been made when Burgin resigned as concertmaster.

Burgin had received permission from Cabot to move to Florida, where he directed an orchestra, as long as he would be available to the Boston Symphony for all touring. I was so dumfounded by the absurdity of this agreement that I failed to ask first why this had been kept a secret from me. "What is to happen in Boston if I get sick?" I wanted to know. I was told that the flight from Miami to Boston was short enough to allow Burgin to be with us for anything but a last-hour emergency, say a 6:00 P.M. sudden indisposition or a broken leg, and in that dire situation, we always had Harry Ellis Dickson right within the orchestra.

This gentleman, whom I valued as one of the finest storytellers and Koussevitzky imitators, had been for many years the associate conductor of the Boston Pops; his credits include his pupil Danny Kaye, whom he prepared for conductorial sallies, but to my best information he had done little symphony conducting of his own. Perry not only was supremely confident that a last-minute emergency would find Harry on the ball, the subscribers indulgent, and everything in the end as "glorious" as always, but he seemed ever so slightly put out by my visible irritation at this entire arrangement, which was, to my blunt thinking, neither appropriate, cricket, or very kind to me.

My personal representative spent many hours in a lost effort to convince Perry that a fully available assistant conductor was an urgent necessity, but the best obtainable result was to let me have, after two full seasons, a person who, without actually conducting, could relieve me of many nonconductorial tasks. By the time this became reality, Burkat had been away from Boston for over a year. He was lured to New York by Columbia Records for a position in which he could rise, commensurate with his abilities. In Boston he would have remained an eternal second. Another two years had to pass for a new assistant conductor to be engaged.

At the time of all my planning meetings with Perry in the spring of 1961, I looked forward to a marvelous tandem of aides in the persons of Burgin and Burkat, not realizing that one would be absent and the other leaving us within a year.

In my second season I spent one of my regular winter rest periods in London and found, to my great joy, a most wonderful assistant, Andrew Raeburn. I can't begin to list all his qualities as a person and as a musician. There was one outstanding contribution among his many: his profound expertise and understanding of recording and all its problems. He had been head of a small record firm, Argo, where he had specialized in baroque music. Without him my constantly increasing difficulties with RCA might have been totally overpowering. When he arrived to take up his duties in the summer of 1964, it was in the nick of time as far as recording problems went.

With my contract the Boston Symphony had given me another document to sign, a declaration that I would abide by the existing agreement that made the Boston Symphony an exclusive RCA performer and therefore myself, now an exclusive Boston conductor, bound to that particular record company as well.

## RCA *and* BSO

Three months after my appointment I became aware that relations between the Boston Symphony and the Victor Company were not good. That summer I had once again been "permitted" by the American Federation of Musicians to record abroad and flew to Rome for a *Bohème*. George Marek, vice president of RCA and man-in-charge of the classical repertoire was, as usual, there too. He loved to assist at sessions and hear the playbacks and treat us all to dinners at Passetto. This time he took several opportunities to speak to me of his grave concern over the "whole Boston situation."

The upshot of his long explanations was that ten annual LP releases were more than RCA could sell. It was his idea to reverse the figures in the existing commitment of eight Pops and ten Symphony releases. When I had fully understood the direction of his thought I asked him how he reckoned the effect of a new conductor appearing for the first time in front of "his" orchestra with the cheerful announcement that he had succeeded in reducing the number of recordings to be made. Even though the personnel of the Pops was about 90 percent identical with that of the Symphony, all Symphony's principal players were missing from the Pops and would lose an enormous amount of money. And what effect would this retrenchment have on the morale of an ensemble at the start of a "new era"? This plan was diametrically opposed to all precepts for success. I took note that George had spoken of "releases," not numbers of disks, and I thought that finding long works needing more than one LP would reduce the bothersome figure without damaging the orchestra.

That was later the rationale behind my selecting the Requiems by Brahms and Verdi, symphonies by Mahler, and, longest of all, a complete *Lohengrin*, which consumed five LPs, reducing for the year of its issue the RCA commitment to five releases. How these grand projects fared is part of the story to be told.

George Marek had barely finished telling me of his worries, complaints, concerns, and desires to reduce our recordings when RCA senior producer Richard Mohr got my ear for a recital of his list of undesirable players in Boston's great orchestra. Mohr was at the time deeply involved with the records of the nonpareil Chicago Symphony and found, when comparing them, that Boston needed twelve key replacements. With that many alarums in my mind I began to listen systematically to recordings made in Boston during the previous five years.

What gave me perhaps the single gravest concern was Mohr's contention that Symphony Hall had not been satisfactory from RCA's technical viewpoint. It seemed incredible to me that this finest of all halls for beautiful, rich sound should be rated less than a recording engineer's dream. Mohr's assertion, however, gave me a chance to ask and obtain from RCA's management an appropriation for one three-hour session during which I would experiment with several seating arrangements for the orchestra. I was certain that some mistake in seating was the cause of the unsatisfactory results and attitude of RCA.

Very early in my first month this experimental affair took place. All the downstairs seats were removed from Symphony Hall, three different sets of music stands and players' chairs were prearranged for the recording, and we selected three very short pieces of music with varying orchestral sound problems to give us, when we reviewed the results, the widest musical diversity. What is good for Brahms may be — and indeed, will be —

acoustically not so good for Webern. RCA sent a panel of producers and engineers to evaluate the tapes, and we added our first desk players to help judge the merits of the options.

When the returns were in, it was not very difficult for the two groups of experts to agree that one seating had given by and large the best results in all three pieces, and the BSO and RCA decided that henceforth we had a new way of recording.

No sooner did we record in earnest our first public issue than some of the placement was changed. This happened so gradually that only a detective could have registered what went on. The engineer would come into the hall, move one microphone just a bit this way or that, which in turn brought discomfort to a player who couldn't see the conductor. The player moved a little in some direction, which upset a balance. This brought back the engineer for another tuck and push. It was as if one had a budget and added sheepishly a tiny sum here and one there, until the entire total no longer had any connection with the original plan.

In approximately two hundred sessions of three hours each we never got a fixed and established feeling. Each start was at square one and there was no end to the troubles and bickerings. Too late in the game I concluded that we needed another producer. Mohr, out of sympathy with the hall itself and unenthusiastic about the orchestra, should perhaps have disqualified himself, since there were four senior producers at RCA, and another might have at least come with a more positive attitude if not with more skill. Ultimately the fault had to have been mine, because I missed the right moment to suggest that somebody else be sent to Boston for our recordings. Very much toward the end, Peter Dellheim and then Howard Scott replaced Mohr, but by that time the future of RCA was with Philadelphia and that of the BSO with Deutsche Grammophon.

To distribute postmortem responsibilities in a complex team effort is very sticky and perhaps of no value. There were so many small factors of great importance. When I had, from my

third season onward, the good help and advice of record expert
Andrew Raeburn, he suggested that it would be a great lift
technically, and for general morale, if a special room were allo-
cated in Symphony Hall for the recording apparatus. As it was,
each group of sessions was preceded by a long, laborious, and
very costly setting up of innumerable pieces of equipment,
which had to be dismantled again after the conclusion and sent
back to New York. A special room in place of the Old Instrument Room at Symphony Hall (which sometimes had to be
vacated between sessions to make it available for its duty as a
foyer-exhibition couloir) would have gone far in making the
RCA people feel more at home. It was simply impossible to
budge Perry, who had to approve whatever suggestions were
made. No sooner had BSO terminated the RCA contract and
signed with DGG than a room was found where the engineers
could park their equipment.

Equally vague were the decisions on repertoire. For any recording company a leading orchestra represents a major "artist,"
and enormous expenses are attached. Each recording session cost
a small fortune. There was more than a year to establish repertoire policy before we began to record. I knew, from hearing
chance remarks by one of the trustees, that there had been a
steep decline in the BSO Corporation's royalty receipts. Notwithstanding the great significance attached to this by at least
one trustee, Perry never spoke of royalties to me in any sense
whatever. Neither did RCA, which was primarily concerned
with them and decided, with the help of some statistics, what
pieces to record. I knew what I wanted to record, and some of
it was accepted, but many suggestions were opposed by the
baffling phrase, "It does not sell." As RCA and its competing
record companies obviously consult the same crystal ball, they
all produce and issue identical titles and never bother with
others. In my first season we recorded Schumann's Fourth
Symphony. I love Schumann very much and have programmed
not only his best-known vintage pieces but several neglected

works as well. Ten days before my seventh year with Boston, the manager of the Red Seal Division, Roger Hall, canceled an already scheduled recording of Schumann's Second Symphony with the surprising explanation, "It won't sell."

What nobody took the time and thought to do was follow a basic contemporary maneuver: build an "image" of the new combination RCA was going to put out. For this a center line of recognizable repertoire is the first necessity. George Marek was so much less au courant in the symphonic repertoire than in opera that he did not attempt it, and when he brought Hall in as the new Red Seal manager, to replace the gentle Alan Kayes, who was thenceforth sidetracked to club operations, our goose was cooked. Hall had been manager of the Philadelphia Orchestra and wanted nothing more than to bring that great orchestra back to RCA, where it had been many years earlier. He accomplished his desire by making such a magnificent contract between the two that it cost him his position with Victor. That was no help to the Boston Symphony or to myself.

I fought with Roger Hall as soon as he was hired. I was very happy with Joseph Silverstein and thought that a musician of his talents deserved not only to regularly play concertos with "his" orchestra but ought to record some of them as well. Alan Kayes had promised we could do an LP, consisting of the Bartók and Stravinsky concertos with Silverstein. Session dates, duly preceded by concerts featuring these works, were all set when Roger proposed canceling the entire project. His novel and original reasoning was, "It won't sell, no concertmaster does." This time I forced the issue by simply stating that this had been a firm promise, that this concertmaster meant a lot to me, and that he was a first-class fiddler, and I insisted on going through with it as planned. I have no way of knowing if I could have established truly good relations with Roger, but that beginning was surely a guarantee for very bad ones.

In his behalf I will say that he never minced words about the slow speed of Boston's recorded output. I must assume that he had been briefed by Mohr and had seen the log of our accomplishments when he faced me with the disagreeable truth that we taped an average of six to seven minutes of music per contract hour, while Chicago taped ten and even eleven. (A contract hour consists of forty minutes' work and twenty minutes' rest.) That conversation took place in my fifth season. I knew from the first moment I recorded with the Boston Symphony that of the principal players two particularly would slow down our progress. It was most important that there seemed to be no way of getting either of them to retire from the orchestra. Both were deserving of pensions, though neither was really old. Their trouble was that they were instinct-performers, which is another way of saying that they did not know exactly how they did what they were doing. In concert one plays once through any given piece or spot or passage and if something untoward happens, it is water over the dam. In recording it is not only occasionally necessary but the rule that everything is performed and repeated many times until a perfect version has been reached. A section player's small mishaps can either not be heard or often don't matter, but when a solo wind player strays from the straight and narrow the whole edifice totters. Some of our fellows in these chairs were responsible for a loss of time that over the years must have accrued to a staggering total.

I did not have to wait for recording sessions to hear their shortcomings and worked very hard in rehearsal to correct vagaries. There was no way in the world to replace anyone for at least two seasons, according to the trade agreement between corporation and orchestra. Naturally I wanted to do the best with what I had. But I had reckoned without the democracy of my president of the trustees. Returning from my second midseasonal two-week break I received a message through my personal representative. "Cabot has phoned with a few minor points and asks you to please stop riding the principal . . . player."

If the usual procedure in orchestras was for the titular conductor to discuss with management and directors what to do when a player proved unsatisfactory, in Boston this custom was reversed. There it was the quaint custom for players to visit Cabot in his downtown office and complain about the conductor. Cabot himself enlightened me with gusto. He told me of several instrumentalists who "used to come to my office and cry that Munch did not like their playing." Judging by their presence and prosperity when I was music director it was Munch who had changed his mind about or given up on the orchestra. Evidently one of our solo winds had been traveling the usual route to State Street and had seen to it that Cabot advised the music director "not to ride" him.

The case of another player was more complex, since he could play with great flair and personality, his trouble being too much lubrication on important occasions. Once he did not show for two concerts on a tour, disappearing after a Saturday evening at Newark and missing the following performances. It was most likely a "lost weekend," and Cabot, when informed of it, decided to be Dutch uncle and speak seriously to the offender. It was at Tanglewood the following summer when Cabot got around to his avuncular role, telling me of the interview before the evening concert. Our chastened player had one of his worst evenings, highlighted by several extremely noticeable accidents, called "clams" in the argot of the American musician, "split notes" in the more international vocabulary of the English. Whatever one calls them, the man, upset or just in bad form, spoiled more than one passage during the half program he played. When Cabot came backstage after the close, he beamed at me and wanted to know if I did not agree with him that the fellow had sounded especially beautiful that night. What could I say? But when I thought this through I understood that Cabot's major motivation was to be a good father to the orchestra, which, if we go along with Dr. Sigmund Freud, meant for him to oppose staunchly the conductor of the orchestra, who has been depicted proverbially as the bad father, the strict ruler, the tyrant.

There was a mayor of Chicago who ran for every election on the same platform: fighting King George III, although it was by calendar count the twentieth century. I felt all through my years with the BSO that Cabot was still fighting Koussevitzky, for whom he had little affection.

This incident with Cabot reenforced my view that no musical organization can stay at the top if its real direction is thinned out by too many vetoes and by having nonmusicians make professional decisions. It was the avowed philosophy that the music director of the Boston organization had all musical matters in his hands, which is a purely theoretical right, since there are no musical issues that do not entail all kinds of other, nonmusical, consequences.

Notwithstanding the protective umbrella that Cabot held over a few musicians, I did get the orchestra into fine shape in a very short time. This was not easy; it took enormous concentration and a great effort to ignore the prominent sore spots. For the rock-bottom minimum of one entire season with well over one hundred concerts and ten long-playing records, I had to perform with the roles as they had been distributed. I was in the same position as a tournament bridge player who plays the cards that are dealt him. Among my cards there were a subprincipal in a string section who made his neighbor, the principal, more nervous than he already was. Each time he turned a page they missed a few bars because of his slowness in getting there. A subprincipal of another string section was hard of hearing. Sickness in a double bass section was so rampant that it was the exception to find a quorum present. Of the ten groups representing woodwinds, brasses, percussion, and other instruments, only three were in first-class condition, the bassoons, the battery, and the harps.

Several gentlemen announced their retirement voluntarily,

others were ever so gently persuaded that it was time to take it easy, and others bargained to be placed into less prominent chairs. Between these methods and other, unfortunate resignations, there were thirty-eight new faces in the orchestra after five years. The unfortunate resignations were the principal violist and cellist, both of whom had offers from the friendly music director of the Philadelphia Orchestra. I could not fault the violist, Joseph de Pasquale, who was attracted to Philadelphia by the prospect of forming a string quartet with three brothers. This is for anyone an irresistible magnet. Samuel Mayes was another case. A personal friend of his financed his recording Prokofiev's Symphony-Concerto, with the BSO as part of our recorded cycle of Prokofiev music. However, around Christmas of 1964, he suddenly announced he was leaving for the Quaker City.

Perhaps the most difficult part of the personnel question is created by the constant shifting within the string sections. American violinists and cellists are a disaffected lot and come and go all the time. Our cello section was so good that five players from the ranks went in as many years to other orchestras as principals. In the violins, too, young people would join after successful auditions only to declare two or three years later that they preferred to switch to teaching. There is a social problem that sees an orchestra member as inferior to a faculty member. The net effect is that from one year to the next the classic repertoire must be re-rehearsed because many new players do not know it. They no longer go into the provinces, because the shortage of good strings is such that upon graduating from conservatories a better than average fiddler can immediately join a first-class symphony orchestra.

It was only in my last two seasons that I could perform Beethoven and Brahms without constantly starting from scratch. Some of our finest concerts were played with either brief brushups or no runthroughs whatsoever. On such occasions I felt the flow of the music as something spontaneous, free, and yet without blemish or sloppiness. Rare as those renditions were, they seemed to make everything worth while to me.

## The Schedule

No matter how complex the issues, or how difficult the principal personalities, I thought many times that all my questions and problems could be handled much more effectively if I had more time. The raison d'être of being a music director is still to function as principal conductor and my calendar left little doubt on that subject.

September 1962 began glamorously. Perry called with an urgent message: Roger Stevens, the theatrical producer and major linchpin of the new cultural activities in Washington, wanted me to drive over to Newport, Rhode Island, to say a few words at a reception devoted to the unveiling of the model for the cultural center to be built in the capital. Mrs. Kennedy, wife of the President, would do the unveiling, and one of the luminaries invited had been taken ill, hence the last-minute call for help.

Perry and I were driven to the town known as the famous "last resort" of a society that has been called a thing of the past. It was my first look at Newport, but I found the assembled crowd, the traditional collection of "important" figures from Finance, Culture, Politics, and Leisure, in robust health, showing no signs of decline. Mrs. Kennedy was shy and somewhat ill at ease. Stevens, major-domo extraordinary, called the party to order and gave the background of the plan for a cultural center, conveying the need of private financing to get America's overdue cultural explosion into Washington, where no appropriate place existed for theater, opera, or concerts. I spoke for a few minutes, endorsing the need for a center, and then the First Lady said a few words, which she delivered very well.

Standing behind her I saw by the constant trembling of her hands how nervous she was. Later, after she had unveiled the model to general "Ohs" and "Ahs," we all went to her mother's home for cocktails and she commented on my lack of nerves when speaking. I explained to her that public oratory was, after all, not my main line and therefore held no anxieties for me. She introduced me to many guests, some of whom I met later many times in the meetings of the Kennedy Center committee. That festive and elegant afternoon was as little of an omen as the blizzard after my guest conducting debut in 1961.

On Monday, September 17, I began in earnest to rehearse the orchestra for the opening program. There were six rehearsals and, Friday afternoon and Saturday night, two concerts. Sunday I flew to New York to be on hand for the gala inaugural of Philharmonic Hall. How obvious the acoustical defects of the place were became manifest when, after the program's final chord, a tall figure appeared on my left, the architect in charge of the whole project, Wallace Harrison. Without as much as a greeting he asked me, "And what do we do now?" Next morning very early Isaac Stern and I were interviewed on a talk show. The violinist had made it his concern to prevent Carnegie Hall from being destroyed and headed a group with the slogan "Save Carnegie Hall." Having a keen sense of humor, he said on television that morning his chief purpose now was to "Save Lincoln Center."

Later we rehearsed in the new hall and that evening performed a brand-new piano concerto by Samuel Barber as the featured work, with John Browning as soloist.

I immediately returned to Boston on Tuesday morning for another concert that evening, the opening of a series of subscriptions called "Tuesday A." There was a total of seven different openings in Boston alone. After Tuesday came the normal four rehearsals for the next program, played Friday and Saturday.

The third week began with the experimental record session. Then four rehearsals and four concerts.

The fourth and fifth weeks featured two three-hour regular recordings on the Mondays, concerts on the Tuesdays, always four rehearsals in between the first days of the week and the weekend pair.

On the sixth Monday we left town for our first of five Eastern tours, after which I conducted one more Tuesday concert in Boston before taking a five-day respite, while Burgin did the Friday-Saturday pair.

Between September 17 and October 30 I had performed twenty-four times a total of five different programs, recorded the Eroica and Bartok's Concerto for Orchestra, and prepared the orchestra in twenty-six rehearsals.

If this had been a mere baptism of fire it would not have mattered, but it was the pattern for the tightest schedule, which went on the same way four times each season, interrupted by one or two weeks of rest for me.

Whatever hours were left of each day, whether after two rehearsals or recording sessions or in between a morning rehearsal and an evening concert, had to be spent preparing the following program.

While I already had a comparatively large repertoire in my rucksack when I first went to Boston, it took up a lot of time studying new scores and restudying old ones. I was always a fast learner, yet I worked constantly at home, neglecting the unexpectedly difficult relations with the manager and president.

There were two world premières in my first week, Piston's Seventh Symphony and the Barber Concerto. Three large scores, Stravinsky's *Symphony of Psalms*, Shostakovich's *Tenth Symphony*, and excerpts from Prokofiev's *War and Peace,* were new to me and to some of the orchestra. Furthermore, I had not conducted some of the "repertoire" works since 1955. Even the best-known, or especially the best-known, classical masterpieces should be reread if one does not want to go stale, and I never had that wish. To me it is one of the greatest privileges to browse through music I have known intimately for decades. I feel, when sitting at home with a Beethoven or Mozart score, like the visitor returning to his native town after a long absence; knowing every passage and every corner, he is getting a new look and new impressions. The joy of this revisiting great and familiar pieces makes for the most revealing discoveries and, I think, leads ultimately to special affinities. I spent most of my time that way, and when I had to tackle the "other" nonmusical topics I was certainly not as rested, relaxed, or patient as I should have been to get my message across to Perry.

With four weekly concerts and an indispensable minimum of four rehearsals for each new program, I had the added complication that the orchestra lobbied, whenever possible, for a five-day work week. With concerts spread irregularly over six different days (only Wednesday was never a concert night in Boston), with constant six-hour recording days, we needed an eighth or ninth day to the week and now the players were pumping for a shorter span. The strangest part of this was that Boston's orchestra did not have much stamina. They showed fatigue pretty often, and I had no intention of letting up on the time needed to improve the ensemble, meaning rehearsing.

This particular hassle over the five-day work week was made still more difficult because diplomacy and delicacy forbade any mention of it. The reason for this was that Munch, as hardpressed as I by an unmanageable amount of work, had taken the road of least resistance by cutting some rehearsals short and canceling others altogether.

When, in the first round of renegotiating their trade agreement, the players' committee complained about overwork, management demonstrated that there had been not one instance of overtime or any utilization of hours not embodied in the collective agreement. "But Munch never used up his time," was the blunt reply of the players. Then, instead of shrugging that off as "tough luck," our management passed the pressure for the five-day week on to me and I, as in so many other issues, had to hold fast without the normal and customary assistance of the administration.

In the winter of 1961, during my guest stint, the players' committee was still negotiating a new contract, which should have been signed prior to the 1960–1961 season. It was not unusual to have this kind of delay, and the general relations within the organization were so cordial that I commented admiringly on them. I was so surprised that there had never been any threat of a strike that I considered the Boston Symphony a model from which the rest of the United States could well take a lesson in labor relations. As I got to know the situation more intimately I saw that these excellent relations were based on a gradual but constant erosion of the managerial position by the orchestra, represented by its committee.

Among the clauses were some reasonable and obvious ones such as, "Each concert must have at least one fifteen-minute interval." The interpretation was in the word *must*. My repertoire preferences were somewhat different from Munch's, and when I planned the Brahms Requiem or Mahler's Sixth Symphony or many other works that last more than seventy minutes, I was told to add a short piece as the opening portion of the program, because the orchestra *must* have an intermission. In most parts of the civilized music world it is up to the program builders, conductor and management, to do the Verdi Requiem as the only work for a concert. Not in Boston. I argued with Perry that the orchestra created for itself not only more work but on each occasion another three-quarter-hour presence on the job by insisting on an opener plus the fifteen-minute interval. One can't play a seven-minute overture and then call intermission. I performed for six seasons in this absurd fashion until I was tired of it and in my seventh year tackled the committee myself. They conceded that we could do Strauss's *Ariadne* (eighty-nine minutes) without adding anything else.

There were other ridiculous points in that voluminous trade agreement, which I never read in toto. Perry's hesitancy to call

the committee was far more crucial on another highly important issue. Whenever we had a meeting with the RCA high command I tackled one repertoire problem, dear to me personally
and musically and, as I was told many times, very important
artistically and commercially for all our recording activities. I
had the reputation, buttressed by the Tanglewood weeks of
Mozart and more Mozart, of having a special affinity for Wolfgang Amadeus. My albums with the forty-one symphonies had
been well received (and have lasted on the market for two
decades). My own advisers pressed me to record Mozart and
Haydn, not only great music but more popular with many
young record collectors than the Brahms and Tchaikovsky repertoire. RCA was more than willing if they did not have to pay
for 106 players when 50 perform. It was a rerun of the Philadelphia story anno 1949, with the difference that I was sitting in
another chair. Each conference took the identical route; I asked
how about more Mozart and Haydn on the next season's recording schedule; Roger or George or Dick would agree and remind
Perry that the cost factor needed adjustment; Perry nodded
and scribbled on a yellow legal pad. To the best of my knowledge no one ever gave an answer, not even a negative one, to
RCA. If there had been any serious representation of the topic
to the committee I might have heard about it. As a result we
recorded a total of one Mozart and one Haydn LP in a seven-
year stretch, not counting the Requiem that was a special issue
of the Holy Mass held in memory of President Kennedy.

## *The Balance*

There was no question after my first season that the live
concerts had made their impact and that we were past the period
of empty seats. I have always been unashamedly pleased by sellouts and have never liked to see the bare wood or upholstery on
chairs. The New York concerts in Lincoln Center were so com-

pletely filled by subscription that I decided to make things a little easier by playing the same program Wednesday and Friday nights at Philharmonic Hall. This gave us the chance, welcomed by the orchestra and myself, to return to Carnegie Hall on Saturday nights and to later add two more Thursdays at the same place in a series called "Visiting Orchestras." In Washington too we soon found that the immense capacity of Constitution Hall was none too large for our concerts. In Boston the problem was less acute, though here too we improved the Thursday and Tuesday series.

Our trees were never permitted to grow too tall. As we seemed en route to the most complete sellouts, the orchestra insisted in its 1964 negotiations that it would no longer play Sunday afternoons. The committee was following the lead of its New York colleagues, unmindful that there are few similarities between Boston and New York. New Yorkers do not depend as exclusively upon the Philharmonic as Boston residents depend on their orchestra. The committee simply insisted that Sundays had to be rest days and that was it, once again without effective protest from management. I received many letters of complaint from Sunday subscribers, suburban and ex-urban residents who could not possibly get to Boston on any weekday.

I thought then that a board of trustees, involved only on the side of privilege, with Friday matinees, old subscribers, and Brahmins, needed to be told of a public that could be with us only Sunday afternoons, one that should not be sold down the river.

In my indignation I made one of my most scathing remarks, and not in camera either: "I expect that the next round of negotiations will rule out all evening concerts to allow our players a more normal home life when the kids are back from school for dinner." I still think that artists should perform when the public has time off to enjoy musical offerings, but evidently the middle-class instincts of the musicians' committee no longer had any feeling left for the real mission of players, which is to serve the public. I know that the step leading to the ban on Sunday matinee concerts was a severe disillusionment for me personally. Without being in the least naive, I have felt all my life that it is a special advantage of the theatrical and musical professions not to be subject to the routine of regular hours, days, and weeks throughout the year. I consider it something out of the ordinary to perform on holidays, when office and shop are shut and when people look to us for recreation, solace, and pleasure through great music. I've always rejoiced because I did not work a routine schedule, and here were people, highly privileged, using their pressure to return to a humdrum pattern of middle-class living from which a special skill liberated them at an early age. It made no sense.

Without waxing spiritual I still consider great music most appropriate to be heard on the day of the Lord. And Cabot, who felt even more strongly about this, did not budge when Sundays were banned.

On the Friday afternoon in November 1963 when President Kennedy was assassinated in Dallas, we got the news at Symphony Hall after the first half of the concert. In my room I witnessed a heated discussion between Cabot and the chairman of the orchestra committee, who assumed that we would go home, while Cabot insisted that a serious symphony program should be continued. He told us of the day he went to Symphony Hall directly from the cemetery where he had buried his father. He considered music that much of a comforting, consoling force.

Apparently not for the subscribers from the suburbs on Sundays.

I could once again observe the precarious balance between players and management when we started rehearsals for the 1964–1965 season. During the previous winter we had performed and recorded Mahler's Fifth Symphony. After playing it at Carnegie Hall a most unusual thing had happened: the

*New York Times* reviewer made a special point of asking how long I could tolerate the playing of the first trumpet. And he used extremely negative adjectives to illustrate the sonorities heard. It is rare that an orchestra member is singled out thus. The following afternoon, Roger Voisin, the first trumpet, visited me in my dressing room at Storrs, where we played a matinee, and showed me the clipping in dismay. We talked for a while and I sent him off somewhat calmer. A few weeks later he told Mazzeo, the personnel manager, that he wanted to exchange places with Ghitalla, the junior principal of the trumpet section. He had had enough of the nervous strain and added that "now when every performance has to be just right" he wanted to let the other fellow carry the burden so he could be more at ease. This was accepted by one and all as a fair solution.

Before I went on stage for my first rehearsal in September, Mazzeo appeared, out of breath, and fairly stammered that he did not know what to do: "Roger is sitting in his old place, refuses to move, and says that he has changed his mind about giving up the senior chair." It is not fun to be faced with such decisions five minutes before the hour. If I insisted he move in front of the orchestra, we might have a confrontation, which would give a few elements the welcome chance to raise Cain. If I gave in I was cooked and Ghitalla was broiled. I thought fast and suggested to Mazzeo that I would not begin rehearsing the Shostakovich First Symphony (with its opening phrase played by the principal trumpet) at all but would replace it with Beethoven's Pastoral Symphony, which does not require any trumpets for the first two movements. During these movements Mazzeo would have enough time to take the entire section of four trumpets to the manager and straighten things out.

While the decision was, as it should have been, to stay with the earlier rearrangement of the principal desks, this little interlude may have added pressure on Ghitalla, who almost instantly got a wart on his lip and was out for nearly the entire season. Since Voisin, not illogically, refused to play principal, we had to make do with guest trumpet players. It was a most unsatisfactory situation.

By the time this contretemps took place I already had the good help and assistance of Andrew Raeburn. I also had been "granted" a secretary, which was not at all a matter of course according to Perry. I never could be sure if it was economy or plain misconception on his part: he wanted me to use his secretary, a splendid and fast worker, for all my correspondence.

The staff situation was more peculiar. When I first came Perry was surrounded by three of the best people anyone could possibly have found: Sally Hempel, Burkat, and Mazzeo. Mazzeo was altogether a wizard, filling four different positions. He played bass clarinet, he was personnel manager, he had developed the orchestra's pension fund so brilliantly that a couple of bankers among the trustees suggested he move into the financial field, and he was the constant loyal supporter of the management, a rare quality in a personnel manager. When a year later he had to retire on his doctor's advice, after thirty-three years with the organization, he asked for a double pension, in consideration of having been a member of the orchestra and of the staff. He was refused and left in great bitterness.

While every one of these problems touched me and the whole formidable task I had undertaken, the single most important appointment had to be made in 1963. Every orchestra has a press department, the effectiveness of which depends entirely upon the incumbent publicity man. We had Harry Beall, whose personality and mental concepts made him a perfect type. In 1963 he was invited to join the newly formed agency of Judson, O'Neill, Beall, and Steinway, a great improvement over his situation and prospects at Symphony Hall.

Perry came up with a replacement who was a gentleman of the finest caliber but who, in my opinion, lacked true professional qualifications.

I never felt that the BSO took a strong position on publicity, and this certainly disappointed me.

## *Tanglewood*

The summers in the Berkshires were the happiest times of my Boston years. They remain a glowing memory, and if there were moments of exasperation they have evaporated and are no longer within my recall. I like the landscape, the shed, the acoustics, the lawn with or without people, the open-car driving to and from rehearsals and concerts, the parties, the restaurants, the symposia we arranged on all sorts of related subjects, the often screwballish contemporary concerts, and even the buzzing mosquitoes. That is one place I shall not readily revisit lest one of my most cherished recollections dissolve into gray fog.

Some of the reasons why all this looks so radiant in retrospect reflect my general tastes in life. All the music-making was outdoors, which I prefer to indoors.

All the concerts in the winter season were for subscribers, but none of the Tanglewood ones were. Only a performer who has experienced both types of audiences will readily appreciate the difference. The simple facilities of the shed made contact between performers and public closer and more intimate than it could ever have been in the formal atmosphere of a concert hall. The few demarcation ropes were disregarded by one and all, the musicians talked with the audience at intermission, people gathered backstage and took pictures. The entire sequence of events resembled a real communal experience, and I wished that we could find ways of transferring that mood, informality, and lively spirit to the whole year. (The Proms in London are the next best thing, but, unlike the shed, the Royal Albert Hall has pretty dry and unattractive acoustical properties.)

Tanglewood's principal problem was the Friday night concert, which was only sparsely attended, no matter how attractive the program. Our public came mainly from New York and Boston for weekends, and not even the fastest driver made an 8:00 P.M. start after leaving his office at 5:00. As the years progressed I found an answer that made some difference. I scheduled a small concert, a recital, chamber music or short choral selections, to be performed for the local residents, who were able to come at any hour, from seven to eight. There followed a one-hour dinner interval, with facilities on the grounds for those who wanted to eat. By nine, when the commuting population could comfortably be at hand, we began the regular Boston Symphony program. I saw to it that the "Prelude" (as the short hour of recital was called) had a thematic relation with the entire weekend.

Each year my major concern was to find for one or two early programs at Tanglewood enough musical "news" to attract the New York press. Their write-ups would, in turn, create more publicity for the rest of the summer's doings. In my first year I had the windfall of obtaining the rights for the United States première of Benjamin Britten's *War Requiem*. In 1964 I featured a retrospective of Richard Strauss, on the occasion of his centenary. In 1966 and 1967 I produced Mozart's *Die Zauberflöte* in a novel manner and Beethoven's first version of *Fidelio*, *Leonore*. In *Zauberflöte*, I used, in place of the spoken dialogue, an English-language narrative which allowed the original language to be sung and the public to follow every turn of the plot. I considered this staging so successful that I want to try it in a theater as well. In 1968 the trustees refused the necessary budget for any "special event," and in 1969 we made up for the frugality of the year before by having two specials: Mozart's *Die Entführung aus dem Serail* and Verdi's *Otello*.

While I was defending these events and their extra cost to the bankers and lawyers among the trustees, I had no support from management, which never admitted that through one splash we got attention and publicity worth a great deal more. Management just did not follow my arguments that we could not expect wide newspaper coverage for conventional symphony programs, which would be far better attended in the long run if every year we had some work that was irresistible to the music press.

The great splurge in 1965 became a disaster for which I have readily shouldered the lion's share of responsibility. I was, however, most ably assisted by RCA. The tale is involved and not a pleasant memory for me.

We planned to perform a complete *Lohengrin* for the three final concerts in 1965, the first act Friday, the second Saturday, and the third Sunday afternoon. At each concert there would be one overture to *Leonore* to round out the program. We would follow up by recording *Lohengrin* in Symphony Hall between Monday and Saturday, with two three-hour sessions each day.

The origin of the project was twofold. I still sought every year one or two titles that would consume more than a single LP and thereby reduce the bothersome ten releases for RCA. I also bore in mind a plea from the president of the American Federation of Musicians, Herman Kenin, who had asked me more than once to use my influence to bring RCA's opera recordings back to the United States.

Here was the ideal plan to kill two birds with one stone.

RCA always worked with a particular group of singers who were supposed to be good for any role. Thus it was a foregone conclusion that they would ask Leontyne Price to do Elsa and they did. Sándor Kónya, then in very fine form, was cast as Lohengrin. For the other men's roles we compromised, because nothing better was available. That Wiener schnitzel was not the best cooking. I should have called off the whole affair then but did not. Who ever scrapped a *Lohengrin* because of the King and Telramund?

Ortrud was to be Rita Gorr, a Belgian mezzo-soprano who had recorded Fricka in my complete *Walküre* album in 1961. (Then she had been in a peculiar mix-up. RCA had issued two contracts for the same role, giving her one of them. After much argument and many tears the other lady was promised full pay and a ticket home, while Gorr held her place as Wotan's strict wife.)

On my return trip from Europe in June 1964, I wanted to show l'Opéra in the Palais Garnier to my daughter Hester and took her to a *Don Carlo* performance. Gorr was Eboli and sounded so appallingly like a foghorn and was so shrill in the high range that I became convinced she could never undertake Ortrud, an equally high and taxing role. This I conveyed to the RCA people as soon as I was back in the States. Neither Marek, nor Hall, nor Mohr believed me. When, in the fall of 1964, she sang Dalilah opening night at the Met, I received immediate assurances from the recording company's executives: "No worry — she was fine."

The trouble with this optimistic verdict was that a voice can be splendid as Dalilah and totally incapable of singing Ortrud, but for this intricate deduction the troika at RCA was not mentally prepared or musically knowledgeable enough.

In December Miss Price declared herself out. Her reason was that she did not want to sing three days in a row, which was perhaps only another way of saying that she did not find the role suited to her. This was the second time I should have called the game, especially since Marek suggested doing so.

I, perhaps foolishly, perhaps honorably wanting to keep my word, persisted in going forward with the whole plan. I was only concerned at that moment with my promise to Kenin and how I would explain a cancellation to him.

At the concert performance Gorr was loud and sounded as I remembered her from Paris. But once a difficult spot is over on stage the music goes on and so does the mind of the listener.

When we moved to Symphony Hall all the weaknesses in our cast were magnified by the cruel objectivity and impartiality of the microphone.

As if our vocal problem had not been enough, Mazzeo had engaged the necessary extra trumpet players (nine of them) according to the union book, which insisted on members of Local 9, the Boston chapter of the American Federation of Musicians. There is little call for classic trumpet playing outside the Symphony in Boston, and from the way these fellows sounded I was sure that they had performed only at clambakes. With a costly loss of time we ended up doing these trumpet calls with our own regular foursome, splicing and using other tricks, while the local Niners were paid and not recorded.

Price's replacement was a reliable singer whose basically very fine voice had never, since her Met debut in 1950, been sufficient to get her above the rank of permanent standby.

The net result was the most expensive five-record album ever produced, unsuccessful with the reviewers and unprofitable commercially.

My recreation after this harassing experience was a four-week vacation mixed with a new activity. John Secondari, a television producer, had asked me to be his consultant for a documentary on Beethoven that he would shoot in Vienna during September 1965. I persuaded him to use Claude Frank playing an original Broadwood from the composer's time and to record all orchestral selections in and with Boston. This was a first on commercial television for us. We regularly did six concerts for the splendid educational station WGBH, which meant much honor but no extra income for the musicians. But a connection with the American Broadcasting Company could spell a great deal of profit for each and every one. It unfortunately became another instance when a mixture of indifference, strictness, and arrogance spoiled a fine opportunity and frustrated my efforts.

To be filmed and recorded for videotape meant playing the music as if we were making a sound recording and later, for the cameras, miming the motions while the music was played back so that there would be perfect synchronization between sight and sound. An entire Monday, from nine to six, had been set aside.

Our orchestra, not used to the early rush-hour traffic, what with regular rehearsals starting at 10:30, arrived quite close to the starting time and eight or nine did not make it, thus holding up the recording for several minutes. These minutes at prevailing rates of commercial television are quite dear. This delay did not prevent Mazzeo from calling the contractually pinpointed first intermission at the exact moment it was due. Secondari blew up and said a few explicit words about "tough unions up here," which was sufficient for me to know that this was going to be our first and last chance with that particular outfit. It was.

Otherwise that fall's opening weeks were among my happier moments, particularly the performance of Beethoven's Ninth Symphony. In the past the Ninth had always ended the season, which meant that only the Friday and Saturday audiences heard it. Now, for the first time, it was scheduled for every one of the seven Boston subscription series, and I was the beneficiary, if for no other reason than the unique experience of conducting it seven times within three weeks. If I had to make a list of only three works that make conducting worth while it would consist of the Ninth, Wagner's *Siegfried* and *Le Sacre du printemps*.

On the negative side was a forthcoming arbitration over the notice given a trumpet player at my suggestion. The entire orchestra, including Arthur Fieldler, the director of the Pops, signed a petition for the withdrawal of the notice. A day or two prior to the arbitration meeting the orchestra's attorney visited me in an effort to avoid a procedure that always leaves a bad taste, no matter who wins. He had tried to make the player resign without succeeding and now persuaded me, with better results, to call off the whole thing. I liked the attorney and his manner and agreed to forget it all. It is ironic that only a few years later this same attorney, an experienced specialist in representing theatrical unions, refused to renew his retainer from the Boston Symphony players. He considered them unreasonable and would no longer act for people demanding the impossible. It made me feel a little better at not being the only one to throw in the towel before the fight had gone the full route of fifteen rounds.

## Carter, Bach, and Zealots

One day early in 1966 Perry appeared with an intriguing proposition. In a long and intricate chapter that might be called "Contemporary Music and Symphony Orchestras," it looked like a new wrinkle. For several years the Ford Foundation had made grants to performers for the purpose of giving them the wherewithal to commission new compositions for themselves as vehicles in which to ride to greater prominence.

One pianist, Jacob Lateiner, had used the money to ask the eminent Elliott Carter for a piano concerto. The composer agreed in 1959 to write the commissioned work, delivering it less than six years later. The Foundation, always a pioneer, was persuaded to give the opportunity for this important première to a young orchestra rather than to one of the Eastern Establishment symphonies. The choice fell on Denver, whose music director after a good, long perusal passed and returned the score. Then somebody called Perry and said, "Leinsdorf is known to handle the most complex scores. Would you do the first performances?" After a good look at Carter's rhythmic modulations I told Perry that I should need three full rehearsals for the Concerto in addition to our normal quota. That, he replied, cost $7500, which the Boston Symphony could not spend. I could not disagree with him on that point and was quite ready and not too unhappy to forget the project when Perry returned a day later and proposed two extra rehearsals, for which "an anonymous foundation" wished to pay.

I settled for two extra sessions, and after consulting Lateiner on his target date, for he had to learn a fiendishly difficult piece, November 1966 was set. First we would do a weekend pair in Boston, then a Thursday at Carnegie Hall, and finally a recording at Symphony Hall on the following Monday. For these four sessions the Martha Baird Rockefeller Foundation granted the funds to pay the musicians, while the Steinway Foundation added money for some other costs. RCA offered to do the technical portion of the job and would issue the record on their Masterworks label, compelled by a condition of the foundations to keep the work in the catalogue for seven years. As it was a work, in the famous words of Marek and Hall, that "doesn't sell," this was a wise clause.

Six weeks before the event, Lateiner revealed that he would not be ready and asked for a postponement until January. What this entailed in shuffling dates for extra rehearsals and recordings and in finding suitable substitutions for the Carnegie Hall program, which had by then been publicized, was an ordeal. We could never find a New York date, and the work remained unperformed there. We also found no recording date, but resolved that problem by taping the Boston performances.

Like any three-ring circus we too seemed always to have two side shows. A very distinguished colleague had engaged Lateiner to play the Carter Concerto with his orchestra, and during my rehearsals he asked me if I considered the work performable. Later I learned that Lateiner had played Beethoven, not Carter, with him.

The cost of recording the work during concerts was higher than it would have been had we done it in the usual Monday special sessions. For services not requiring any extra time, playing a concert as part of a regular contract, simultaneous taping pays at a higher rate than if the musicians had to journey specially to the studio. The logic of our industrial age is overwhelming.

*

Bach is a special composer, and performing his music poses special problems for a symphony orchestra that is a nineteenth-century institution, generally unsuited to tackle music written before 1750. After having heard some of the Tanglewood Bach performances prior to my incumbency I decided to give Johann Sebastian a rest. I concentrated on Mozart and on Haydn, as every summer for the first six concerts I had only half an orchestra available, the rest playing on Boston's Esplanade. By 1966 I wanted to bring Bach back, especially since the great Swiss tenor Ernst Haefliger was available for one weekend. I chose, together with instrumental works and a solo cantata on Friday and Sunday, the *St. John Passion* for the Saturday night concert. A most happy collection of fine singers, with extraordinary gamba playing by a retired cellist, Alfred Zighera, made that evening moving and rewarding in the best sense of the words. Then and there I decided to repeat the work during Holy Week 1967 at Symphony Hall.

The Friday afternoon performance was tremendous but even before starting Saturday night's repeat I got an inkling that something was afoot when I was told that none of the wives of the Jewish orchestra members was using her ticket that evening.

All was clear when on Monday I received a long letter from Rabbi Roland Gittelsohn, head of a large Brookline congregation. He protested vigorously against performing a work so anti-Semitic that each hearing would renew and increase the hatred against Jews. My rebuttal that an immortal composition had its own laws and could not be judged by the yardstick of a political tract brought forth another note from the rabbi with the comment that he had hoped, after similar fruitless exchanges with Munch, to have better luck with me, considering my background.

A few weeks later the season was over and I left, more vexed and irritated than ever before. My trip to Israel that spring was cut short by a phone call from the United States Embassy, admonishing me to leave as quickly as possible because of imminent war. I returned to the States, where in June I was photographed in cap and gown together with two of my sons, similarly attired. My oldest graduated from law school, my youngest from college, and I was going to receive an honorary degree, all at Columbia University.

Less happy was a long phone conversation with Cabot. I had asked for consent to leave Tanglewood one week early in 1968 to accept an invitation from the Edinburgh Festival. It was my first such request in five years, and it was refused. I had to be at the Berkshires for the entire eight-week period.

Then I wanted to know if after the 1967–1968 season, my sixth, I could have a leave of absence without pay. Not possible.

Finally I offered Cabot my immediate resignation, effective as per contract two seasons thence. Also rejected.

This was in June, and after that it took until Thanksgiving for the actual break. A blowup at Tanglewood was the spark plug.

The "special event" for the summer of 1967 in the Berkshires was *Leonore*, the generally unknown, original version of *Fidelio*. Because of repeats from the previous winter's selections, I always managed to get enough rehearsal time for new performances. It is self-evident that an evening-filling work with a cast of singers, a chorus, a narrator, and an orchestra must have one runthrough to give all participants a chance to know waits, cues, what comes when, and all sorts of details that are unknown in a rarely or never played work. The uninterrupted dress rehearsal is an elementary condition for a decent show.

That was set for Friday morning. Before starting I announced that there would be no interruption, whatever mishaps occurred. Corrections would be made at intermission and at the end.

The first part went well enough. After making two or three comments we all recessed for the regular break. Looking at the clock I saw at once that even with an uninterrupted play-through the second part would not be finished by 1:00 P.M., the regular hour to terminate the rehearsal. I called Bill Moyer, personnel manager since Mazzeo's retirement, and informed him that overtime was inevitable. I was sure that it would be less than a half-hour. "It is perfectly fine to go over," Moyer allowed, "but there has to be a five-minute break within the first fifteen minutes of the overtime period." "Surely not in a dress rehearsal," I said. "Makes no difference, the book is clear on the subject." "How can I stop in a runthrough when I have specifically stated that it is to be uninterrupted?" "Trade agreement has it." I was boiling inside but fortunately spoke very quietly. I still remember every word: "Bill, I shall not stop until we are through. If it is your duty to force an intermission you will have to come on stage and tell me in front of two hundred performers and a handful of rehearsal watchers to halt for the five-minute break and I shall do so without fuss, but I will not abide by such idiotic rules voluntarily."

The second half of the rehearsal was not interrupted or disturbed by any incident, but the orchestra committee's visits to Perry went on for the balance of the summer and continued into the fall after vacation. Except that the word contract violation was frequently used I do not know what was said in these visits. Judging from my meeting with the trustees in November, when any consideration of special-event money for 1968 was flatly rejected, there must have been hell to pay.

My return from that gathering was enhanced by one of the bankers, who suggested that I place my investments through him.

My own thoughts were in turmoil. What was the point of holding on to a situation where Beethoven is expected to yield to the five-minute rule?

## A Boston Postscript

The actual dialogue with Cabot that ended with my formal resignation and the written confirmations was calm and even pleasant. Perry seemed particularly delighted when Cabot called him to my room at the hall and "revealed" the outcome. Like a good headmaster he had a fine compliment for both of us.

When the smoke settled down and I appeared for my next rehearsal after a one-week rest, an embarrassed silence from the usually chattering players surrounded my entrance. I smiled and said that I expected for the twenty months remaining to make music as freely as one should when all sorts of cares and heavy burdens have been lifted. This intention was carried out by the players as well as by myself, and we had possibly our best time between December 1967 and the concluding Ninth on August 24, 1969.

At the outset of this book I told something of my personal problems coming to a head at the same time as my professional crisis with the high command of the Boston Symphony. I shall never know which was the chicken and which the egg. For nearly fifty-six years I had accepted the common values of family, career, honors, success, acquisitions, important people, an interesting social life, vacations in the mountains and by the sea. Having experienced all these I still did not feel any conspicuous sense of having grown more mature. The outer image was no reflection of the inner reality.

Once every twenty-four hours there is a short period of time, maybe no more than five minutes, before sleep comes. This is the moment of reckoning. Applause — no matter how cordial two hours before — has given way to silence; people with autograph books, well-wishers with a nice word, youngsters with a

query have all gone; lights are turned out, the wine at supper
has worn off. If it had not been for strains of the evening's
music floating through my mind, I would have felt only that
"Every third thought shall be my grave." Getting older means
more frequent returns of this third thought, which makes it
rather desirable that the other two should dwell on better things
than Hell.

After a winter vacation, part of which I spent conducting
in Paris, I returned to the States at the end of January 1968. A
cable had asked me to stop in Washington to see Douglass Cater,
President Johnson's assistant for cultural affairs. He invited me
to lunch with him in the basement staff dining room at the
White House, and after telling me of my appointment as a
director of the PBC (Public Broadcast Corporation), he suggested we go upstairs and say "hello" to the President, who
wanted to see me.

We were shown in at once, pictures were taken, then I
thanked the President for my appointment, and he asked about
my plans for the future. It surprised me how much he was up
to date on my professional affairs. I had not seen him in some
time. He did not look well, but was, if that were possible, even
more cordial to me than ever. He asked about our mutual
friends and spoke of his little grandson. After this most informal and particularly friendly visit I left with a political
appointment (I returned later to Washington for an appearance and Senate Committee confirmation) but with an inex-
plicably bitter taste. It was a gray but mild afternoon, and I
walked the few blocks from the White House up 16th Street
to my hotel. I can still feel now, years later, how deeply de-
pressed I was as a result of having seen the President. I did not
know that this would be the last time I spoke to him or that on
that same day the Tet offensive in Vietnam began. But what
I felt was that behind the glamour and the mansion, behind
the power and the worry of that highest office, the man Lyndon

Baines Johnson did not exist anymore. It was less than thirty years and only a few blocks from the time and place of our first meeting.

On that same afternoon, between the routine chores of packing and taking a taxi and a plane to my next stop, New York, I promised myself to do things my way and not abide anymore by notions of what was expected of me. Since the fall of 1965 my wife and I had seriously discussed separation. We had tried the patching-up remedy, which looked to me more and more like the easy way out. The youngest of my children would be seventeen in six weeks, and my wife and I were still of an age when we would have better chances to restructure our lives than we would if we waited or did nothing.

In New York I met the orchestra — the first five days of that tour having been conducted by a guest — for a brush-up rehearsal on Saturday morning, February 3, for that evening's Carnegie Hall concert. If I should ever be compelled to call one single performance my best, I must select Bruckner's Seventh Symphony that particular evening.

Three months later we had our Mexican divorce.

What I did not know either after my visit with the President or even a month later was that I should be remarried in August of the same year.

Following the summer at Tanglewood, as full of carefree music-making as any, we spent the weeks between the seasons in California. Returning to Boston earlier than necessary, we had to decide our whereabouts.

It did not seem worth while to start a household of our own for my final Boston season, a mere thirty weeks interrupted by half a dozen trips. We rented, but the best we could find was a flat in an apartment-hotel resembling a nursing home for the affluent.

When I learned that William Steinberg, my successor as music director of the Boston Symphony, would maintain his affiliation, in the identical position, with Pittsburgh, I wondered if Cabot remembered that neither I nor my predecessor had been allowed to conduct any other American orchestra during our tenures — a total of twenty years. From 1969 on, Cabot's beloved BSO would be a conductor's second band. And Tanglewood's summer festival and school would be headed in 1970 by a troika.

## About Music

If I have made it appear that side issues and office cares at the BSO took up most of my time and energy I have given a false or incomplete impression. Perhaps once in a while fatigue might have got the better of me, but not even in my gloomiest moments, of which there were quite a few, could I lose sight of what was most important. Music was the reason for all the chores and labors, for all the vexations and frustrations, and it provided a reason to bear up under the pressures of this position.

Life runs on two tracks that are rarely parallel. Since the age of fifteen, when I became seriously involved with music, I have never changed my basic purpose of getting as close as possible to the great masters and their compositions. But fairly soon I discovered that for a conductor this involved a career more complex than that of the instrumentalist. It is always easier to obtain the use of a first-rate piano than of a fine orchestra. There are more vintage Guarneri and Stradivari than comparable symphony ensembles. Thus, a musician like myself, who intends to dig deep into the great orchestral literature, needs from time to time an orchestra that can realize in live sound what private study and reading have revealed.

My years with the Boston Symphony gave me altogether a clearer idea of what the whole complex interpretation of music meant.

I felt that I was rather fortunate to be successor to two men who, though opposites of one another, happened also to be

antipodes of myself. The difference between Koussevitzky and
Munch was simple and well known to all inside observers. The
one worked like a fiend on every aspect of his music-making,
while the other relied on his genial and apparently carefree flair
for improvisation. The one had to see every little detail exactly
as he wished, while the other was both generous and cavalier
with the music. Their similarity was a fairly total unconcern
with authenticity and a reliance on their individual tempera-
ments to guide the spirit of performance.

My concept of the interpreter is rather the opposite of theirs.
I have always rejected the term objectivity for my approach,
but it has stuck to me for some time, perhaps because I did not
grandly broadcast in words my philosophy. I believe that the
best performer is the one who is medium rather than overlord,
especially when undertaking the perfect masterworks with
which our repertoire abounds. To me the triumph of the great
actor is complete when he passes unrecognized after donning
costume and mask.

In my first interviews after the Boston appointment was
made public I was asked regularly, "Will the orchestra now get
a German sound?" To which I replied that my aim was to make
it sound as each score should. But the question itself was symptomatic of a certain approach to orchestral sonorities, which I
call the Philadelphia school, where everything sounds more or
less the same.

Opposing this monolithic approach as well as the freewheel-
ing school of the ego trip, I am by no means alone: my supporters are the composers themselves. Wherever I have looked,
I have looked with much care, and I have found ample evidence
of how distressed composers of all eras have been by willful
performers, regardless of success. Carl Czerny once published
a letter he had received from Beethoven: "Yesterday I burst
forth so that I was sorry after it had happened, but you must
pardon that in an author who would have preferred to hear his

work exactly as he wrote it, no matter how beautifully you played in general."

Nearly one hundred years later Richard Strauss complained in a letter to his parents of Arthur Nikisch, a superstar conductor even in the days when the word itself did not yet exist. It was after a performance of *Death and Transfiguration* that Strauss wrote: "To-day, at the public dress rehearsal, the prima donna Nikisch chopped up my *Death and Transfiguration* in such impertinent ways that I was wondering why the public didn't cause the work to fail. But no. Raging applause. It seems to be immune to strangulation. He really conducted only the instrumentation, underlining every sound effect in the silliest manner; where I put *tranquillo* he played blithely agitato and vice versa — in short the most repulsive podium virtuosity, which for vanity's sake no longer respects any will of the composer; yet in spite of it, mad success." The editor of the volume adds wistfully: "Strauss later changed his tune, considering good will from an international conductor too valuable to alienate him by being critical."

Long before I ever dreamed of Boston and its orchestra I heard from composers what highly idiosyncratic versions of their works Koussevitzky presented, which did not diminish gratitude and appreciation by these composers for the yeoman services of the conductor. Yet neither moral support nor material help could corrupt authors to accept changes in their work.

There is also good documentation that Bartók and Stravinsky were appalled at some of the Symphony Hall premières of their works, all of which convinced me long ago that the masters of the past might on many an occasion rise up in wrath on hearing what is being done to their work under the guise of individualistic liberty of interpretation.

The two approaches to performing music have their origins in the very dark precincts of motivation. My belief is that —

consciously or not — the eccentric ways of musicians, conductors, and virtuosi represent frustrated composition.

It is good to remember that any well-tutored student takes at
least three years of composition as a classic part of the curriculum. I know from my own experience that this is heady stuff
for a young person. After doing reams of exercises in a conservative vein, chorale harmonizations, and three-part counterpoint, the disciple must deliver original compositions to the
teacher, a process in which the methodical and the creative
overlap and during which most talented people discover their
nostalgia for immortality.

After my own apprenticeship I decided that I was better
suited to perform than to compose. I had a fine teacher and
learned how one composes music. This itself is, as Hindemith
correctly named it, a craft any intelligent person can learn.
Notwithstanding some encouragement, including a commission for a cantata I did compose and perform, I realized soon
enough that my "craft" was not buttressed by the distinctive
creative originality without which composition is a mere per-
mutation game.

The difference between myself and others like me is probably
that they did not make peace with their lack of originality and
applied it to the scores of Beethoven et alia.

How much free-floating imagination is necessary to understand the text and content of great scores will be in future years
part of my teaching. Even composers as their own interpreters
may be at times of questionable authority. I became aware of
this through Ansermet, who told me of his bewilderment with
Stravinsky when that composer made it known that Monteux's
and Ansermet's tempi in the early ballet scores were not authentic. Ansermet was incensed by this, claiming that he and
Monteux had conducted these works at a time when Stravinsky
had not yet discovered his own proficiency with the baton and
that the composer's limited dexterity as chef led him to change
for his own good (or bad) reasons the tempi he had composed.

It was Ansermet's firm belief that a great composer knows best what he wants when writing it down in the final draft. It is certainly true that Mahler the conductor found so much to change in the scores of Mahler the composer that it has become totally impossible to find a truly authentic version of his work. Who knows what kind of a band Kassel had for the première of Mahler's Fourth Symphony?

As I grew older I found reading and rereading great compositions as stimulating as any journey into the unfathomable. It is totally insufficient to be literal and punctilious. The reading of any master's text requires profound knowledge and even more imagination. The symbols that serve composers are not only limited in number, they are not and never were intended to be explicit. To make this an excuse for waywardness shows only how little the excitement of discovery is appreciated.

At Tanglewood I arranged for various symposia on important musical topics, including notation. In one meeting our principal oboist suggested that more signs were needed to guide the musician explicitly. My reply that the existing signs were already insufficiently understood led to a heated discussion. I finally promised to produce a simple example to prove my point. Brahms often abbreviated directions to save time in writing the same thing for every line of the full score; then a dutiful copyist repeated literally what he found in the score in each part. When I showed our oboist a "pf" in one of his own parts he had played numerous times, he was unable to identify what it meant. He was disappointed when I told him that this was shorthand for "poco forte," one of Brahms's favorite markings.

The frequent use of the word "poco," meaning "somewhat" for tempo and for dynamics, is typical of the antiemphasis Brahms favored in many of his subdued and melancholy pieces. From the full understanding of such a small symbol many new discoveries can result — which in great music never cease to astonish me.

The sheer size of the repertoire I performed in the seven years with the Boston Symphony — an archivist counted 429 different scores — taught me that the first task is to distinguish among compositions that are great, good, and less than good. This expertise is comparable to that of the wine taster who knows after a few drops if he is sipping a sample of a vintage, an average harvest, or a poor year.

Many of the untried works I chose for premières were selected without illusions. Diplomacy has been and still is part of a music director's lot. I did not have to be an especially sophisticated score-taster because there had been few vintage harvests in symphonic music since the end of the war in 1945. I often wished it were possible to fill season after season with nothing but the best, a point on which I saw eye to eye with Cabot. But he could be openly conservative in his taste as a member of the audience, while I had to be, at least ex officio, liberal, progressive, and confident that we in the United States had the most gifted school of composition.

The fluctuations of quality in the scores submitted and accepted were enlightening to me. I began to realize that second-rate music cannot stand study in depth, as it reveals whatever message and content there is to a good reader on a first or second perusal. Gradually scores began to assume human characteristics for me. There are shallow people whose thinking and conversation can be foretold after only a brief acquaintance. They are to me, like shallow scores, boring in their predictability.

What has remained a mystery is the wide range of quality between two works of one and the same composer, e.g., Opus 25 may be a work of genius and Opus 26 one of conventional routine. Perhaps Toscanini had the final answer to this one when he said that "nobody is a genius for all the twenty-four hours of the day."

Not every lesser composition was picked for reasons of diplomacy. I made many genuine mistakes, which I recognized readily but most often after it was too late to withdraw them. The pressure of making so many different programs did account for some of these errors, since I was convinced that the popular perennials needed longer intervals between repeats than they were getting. When I first went to Boston and studied the program patterns of the preceding seasons, I found such a plethora of *Symphonie Fantastiques*, *La Mers*, and *Daphnis et Chloés* that I never did any of these in 721 concerts. I also decided to space the great symphonies of Beethoven and Brahms, which can so easily be taken for granted that to do them often is fatal in the long run.

Even with the enormous number of new pieces, I got enough time to constantly restudy the great works of the past and found much gratification when I rediscovered an old work and it was recognized by some like-minded souls. When a discerning observer once noticed a few of my findings, we discussed the large complex of "meaning in music." I am convinced that all great music means something and that music without meaning is not great music. The difficulty lies in verbalizing this without getting into muddy waters. Our language has a terminology for musical analysis but not for meaning. This is unfortunate, because the stuff of which program notes are made consists basically only of analytical terms that give nothing to the green listener.

I also found that the professional orchestra player is not helped much by the analytical knowledge of his own student days. Through sheer chance did I get confirmation of this. We made a Southern tour in March 1969, and I planned to include on the program a piece by Edgar Varèse, which needed too many percussion instruments for accommodation on one truck. Perry suggested that the extra $1200 to play the piece might be too much. I agreed with him, took Varèse off, and substituted Schönberg's Variations for Orchestra.

In Atlanta, where we were to play the piece, I saw the otherwise amply endowed program booklet without one word of guidance or explanation on this twenty-minute piece, which is a formidable challenge to any listener, green or not. What can an audience make of the listing "Arnold Schönberg (1874–1951) Variations Op. 31." Not another word. In every program when a nine-hundreth repeat of a Beethoven symphony is given, the four movements are listed with their tempo markings, but there were no subdivisions for this dodecaphonic encyclopedia of a work. I decided that I had to say a few words of introduction, which I did without a single reference to the system of composing with twelve tones or any other analytical terminology. The next morning, as we enplaned for Florida, several musicians stopped at my seat to suggest that such introductions were helpful to them as well and asked if I would do more of them. (I am sure that these kindly people were not conscious of the overt irony in making such a suggestion while we were on my final tour as regular conductor.)

For many years I had been loath to use anything but strictly technical terminology when rehearsing an orchestra. Only gradually did I understand that orchestra members are, with very few exceptions, undertrained in musical knowledge and are often as unsophisticated as the people in the ninth row. Traffic signals are about all the players ever see, and their interest can be easily aroused by making them more aware of "what goes on." My reluctance to explain was due for a long time to my horror of the cute clichés used in music appreciation, to misleading comparisons, and to revolting sentimentalities. But I did come around to the conviction that even a wrong word can at times be more serviceable than no word at all.

It started once when I rehearsed Beethoven's Third Leonore Overture with a French orchestra. The backstage trumpet player was outstanding, but the bugle call sounded as if it had been intended as a cadenza in a trumpet concerto, void of any dramatic significance. I called the man out from the wings, thinking that the whole orchestra might as well hear what the passage meant, and told them of Pizarro, who wished to be

warned as soon as the lookout on the highest tower spotted a
carriage coming from the direction of Seville. I also told them
what that same call meant to the four people in the dungeon
at the height of the tension and the attempted murder of
Florestan, the revelation of Fidelio's identity, and everybody's
shock at the recognition that the solution is near. This explanation was no longer than these few sentences, but it gave some
content to the player, who not only improved but couldn't
stop thanking me for something "he should have known but
didn't," as he himself put it. This may have been a relatively
simple corner to illuminate, but I was encouraged to do more
of it, and whenever I find such an occasion it meets with warm
acknowledgment.

Altogether I find it an ever greater privilege to spend so
much of my life in the company of great composers. It has
made me most assuredly less tolerant of the ordinary grind of
daily trivia and has made me more impatient with the abrasive
problems of time limitation and the concerns of the purse. But
it has also given me a blissful perspective to many prosaic aspects
of my profession, which cause many of my colleagues sleepless
nights.

Since leaving the hub I have phased out (to use a modern
term) even the occasional three-quarter-grain Seconal I needed.

# PART IV

# Wanderjahre
Free-Lance on the Road

## Years of Travel

Without sharing Thomas Mann's lifelong ambition to emulate Goethe I still dare to call what follows my *Wanderjahre*. The original meaning of the word goes beyond the literal translation. The young craftsman of preindustrial days, after three years as apprentice to a master, wandered across the land to acquire knowledge of life and people, eventually returning to base, a master himself.

I now did the unorthodox and embarked, aged fifty-seven, on a life that should have come thirty years earlier. At twenty-seven I thought that I had become a fixture in New York's opera, until my dissatisfaction with unavoidable routine drove me on.

For three decades I had tried to reconcile the conflict between family and music; I was intensely aware of their near incompatibility.

Whenever I see an artist's family clan assembled backstage I feel pity because they're being used as stooges. Children especially should not be part of a court. A dressing room becomes that as soon as the curtain is down and the crowd gets in. This at least my children never had to suffer.

In 1969 I could confidently give up my permanent address. My offspring were grown-up and could forgo the schoolwork consultations with father. I am lucky that all five turned out well. There had been a few minor problems, yet when I hear the tales of contemporaries I feel grateful to my family for having given me so few anxious moments. What I now anticipated most was an absence of middle-class living.

To be blunt about it: there is too little artistic spirit around our whole profession and too much concern with supermarkets, mortgages, and PTA meetings. With most musicians it is the exception rather than the rule that music is the topic of conversation. Perhaps I had also been impressed out of proportion by the ban on Sunday concerts, which struck me as an arch bourgeois act and contrary to our mission. I never ceased to believe that we have a mission and an obligation. Not only *noblesse oblige,* but talent too puts the carrier under a manifold obligation. I say "carrier" rather than "owner," because I believe that whatever gifts we may have are lent to us for the best use and are not to be treated merely like the milk-giving cow.

For twelve years, from 1957 to 1969, I had been associated with one of the world's great opera companies and one of its best orchestras. No matter what my own fanciful mental reservations, Boston's orchestra is unquestionably on the list of the "ten best" in the world. Having breathed such rarefied air for a fair stretch of time I knew now with assurance that I did not care to repeat the experience at other latitudes. Highest excellence of an orchestra can be developed and maintained only at the expense of a conductor's freedom. This is a subtle problem and one that many of my young colleagues are solving in a novel way. They hold two "permanent" posts, though this is a contradiction in terms. I have watched them tearing from California to the Middle East and from Berlin to the Middle West, combining music directorships in Texas and Manchester, in Amsterdam and Los Angeles, dropping dead of heart failure. And why? Because they do not want to be eaten up by cares and yet want the fixed income of a firm position. What then is safer than one job? Two jobs. A conductor who was not bothered by such fears summed it up neatly when relinquishing his permanent situation with the statement that he had ambitions other than those of a "curator."

To increase power and influence, it is of advantage to "have" an orchestra; to be independent and live as a musician and an artist it is far better not to "have" an orchestra. To be honest means undivided devotion to one organization only. In the case of the Boston Symphony the double music directorships collapsed, not only with my successor but with his successor as well. I knew these problems and their answers and wanted no part of them.

In 1969 I considered my situation among these reflections and decided to embark on a free-lance career, with no strings attached. I still remembered one of my mother's homilies: "No man can eat more than one roast beef," which translates: "Don't be greedy." If I look analytically at my profession I can observe that with year-round contracts for musicians, summer festivals everywhere, and increased intercontinental travels for orchestras, symphony concerts have perhaps doubled in number. For many spotlighted events, particularly foreign tours, impresarios and managers forget all their patriotism, nationalism, chauvinism, and jingoism to get a conductor of note. Of these there is a shortage. I got several of my most attractive engagements because of this prevailing condition or because of the two-headed music directors.

From earliest childhood on I dreamed of travel. My interest in all forms of transport, trams, trains, ships, and planes, was never inspired by any mechanical bent, it was only an expression of my desire to move. That wish has been amply fulfilled. The French proverb *"l'appétit vient en mangeant"* holds for travel as well as for eating. The more I saw, the larger loomed that part of the world I had not visited. It began to look as if I knew only the handful of places to which my voyages had led me over and over again. My lengthy periods of making records had given me a most intimate acquaintance with Rome. In

London I had become a connoisseur not only of the historic sights but of the motor routes to Watford, Wembley, Walthamstow, and Barking, all hour-long trips of unrelieved ugliness. On vacations I had seen spots of incomparable natural beauty, the sea at Taormina, the Corniches, the Dolomites, the mesa at Santa Fe, and more. In my professional touring I learned a collection of data on Pottsville, Pottstown, Greensburg, Rockford, Lewiston, Bangor, Lansing, Marietta, Sandusky, Saginaw, et alia.

These last visits I hoped to have shed for good when I joined Boston's distinguished band, especially after reading their press book, with its references to journeys in the Soviet Union, through Europe, and to the Far East. What I did not know was that the last trip to Japan in 1960 had led to a long-drawn-out conflict between management and the orchestra members. Maintaining good health had been a problem, and on one date, when thirty players were hospitalized or hotel bedridden, *La Mer* was performed with two trumpets in place of the regular five. Neither players nor manager wanted to hear of foreign travel now, and they kept their resolve for exactly eleven years, enough for me to miss it all. There was a period when I would have loved to show the Boston Symphony to the European public. When I read every year of two or more American orchestras going abroad, I was highly displeased and, frankly, envious. Musical imperialism during my tenure consisted of one transcontinental tour in 1963, which was fun, and a Southern trip in 1969, which was not. Other than that we returned regularly to Storrs, New London, New Haven, Hartford, Springfield, Northampton, and occasionally to Newark.

In the first four years after leaving Boston I went, always with my wife, to Rio and Buenos Aires, to Lisbon, Madrid, Seville and Granada, to Teheran and Mexico, to Hong Kong, New Zealand, and Australia. Except for Rio, which, as a way station to Buenos Aires, gave us a short holiday, all were visited with orchestras.

It is a fun lesson in musical geography to contemplate that I played Lisbon with a Dutch orchestra, whose conductor at the time doubled in Melbourne. My visits to the Spanish cities were with two English orchestras whose regular chefs were busy in Germany and in Texas. I went to Teheran and Mexico because the titular heads of the orchestras involved were busy elsewhere with their "other" ensembles. Could I have been the beneficiary of musical bigamy?

We are neither discerning collectors nor simple-minded hamsters, but we still brought back attractive souvenirs, the best of which were new friendships. Hospitality in Hong Kong and in Oceania was such that we are impatient to return at the first opportunity.

My disposition changes as soon as I am on the road. Bernhard Paumgartner, my Salzburg mentor when I was eighteen, quoted his mother — herself a famous singer — as saying, "My Bernhard was born on the green wagon." I don't suppose that my mother would have liked the image that she was delivered of me by the midwife of the gypsy band or the *accoucheur* of the circus troupe. She was a sedentary type, but my father, whom I hardly knew, traveled constantly in his business capacity and got as far as Varna and Constantinople. Perhaps he had that same wanderlust that is so much part of myself.

Let nobody think that musical values are shortchanged on tours. As long as the sound in a hall is better than average I can get performances that rank with the best. Live music is always an interplay between performer and public. Most visits of orchestras and even more of opera companies are singular events in the lives of the local populace and expectations run high. This creates an excitement that is felt upon arrival in the hotel lobby, in shops, on promenades, and backstage before the first oboe gives the A to tune by.

A *Fidelio* in Lisbon ranks among my biggest surprises of this kind. The Gulbenkian Foundation had arranged for a Beethoven bicentennial series of events to be climaxed by two concert performances of the composer's opera. A cast of fine singers from the Vienna Opera and from Covent Garden, the Residentie Orkest from The Hague, a local chorus, and I were the disparate elements. I spent several days forging these into an ensemble, and on Thursday, May 21, 1970, we performed in the Foundation's beautifully elegant auditorium. It was, following my Tanglewood pattern, a semistaged rendition with singers indicating the dramatic outline in stylized action on an elevated platform behind the orchestra.

For Saturday night a repeat was set in an arena holding five thousand. To give the widest possible access, prices were low. It was an unlikely spot for the Prisoners' Chorus or the starving Florestan's arias — as if the theater in Drottningholm had been turned into a corrida setting. We had a ramp behind the orchestra for singers to come on and get off and a narrator to tell in Portuguese what normally passes in the spoken dialogue between numbers. The Brazilian-born wife of our tenor sat among the violins with a script to cue me when the narration ended, as I could not follow the language and would not have known when to bring in the orchestra for the next piece. What happened that night between the mounting enthusiasm of the packed house and the excitement of the performers made for a memorable happening, which none of us had foreseen after Thursday's muted cordiality of Lisbon's "best people." Sena Jurinac, our Leonore, after an international career of more than thirty years, said to me as we stood and bowed in a line with held hands that she had never, but never, experienced anything like this. If I thought that the audience was perhaps easily pleased and satisfied I was taught better; the night before a concert had been roundly booed.

Ever since my summers at Tanglewood I felt that the purely musical values of great opera scores were better served in concert form or what I call "semistaged" versions. As soon as there is a pit for the orchestra and make-up and costumes for the singers, as soon as there is lighting of sets, something else happens and takes the upper hand. It is undoubtedly more romantic and colorful to the public mind when opera is given its due as a spectacle, but for the composition as such the concert with well-indicated dramatic movement is more representative.

I have tried to steer clear of opera except for one essay at the 1972 Wagner Festival in Bayreuth and three short guest stints at the Met. This laudable resolution was reinforced by my first excursion to the Teatro Colón in Buenos Aires, where I started my years of wandering with fifteen performances of three operas.

The incidents and folkways could easily fill fifteen chapters and three volumes, but then it may be the better part of valor to learn from the success of an enterprise based in Pleasantville, New York, where the system of digesting words has blossomed into a popular way of reading.

## *El Teatro Colón*

My experiences during nine weeks in Buenos Aires were enough to prepare me for any and all of the political and economic pranks that are ruining the Argentine republic. The opera season there is called *temporada*. Its organization in 1969 must have been along the lines of the Met's in 1923 if reports have been accurate. Importation en masse from the mother countries for leads and subsidiary roles, for conductors and helpers, for assistant stage managers and auxiliaries left a talented contingent of natives bitter and justly resentful. While in other parts of the world reasonable concern with one's own compatriots grows, in Argentina the import business reigned supreme. There was a reason.

Payment to all foreign artists was in United States dollars, as the obviously unacceptable peso would not have done as legal tender to lure Germans or Italians or Americans. One agency was the principal intermediary between the municipality of the city, which pays for the whole Colón, and the artists. That agency advanced to us, as to every client from abroad, the necessary funds to cover rent and daily expenditures. They also were kind enough to escort any artist on shopping sprees, with much encouragement and good advice about where to find the specialties. Artists never tired of paying for these purchases — in the local currency. When the artist's engagement drew to a close the final accounting, which was meticulously accurate, would still leave the agency with dollars calculated on the official rate of exchange to trade on the black market. Or did the agency perhaps return the unused dollars to the city treasury?

The native artists would be paid in pesos; hence, the interest in promoting them was not on top of the agency's agenda.

There were other side shows. The orchestra was the first and only one I ever found that loved to rehearse, which puzzled me until I learned why. The basic salaries were miserably low and only overtime was well paid. There was a tacit understanding between employer and musicians that every *temporada* should include suddenly needed extra rehearsals to bring the take-home pay to acceptable levels. That was why my first rehearsals went at a snail's pace and I nearly went out of my mind until I was enlightened. As soon as the schedule with the overtime additions was issued to the orchestra our progress became far more rapid.

I still have never seen such possessive feelings of musicians for their instruments and chairs. One evening, half an hour before a *Rosenkavalier* was to start, I was informed that the bass-clarinet player was ill. In the opera the player must double on basset horn, which the substitute was unable to do, for the simple reason that the one and only available instrument was safely and inaccessibly locked in the sick man's closet. No arguments, I was told, could budge the key holder to let us in. There was no time to copy the possible transpositions into a clarinet part so I presided over a unique performance that omitted every note written by Strauss for the basset horn.

Another tenacious incumbent, the principal trumpet player, had to fly to Montevideo to be with his "dying mother." When I was about to start the first general rehearsal for *Parsifal*, with stage and chorus and the entire cast, involving hundreds of people, the first trumpet's chair was empty. No word, no plea, neither promises nor threats could induce any of the present contingent of buglers — and there were quite a few on stage for the brass band — to assume the vacant chair in order to help out. One of them, a young fellow who had done a magnificent job of filling in for the absentee in the preceding night's *Wozzeck*, was the reason for the blanket refusal of the lot to cooperate. It was a fair assumption that the "titular" in Montevideo had laid down the law, *"Sans moi pas de trompette."* I decided that I would not buckle under to such tactics and sent everybody home rather than do *Parsifal* without the principal trumpet part. Mother must have recovered rapidly or risen from the dead because the next day her son was back and present at every session where his services were required and desired. He never again budged as long as I was there.

After seeing the remains of a decaying social order and a corrupt set of arrangements, I was astonished at the quality of the performances as a whole. Casts were mostly superior, and the house itself has no peer for elegance, architectural perfection, and beauty of sound.

## Rehearsals

Among the vexing questions and problems in a musician's life, the least understood is the rehearsal issue. I have met people, quite intelligent and knowledgeable otherwise, who asked me seriously if I did any practicing prior to a concert with a new orchestra. Others think we meet at six and play for the public at eight. Still others want to know if I use the same orchestration as another conductor. This could be a language error, because what a musician calls "orchestration" is an instrumental setting of a composition sketch, while often the same term means only the orchestra material. If the latter is meant the answer would have to be "Yes, whenever available for purchase." To travel with complete sets of parts saves a great deal of time in rehearsals, which are ideally devoted to acquainting the players with at least the conductor's musical ideas for the well-known repertoire. Here I found one of the fundamental weaknesses in all but the very finest orchestras. I can count on the fingers of one hand the orchestras on both sides of the Atlantic whose acquaintance with the classic, romantic, and modern perennials is intimate.

My proudest moment in 721 concerts with the Boston Symphony came after a New York performance of a Brahms symphony we had not touched in fifty days. It is the deepest sense of permanent conductorship to arrive at a stage of such fusion between ensemble and chef that the approximately one hundred basic works can be played in public with a minimum of rehearsing and a maximum of improvisational joy. It is difficult to achieve this, because there are too many changes of personnel and not enough permanent conductors with that particular goal.

When I visit orchestras I notice within an hour of the first rehearsal session how "together" the "ensemble" is, usually by the similarity — or lack of it — in the execution of ornaments by different instruments. If everyone phrases the same way I know that I am standing before a great orchestra.

Within five years after leaving Boston I conducted forty-two different orchestras, two of them consisting only of young people in their preprofessional stage. My experiences with the students at the Berkshire Music Center had been so exhilarating that I wanted, if possible, to do more musical work with youth. At Tanglewood I had gradually increased the scope of the student orchestra until we tackled in 1968 Arnold Schönberg's *Die glückliche Hand* and, my major accomplishment, two performances of the complete *Wozzeck* in 1969. This last was such a success with participants and visitors that it encouraged me to take on Stravinsky's *The Rake's Progress* at the Juilliard School in New York for the opening of their new beautiful opera auditorium in April 1970.

I found Juilliard a bit different from the Berkshire Music Center, where the enrolled members had nothing else to do but play music and no other place to do that. The competition of New York City posed problems new to me. In my second rehearsal I found a largely different group of players, and when on the third day still another batch of new faces appeared I asked for a meeting with the president of the school and his dean of students. "Where are we," I wanted to know, "at the Paris Opéra or at the Juilliard School in New York?"

In Paris it is the rule for orchestra members to send substitutes when there are more interesting or more lucrative alternate possibilities. A famous story tells of the guest conductor who singled out in his final rehearsal one man hidden on a back stand for this compliment: "You, dear sir, are the only member of this orchestra who attended every rehearsal from start to finish and I thank you." "*Maître*," replied the highly flattered musician, "I am honored by your recognition, yet for tomorrow's première I must send my brother to play in my place. I am unavailable." Never having put up with the Parisian system I had no intention of putting up with it now, especially in a conservatory.

The dean, I noticed right away, was afraid to tackle the issue, which did not appear to surprise the president. It was explained that most of the good instrumental students had outside jobs enabling them to pay tuition, which of course pleased the school's administration. "If that is so," I told them, "perhaps a more pliable conductor would be better cast in the role." Peter Mennin, the president, would not hear of this and insisted that dean and students settle on one crew of top players who would make firm promises to be at all rehearsals and performances. From that moment on things went well, and with this high caliber of players we got an instrumental rendition of the score that could hardly have been bettered by any ranking opera-house orchestra. *The Rake* is grist for the mill of the virtuoso-type musician who emerges from the music schools in the United States.

With the singers, who were not nearly as talented, I also had problems of availability. Honest student status seemed a thing of the past. Even the moderately gifted were already full of outside engagements here, there, and everywhere. Our stage director told me some story why the best of three bassos would sing the second performance only. His tale made no sense, his explanations seemed lame, until a third party informed me that the young man had a longstanding engagement in Texas for the night of our première. In that one respect the Juilliard singers were of Met caliber.

The very good first horn of the *Rake* orchestra turned up as a full-fledged member of the Chicago Symphony only a few months later. This direct jump from undergraduate status to top professional position is symptomatic of the American scene. In my years in Boston I had learned with amazement that aside from New York and Los Angeles no city in the United States has any pool of good musicians. One finds talent enough to play at a clambake but not to help out with Claude Debussy. Almost every orchestra member has been imported, and the best of the great orchestras are grateful to get youngsters straight from school such is the shortage of experienced professionals. This fact illuminated for me a complex picture of orchestral music in America.

Between this meager supply of talent and the progressive and effective union attitudes, the age-old differences of quality and experience get blurred and often totally erased.

My visit with the Houston Symphony in 1971 was a good illustration. This is a far better than average orchestra, potentially of first rank, with a good mixture of older musicians who like the easy life in Texas and youngsters fresh from schools and conservatories. They had been playing for years under such conductors as Barbirolli and Stokowski whose systematic influence showed fine results which I had seen in 1961 when I first conducted there.

Now, ten years later, I had been asked and agreed to perform Mahler's Fourth Symphony. Progress was on the slow side, as the style was unfamiliar and we simply needed more time to have the music fully absorbed by all and sundry. The concertmaster, conscientious, cooperative, and anxious to please, came to me during the intermission of the final rehearsal, when I probably looked rather unhappy, and offered his help. "What can I do?" he wanted to know. "Get me six rehearsals instead of four" was my answer. It was not at all management's economy drive but the master contract with the musicians that specified four rehearsals as the quota for a symphony program. I said, without any heat or indignation, that it made no sense for Houston to pretend that they could learn and prepare difficult music in the same amount of time that New York's and Chicago's orchestras allowed. It was alarming to me, because one of the basic tenets in any of the performing arts is that young and less experienced talent should grow with the years to maturity and mastery. It looked to me as if the concept of equality had been misunderstood and misapplied. On graduation day we have perhaps talent, aptitude, drive, ambition, and skill. After that come the years when we acquire the subtler qualities a musician must possess to be an artist. These values appeared to be denigrated by the rule that one hundred players must learn the Mahler

Fourth in four rehearsals. Each hundred players may be a different lot.

I often think that the most frequently found hang-up in conductors is the problem of "insufficient rehearsal." Musicians, when they hear these notions, regale me with chapter and verse — meaning names and score titles — of what they go through with certain maestros who have memorized their music but are still unable to offer guidance beyond conducting a runthrough from A to Z. I am told that they wouldn't know what to do with a second, let alone a fifth, rehearsal. Such are the opinions of the sufferers on both sides of the ocean.

In Boston the older orchestra members spoke to me of the "bloody Mondays" — not a movie but the nickname for Koussevitzky's long rehearsals before the New York tours. On such occasions he would take six or seven hours to file and refine pieces that had been played already. The orchestra then was still nonunion (it was the last to join, in 1942), but its music director well knew the length of time and amount of practice necessary to achieve his brand of top-flight quality. After thirty years and many master contracts the members of the same orchestra made sure that this kind of perfectionism could never happen again by severely limiting rehearsal time. No rehearsals were allowed on road trips, except for an occasional one to allow a fleeting acquaintance with the acoustics of a new hall.

Rehearsals have ceased to be a purely musical issue in America. Somebody invented the term "service," which for a symphony orchestra denotes either a rehearsal or a concert. Need I underline that management, hard-pressed to make ends meet, will also prefer a concert to a rehearsal, the one producing income while the other produces only expenditure? As I began to tour the world regularly it came home to me with full impact how uniformly this entire complex is treated by the great and the not-so-great. The end result is that the great orchestras, those able to afford it, can still be great, while the second and third rank are more or less condemned to remain where they are.

England, where the situation is economically tighter than elsewhere, has, at least in London, another problem compounding the difficulties of rehearsing. There are five orchestras plus a couple of chamber orchestras vying for the same Royal Festival Hall, and therefore two out of three rehearsals take place in wretchedly ill-equipped places where acoustics, light, and heat are of such low quality that no American or Continental orchestra would put up with it. Musically the London orchestras start out as if they will give the best possible performance such is the schooling and first reading of these musicians. All questions of intonation and synchronization can be taken for granted and will cause no interruptions as in most other orchestras. The English all appear to have studied with the same solfège teacher and their A's are the same and so are the dotted rhythms that present such problems in many another group. In London my expectations run high after the first three-hour rehearsal. And then I find that all metamorphoses have stopped then and there and no further progress is made. In performance something else may appear, emotional dynamism, the essential difference in attitude between practice and public show, yet the nuance of orchestral superquality is no different from the first runthrough.

What I had taken as interim makeshift patterns on my first postwar visit to London in 1946 proved, alas, to be permanent arrangements. The two self-governing orchestras, the Philharmonic and the Symphony, were augmented by two privately financed ones. In 1948 Sir Thomas Beecham founded the Royal Philharmonic, and in 1951 Walter Legge, an EMI big wheel, established the Philharmonia, in order to have a perfect instrument for record-making. When Beecham died and Legge left the company, both orchestras were thrown to the wolves, but neither gave up. As an end result London has four self-governing orchestras struggling for survival in an otherwise terrific setting. The tragedy is once again the uniformity of rehearsal patterns. No matter what the program, no matter what changes of personnel, there are three three-hour rehearsals for each Royal

Festival Hall concert. Sometimes this is sufficient and sometimes it is not.

I have made my own adjustment by doing programs that I think can be prepared in nine hours with musicians I know, but I made at least two terrible mistakes, resulting in one case in a rather thin performance: Nobody told me that the London Philharmonic had not played — at least not in a decade — either Mendelssohn's Scotch Symphony or Prokofiev's Fifth Symphony. The Mendelssohn is so idiomatically set for the orchestra that we encountered no trouble in learning the work, but Prokofiev, having been a pianist, often wrote for orchestra tonalities and passages not born out of the instruments, particularly as far as the strings are concerned. By the time I found out that the orchestra did not have any previous experience with that well-known piece it was too late; the proverbial backs were against the proverbial wall, and we scrambled through a poor three quarters of an hour. The relativity of rehearsals was manifest when I performed the same Prokofiev work with the Czech Philharmonic, which knew every twist and turn so well that the first five minutes of the first rehearsal were superior to the entire London performance.

The European continent offers another set of variable conditions. There it is possible to get different allotments for music of different complexity. In some countries the ample supply of time is frivolously wasted while in only a few the music is, as it should be, the beneficiary.

The Italian scene resembles a generous anarchy. "Generous" because ten three-hour rehearsals for a not abnormally complex program are more than one can ask, "anarchy" because the prevailing lack of organization throws away 40 or 50 percent of the time. My most memorable experience along those lines occurred in Milan when I wanted to begin my first rehearsal with the most difficult work, Alban Berg's Violin Concerto. Looking over the placement of the instruments, I searched for the saxophonist but was unable to find him. To my repeated question, *"Dov'è il sassofono?"* there was silence and shoulder-shrugging. "Where is the personnel manager?" Loud shouts of "Roberti, Roberti" — who comes on stage after a considerable wait. He smiles at me beatifically and asks most courteously: *"Prego, Maestro?"* My mention of the missing saxophone produces a barely noticeable shock in Roberti's countenance, which almost immediately assumes again that beautiful smile and what is called an unflappability. *"Ci sara domani."* Firm assurance, without explanations. I was positive that nobody even knew that such an unorthodox horn was in Berg's score.

*Domani,* the next day, there was a player with a saxophone present. When I asked if he had brought his clarinet, which he also has to play, he shrugged, as if that were something totally new and unexpected. It was futile to point out that a list of necessary instruments appears in clear, big print in the score where in a play the dramatis personae are listed. "I will have it tomorrow." *"Domani."*

In Italian it was *"dopodomani,"* the day after tomorrow, when I finally had the quorum and their correct equipment to begin the Berg Concerto in earnest. We got on and made some progress until I had to stop and ask the bass tuba player to please use the mute — *la sordina* — in a passage, as directed by the composer. The player smiled indulgently as if he had not expected anything but idiotic requests from the conductor and stated mildly: "Maestro, *non esiste"* — "it does not exist." I was nonplussed and asked the man what he thought had happened between 1935 when the score was published and performed and now. For a considerable time we argued back and forth, I trying to relate reasonably that in every country and orchestra the tuba used at times the mute, the player insisting in a forgiving tone that such a thing did not exist in Milan. Short of manufacturing one myself on the spot I had to enumerate details of size and shape and material to convince not only the tubist but his confreres as well that I would not be hood-winked. Time passed and after the rehearsal resumed the spirit somehow had gone out of the crowd.

The next day the mute was there, and the fellow played and used everything as prescribed and desired. My guess was that his small Fiat would not take tuba and mute, so he preferred to leave the mute at home. It is also a nuisance to figure out the new pitches of the instrument's response with the mute on. By then it was rehearsal number four, and ten did not look as extravagant to me as a week earlier.

The Parisians utilize their rehearsal time differently. Not willing to rely on memory for an example I dug through my diaries until I found an entry for March 30, 1971: "Rarely have I loathed rehearsals as much as here. The lack of working discipline is appalling. At nine fifty-five they start ringing the bell to go on stage. The tinkle goes on continuously for minutes, a disagreeable assault on the nerves, which neither wears off nor produces the result of getting the orchestra members seated. To accomplish that feat a more old-fashioned method of shouting and hand clapping by the personnel manager is used. The ringing continues optimistically and repulsively all the while until I for one am ready to go out of my mind even before beginning the rehearsal. Two days ago I gave new bowings for the adagietto to the violins, whose leader graciously agreed that they were very good; he would have them copied into the parts. Nothing has been done by this morning because there is no mechanism for doing such arcane things as writing new bowings into the string material."

The resident manager of the Orchestre de Paris suggested for my concerts in 1973 a performance of Mahler's song cycle "Des Knaben Wunderhorn." Two very fine English singers were engaged, and they sent an exact listing of the key signatures for their numbers, orchestrations being available in several tonalities for different voice ranges. When I officially confirmed sequence, key relationships, and titles to the management it was eleven months before the first concert. Ten months and twenty-five days later, at the first rehearsal, four of the ten songs were in other keys and one was missing altogether.

If it had not been for the sportsmanship of Helen Watts and John Shirley-Quirk, who gamely sang a few songs in ranges not really theirs, the whole cycle might have been called off, perhaps on second thought a better service to Mahler than performing it as we did at the second of three concerts, when the musicians felt like making wrong entrances and choosing B-flat clarinets when instruments in A were needed, and other such niceties.

Then I decided that in Paris it is the better part of wisdom to consult Michelin for the bistros, leave to the orchestra their simple ways of bowing and wrong transpositions, and let somebody else conduct.

In October and November 1974 I had two rehearsal experiences that not only encompassed the gamut of possibilities but also demonstrated how things should be. The Hessian Radio Network had arranged for two concert performances of *Gurre-Lieder* as a centenary commemoration of Schönberg's birth. The mammoth work, while traditional in musical language, is exceedingly difficult to play. Balances, intonation, technical complexities, and an ensemble complicated by many extra instruments necessitate more than the usual time for preparation. Frankfurt's head of music made a determined effort and allowed a whole week of the orchestra's services to be used exclusively for *Gurre-Lieder*. That was in addition to a normally already ample rehearsal schedule. Regular and extra rehearsals totaled forty-six hours, with the result that an otherwise just fair orchestra could produce two performances to such effect that one of Europe's leading recording companies wanted to issue the tapes made from the broadcast as a commercial recording, in today's music world one of the highest compliments.

Four weeks later I was guest with the Berlin Philharmonic, an orchestra of unusual caliber in every sense of the word. It had returned three days earlier from a tour of the United States, and its *Intendant* — what we would call general manager — Wolfgang Stresemann, a son of Gustav, the Weimar Republic's great statesman, expressed his sincere regrets that we had inadvertently agreed on Brahms's Fourth Symphony as our major work, since, unfortunately, it had been added to the tour repertoire for America and had been played as recently as five days ago under the regular chef of the orchestra, Karajan. All of this tended to make my task with an already fatigued group more complex. Stresemann seemed to pity my lot and couldn't say enough in advance apology.

I rather enjoyed the prospect for a variety of reasons. It so happens that I respect Karajan musically and had no apprehensions about doing with his orchestra anything at all, familiar or unfamiliar. It intrigued me to have a little artistic tournament competition, and the condition under which I should have a go at it would test my applied psychology.

The first rehearsal was on a Sunday morning, the first of three concerts Monday night. Before we began I said to the assembled musicians: "I have some reliable intelligence attesting to your faint and vague familiarity with this symphony [laughter and snickering]. Still, we have to get some agreement on doing it together. There is my own material clearly marked to help and I feel that a kind of musical checkup will not take too long and that afterward all those who do not play in the other two works on the program should come back Monday night in time for the Brahms Symphony." With this little announcement I showed my confidence and my intention of not keeping at it longer than necessary. I also demonstrated that I intended to go my own way. Not having been willing to merely imitate a predecessor at age twenty-six, I was an unlikely candidate to do it at sixty-two.

The checkup took fifty-nine minutes. After the Monday concert Stresemann assured me that he would not have believed anyone who told him what he had heard with his own ears: a completely fresh-sounding orchestra playing a totally different Brahms from that which it had performed with its own chef six days earlier in New York.

Forty-six hours for *Gurre-Lieder* and seven hours for a program of Brahms plus Stravinsky's *Symphony of Wind Instruments,* which was quite new for the players, are perhaps the limits of rehearsal time and its uses. It sounds simple to have as much time as the music requires and to use as much of it as the brilliance and versatility of the musicians suggest, yet it is so very rare to find conditions such as these.

The end of the Berlin triple concert was even more gratifying personally. After the finale of the last evening the principal oboist thanked me in his and his colleagues' names in terms that nobody at the Juilliard School had found in the dictionary.

## Name Dropping

Whenever a reference volume in which I am to appear is compiled, the editor sends me long questionnaires asking for a list of honors, awards, decorations, and titles. Since I never chased after them I have very few and do not attach any great significance to them. By the same token I have not found much pleasure in collecting famous names. My greatest treat in personal exchange is to talk music with musicians. It has been surprising and disappointing to me how difficult this is. That I am not alone with such regrets is shown by the following story:

A pianist friend of mine played a round of concerts in a setup where the participants met in their free hours at poolside in a relaxed and friendly atmosphere. He is deeply involved with many questions of textual accuracy and broad interpretive problems and looked forward to getting the views and opinions of the conductor, whom he respected. When the pianist and I met next, it was in a European capital just after that tour, and he was terribly puzzled by his experience. Each attempt to involve the conductor in a musical conversation met with a rebuff, while all other topics were debated freely and in great friendliness. I too have felt this lack of regular shoptalk ever since my visits to Toscanini stopped. Maybe the fault has been primarily mine since I have never led a life of late hours and perhaps tongues loosen only after midnight. My guess is that prevailing inner insecurities, not uncommon in highly successful people, prevent substantive talks, lest somebody's slip is showing.

And then — what bores some well-known people are. For many years I had admired Edmund Wilson and had read nearly all his collected essays. When I found him living in Cambridge during my Boston years I made an effort to strike up a personal acquaintance, which I enjoyed greatly. Once, when the Wilsons asked me to dinner, I was so full of anticipation that I arrived seven days early. On the correct evening, for which I returned after my mishap, the party was graced by the tall presence of another Cambridge resident, who brought with him a tiny television set, which he connected in the dining room opposite his place at table. He explained, not being a man to apologize easily, that he must watch a program. Was a taped interview with him being shown? No. Was one of his books being reviewed? No. Was his academic subject perhaps being discussed by someone he wished to scout? No. Nothing as unimportant as all this. He had submitted gags to a fun show and wanted to check which of them, if any, were being used. This paralyzed our dinner conversation.

When I first met Stokowski, who is my senior by thirty years, I hoped to get a few answers to important musical questions. I asked specifically how much rehearsal had been necessary in Philadelphia to master the complexities of *Wozzeck* when he gave it in 1931. His reply was that the light cues proved to be most difficult, but the music quite simple.

I regretted that my encounter with Ansermet was a one-time event in the bustle of a large party, for I felt great empathy and ease of communication with him. He appeared to be past the stage of running and treading the mill, which gave to his words a feeling of superior detachment, not cold disdain but Olympian maturity.

In the official world I found several United States ambassadors of such engaging and attractive personality that I was under the mistaken impression all our representatives were of that top caliber. Certainly those whom I met personally went out of their way to be kind to me and were a credit to their countries. When I conducted in Israel in 1960, Ogden Reid, then quite young, with a most attractive wife, made a particularly fine impression. Both the Reids took Hebrew lessons, which he made use of when making his public addresses on ceremonial occasions in that language. At a luncheon he gave, the conversation was far more substantial than is customary for such courtesy affairs and revolved around fairly ticklish political subjects. It is always a shock to me when such fine people are recalled as soon as the other party comes to power in Washington.

John Cabot Lodge in Buenos Aires gave a splendid dinner toward the end of our stay. I was particularly grateful not only that we were personally feted but that the whole show was not left to the German and Austrian ambassadors, who fell all over themselves paying attention to the artists connected with the *temporada alemán.* Lodge, musical or not — I could not really decide — accepted the invitation to be in our box a couple of times and threw a magnificent shindig at his Argentine palace.

Visiting Tokyo in 1966 I was myself on a kind of diplomatic mission with the blessings of the State Department. An exchange of musicians between a Japanese orchestra and the Boston Symphony had been proposed and was then to be put into operation. It was a somewhat ticklish issue that necessitated my trip to Japan. I had refused to accept anyone as a member of the orchestra for a year without hearing them in audition. This, however, is to the Oriental mind a loss of face and not accepted

as a legitimate procedure. I still do not know exactly how I got
to hear the candidates, but it was with very good help from the
United States Information Service. I concluded my stay by visiting the ambassador, Professor Edwin O. Reischauer, an unusual
and fortunate choice for a diplomatic post.

To me the most appealing of all was John Humes in
Vienna. First he sent word to find out what kind of a luncheon
party I wanted, large or small, with VIPs of Vienna's musical
Establishment or with the VIPs of the United States colony.
When I asked that it be very small and limited to only our most
intimate personal friends, the ambassador obliged and made it
for ten people, which meant real conversation and one of the
nicest two hours ever. The ambassador's wife was absent, as she
was a medical doctor and working at the time, so he was assisted
as co-host by the cultural attaché, who confided to one of my
friends that there were two unusual things about that luncheon.
First, it was a personal affair without any career aims pursued
by the guest of honor, and second, it was not an autobiograph-
ical soliloquy by the honored guest. Humes made a splendid
toast, commenting on the cross-fertilization between the émigrés and the host country in a way that was most personal and
quite moving. He too was recalled as soon as his former boss
was replaced in Washington.

I collect coins in a desultory way, and when I stop from time
to time in front of a window to look at the numismatic beau-
ties, I gaze in some amazement at the medals, which are often
exhibited with the ribbons ready to be pinned on to the dress
uniform or hung around the neck. I have a sufficiently skeptical mind to wonder on such occasions how many times at parties
and receptions one sees decorated people who have just acquired
their honors in one of those coin stores. I am unimpressed by
the costume ball performed in many quarters as if it were the
real thing, and I itch at the sight of a decoration to ask the
wearer exactly how it became his. On the other hand, I marvel
at the largess of some monarchs and princes who gave diamond-

studded snuffboxes or rings in lieu of their recognition to an
artist. If such generosity were around I too might have lobbied
as some of my acquaintances did for the cheaper metals of their
medals.

It is the personal factor that makes a friend of note or an
acquaintance in high places valuable to me. I appreciated President Johnson's many invitations because of the closeness of our
connection for many years, even though it was no fun and very
expensive to go to the White House. In the summer of 1964 I
even chartered a small plane to fly with my daughter Hester
from Pittsfield (near Tanglewood) to Washington between my
duties at the Berkshire Music Festival. It was certainly a wonderful experience for my sixteen-year-old girl to dance with the
President of the United States. Earlier, when we stood in the
East Room with all the guests awaiting the President and his
guest of honor, an alphabetical neighbor (one is lined up in order
of the last name's first letter), Herman Kenin, the head of the
American Federation of Musicians, spoke to me with some ur-
gency about bringing back operatic recording to the domestic
orchestras. That discourse led to the questionably successful
*Lohengrin* recording and such ramifications that the price of
the charter plane dwindled into insignificance by comparison.
Only when we were not in a crowd was it fascinating to be and
talk with Lyndon Johnson. When sitting near the President in
his box at Constitution Hall at the preinaugural concert or right
behind him at the ground-breaking ceremonies for the Kennedy
Center, I confess that I found my apprehension at the chance
of getting shot more forceful than the pride of place next to
the first citizen.

Prizes and awards for having done the best or the worst, or
for having the biggest or the smallest record sale, and nomina-
tions for an Oscar or Grammy or Tilly or Becky are commercially arranged within the "industry." They are part and parcel
of one's box-office success. Not that they create it, for they
are made only after it is clear that box office has been more than

favorable. This is the basis for the most mundane kudos —
awards are made to appear as something leading to practical
acclaim while in reality they merely confirm that the practical
acclaim has already been yours. It is quite the same with the
social game. The young artist is told that it is essential to go
to the "parties," which is true. The only small difference is that
the importance is not so much the advantage to the young artist
as to the party-giver.

Looking through some of these confidence tricks did not make
me indifferent to the real honor of meeting a great person. In
the summer of 1971 I conducted a concert of an International
Youth orchestra in Copenhagen. The honorary patron was
King Frederick IX of Denmark, whom I met again on that
occasion. "Again" because I had been introduced to him long
ago, in May 1939, when as crown prince he had opened the
Danish pavilion at the New York World's Fair and Melchior,
his compatriot, had arranged for a *Lohengrin* performance at
the Met to honor that visit. As conductor of the performance
I was included at the supper party afterward and was introduced to Frederick, who spoke with me at some length. He was
an enthusiastic amateur musician and even conducted for fun at
benefits. The conversation had been better than the usual exchange with a potentate. But then this was no usual prince
either.

As King of the Danes at the time of the Nazi occupation he
was the first to don a yellow armband when it was demanded
of the Danish Jews for their public identification symbol. To
stand in front of this man thirty-two years later was a special
moment in my life. It is not every day that one may shake
hands with a real and true King.

Meeting the Shah of Iran earlier that same year had been
another type of encounter, better perhaps for the book of good
stories but much less warming for my soul.

In January of 1971 I had been in New York, recuperating
from the aftereffects of a silly accident. A surprise call from

Paris had on a double extension my French agent and the manager of l'Orchestre de Paris with an urgent, if not to say anxious, request that I consider making a trip to Teheran for two concerts of French music, which to me was an attractive thought since I loved the idea of stuffing all possible Debussy and Ravel pieces into two evenings. For a short moment I wondered why they were asking me to take the orchestra to Iran. But then my mind reviewed a short history of that organization, after which I was no longer puzzled.

In 1967 André Malraux, then minister of culture for De Gaulle, was persuaded that France needed at least one musical organism to lay to rest for good the old jokes about substitute musicians and generally anarchical conditions. On the ruins of several orchestras, Lamoureux, Colonne and du Conservatoire, Malraux's deputy formed a new symphonic combination, invited Munch to be titular and regular head conductor, and issued firm contracts making musicians' services exclusive in exchange for better than customary pay scales. Press and radio publicity was enormous, great sums of money were spent and greater ones committed, official sanction was so pointedly manifest that even before its public baptism the new "Orchestre de Paris" was nicknamed "l'Orchestre de Prestige." (When in January 1968 I heard it in Paris for the first time I noticed that the prestige did not yet contribute to playing the slow movement of Brahms's First Symphony together.)

After Munch's passing it was now incumbent upon the guiding spirits to obtain a conductor of prestige, which led to the appointment of Herbert von Karajan. After much fanfare the reality was anticlimactic because the new chef was rarely with the orchestra, preferring for his musical sallies and recordings his other band, the Berlin Philharmonic. I sometimes wondered what happened to a pair of ears that had to listen for many hours to the Parisian group after the nonpareil Berlin orchestra. The disappointment of not seeing much of the new man did not diminish the wit of the French, who named Karajan *le chef fantôme.* (If Joyce had been author of this phrase, it might have established any number of free associations: Karajan flies his own plane and the French title for Wagner's *The Flying Dutchman* has always been *Le Vaisseau Fantôme.*)

My quick recall had told me as much as this: Karajan was unavailable or unwilling to make the tour and they wanted on this international trip to put their best foot forward. Whatever French feet were available did not appeal to the promoters and organizers of the Iranian visit, hence the call to me.

A few days before the start of our journey I arrived in Paris for rehearsals. The soloists were flautist Jean-Pierre Rampal and pianist Aldo Ciccolini. The latter found his fear of flying stronger than his desire to buy caviar cheaply and canceled one day before our departure. Gabriel Tacchino, who had played his United States debut with Boston in 1964 and whom I liked, replaced him.

Iran Air, whose charter we used for the journey, underestimated the thirst of musicians so that two hours out of Paris there was no more champagne left and the stewardess regretfully told me I had to make do with Chivas Regal. Not a real hardship.

After a day of rest and sightseeing we gave two concerts, both of which were preceded by full rehearsals. The morning after the first night, a loud and boisterous evening, I arrived for rehearsal to find the entire orchestra milling around in front of the opera house. They were locked out by a contingent of soldiers armed to the teeth, who stopped anyone attempting to go in. Disgruntled and offended members of the orchestra spoke darkly of a strike (une grève) and a cancellation (une annulation), and only after a bilingual intermediary had been called to settle the dispute were we allowed to have our rehearsal. An apology from the local bigwig explained that all this was due to the security arrangements preceding the Shah's announced attendance that evening. And there was more to protecting His Imperial Majesty's safety.

Eight-thirty was the announced time of the concert; a kind of local sage informed me that the Shah's arrival was set for 9:00 P.M. The public had to be present and seated as a matter of subjects' basic courtesy; then the doors to the opera house were closed and everybody sat and waited. When I got to the stage door it was also locked, but the Cerberus had been briefed and my admission went without a hitch. The one moment of fear and trembling on any sally into unknown territory is the national anthem. Of such anthems as the Iranian, nothing is known in our latitudes, and I depend on an arrangement of the music with perhaps verbal advice from a local musician. We had tried the anthem in Paris and found it so wretchedly orchestrated, so clumsy in voicing and harmonization that I wanted to ask the local conductor who attended to our needs for help. By a sixth sense I made my intention known to our impresario, who warned me that the concoction to which I objected was precisely the work of the maestro from whom I wanted succor.

The gala was as elegant as such events are and, also true to form, less lively than the evening before. Something inhibits the elegant crowd from letting itself go. Perhaps it fears that make-up will flake off and leave it bare. Afterward, a small group, soloists, managers, delegates of the players, and I, were escorted to an upstairs salon for introductions to the Shah. He stood with his beautiful and elegant wife surrounded by a cast worthy of a classical Viennese operetta: bemedaled and beribboned uniforms and long and heavily decorated evening gowns with uncomfortable-looking people inside. It cannot be a cinch to stand as one of a coterie.

After a number of appropriate compliments the Shah asked me: "How do I go about creating such an orchestra for Teheran?" My reply was for him to "kidnap" twelve outstanding instrumental teachers for the different orchestral sections, set them up in his city, and within a generation the students would be ready to form an orchestra. That was much too long a wait

for him. Why couldn't he duplicate Malraux's feat and make
an orchestra as had been done in France — within only four
years. He had evidently read and believed the blurb in the program or the pressbook. It was no secret to insiders that this was
a reconstructed orchestra from three defunct ones, but how
could one explain this to His Majesty?

After we left and prepared our voyage back I thought myself very witty when I named the expedition our "oil concerts."
Two and a half years later at the time of the embargo, this did
not sound like a joke any longer.

It is common courtesy to tell a few selected intimates in advance any important news before it hits the papers, and when I
had decided to leave Boston I phoned Bing. His reflex, like a
flash, was "When will you be back at the Met?" Even though I
had no such desire it was nice to get such a spontaneous welcome. I explained that there was still a stretch of twenty
months with many concerts to digest and that I would eventually be happy to return but only in a big new production.

In May 1969, while guest-conducting in Frankfurt, I received a cabled offer with a firm set of dates for a new *Tristan*
production planned for November and December 1971. It
suited me perfectly and I accepted. It was odd to contemplate
that after having spent thirteen seasons wholly or partly with
the Met it would be the first time I would have Wagner in a
new production. In my early years at the opera there were no
new productions, and Bing during his regime had underplayed
Wagner, whom he did not love. There always have been opera
lovers and music enthusiasts with a deep resentment of anything
Wagnerian. This is a combination of many strands within a
person, too complex for quick analysis. Bing belonged to that
group and made no bones about it.

When in November 1971 I reentered the administration offices that I knew so well from my years in the old house, I noticed a tension, which I ascribed to the presence of Bing's

successor-designate, Goeran Gentele, one floor above. It was known by then that none of the assistant managers, Gutman, Herman, or Krawitz, would be retained by the new regime, yet they all had to work hard on planning the first season of a management to which they would not belong. It was tough and had to be borne with a stiff upper lip. Some lips were looser than others, giving away sufficient resentment to warm the air to a volcanic temperature. After having sampled some explosive conversation I went downstairs to the rehearsal rooms and concentrated from then on on making the new production a success.

Detailed accounts of successes are boring to read about. I find it hopeless to re-create that atmosphere which spells success in show business, and I think that I have been economical and sparing in telling such stories. This one time I am breaking my vow because the singular reception of this new *Tristan* tells a lot of the inner mechanism and the making of a smash. I was amazed myself at how a famous, well-known masterwork could create the kind of stir usually reserved for brand-new discoveries. I thought quite objectively that Wagner has to begin with a most receptive public, who are more like addicts than spectators, who are "sent" into ecstasies even by mediocre renditions. Allowing for all of this our venture was still quite out of the ordinary because for once the three elements, singing, staging, and ensemble, were what they always ought to be but rarely are.

Dress rehearsals for long and taxing works take place on the third day prior to the première to allow two full days of rest for all participants. The Met's dress rehearsals of new works or new productions are like previews in the theater, not for sale but attended by four or five hundred people who either have relatives in the cast, orchestra, chorus, or management or who know how to get into anything worth while without paying. It is an in-crowd, blasé, experienced, knowing everything and everybody, and quite able to demolish any effort by word of mouth before the opening-night curtain. When we finished our dress rehearsal it was four in the afternoon. There are neither curtain calls nor bows nor spotlights after these affairs; the dimmest house lamps go on and nothing more. Yet that afternoon the small audience began to applaud, and while I spoke with a few musicians the heat in the auditorium began to rise. When the concertmaster reminded me that this was quite unique for a rehearsal I went back to my podium and bowed, but the crowd would not leave and continued its clamor. The asbestos curtain came down, but the clapping and shouting continued. We all know that ovations, like most fires, need fuel, which is supplied by the bows, the kisses thrown, the gratitude of the honored artist. They are, like most mass manifestations, a mixture and a cross-relation. This one had nothing much to feed on and yet, to the amazement of the experienced orchestra, it was something that went on and on, as if the few hundred people did not want to leave.

In 1971 the Met's subscription list was no longer what it had been, and plenty of seats were usually available. Between that afternoon of the fifteenth and the start of the première on the eighteenth, all seven repeat performances were totally sold out. When the general verdict of the experts in the press matched the public's enthusiasm the name of the opera was irreverently changed inside the house to *Bing's Fair Lady*. The old Wagner-hater himself went through something like a reconciliation with the magician. He came into my dressing room many times during the eight performances, musing on his final season as general manager and greatly rejoicing over what was perhaps his finest production.

The première was hardly over when I had to spend some time and effort to settle my relations with the incoming regime.

Six months earlier I had met Gentele in Munich. He asked me to help him with the Met's interrupted *Ring*. The first two parts had been produced in 1967 and 1968, but the big shutdown of the Met in 1969 affected the continuation. It offended permanently producer-conductor Karajan, and Bing had not found any way to produce the last two portions of the tetralogy. Gentele felt that his earliest chance in 1972 to have the new *Siegfried* realized would already be four years late, and he pleaded with me to take it on, adding for good measure a few repeats of *Walküre*. When all was said in that first meeting I accepted Gentele's package. The trouble was, however, that not all had been said to me. There had been a secret, which came to my attention in October 1971 when I toured with the London Philharmonic. A letter from Rafael Kubelik, newly appointed music director for the Met, revealed quite openly that after the 1972 performances he would take on the final *Götterdämmerung* production, and the entire cycle during the following season. In plainer words, I had been used as a stopgap without being so advised. I considered this devious, offered Kubelik the 1972 productions, actually giving him a better start for the complete *Ring,* and returned my contract to Gentele.

After the *Tristan* première, when everybody was in New York, well-meaning advisers on both sides wanted things settled amicably and arranged for a luncheon at which Gentele and I could be alone and away from the telephone to straighten out whatever had gone crooked. By one of life's weirdest coincidences we sat for our meeting in the Oak Room of the Plaza Hotel, next to a table at which Gentele's second-in-command, Schuyler Chapin, negotiated with a record company executive terms for *Carmen,* the grand opening production to be staged by the new general manager himself. As we sat there in the elegant room with people stopping to say a pleasant word, others looking and discreetly pointing, everybody full of smiles and plans and projects, it all smelled, sounded, and looked like Success, a New Era, a Different Style, with all the optimism and dynamic energy rightly expected from an incoming group. None of us could possibly have seen the doom and disaster awaiting this attractive Swede. Our differences were laid to rest, and we parted on friendly terms.

My regular involvement with the new *Tristan* ended a few weeks later, before Christmas. At the close of that season, after the 1972 spring tour, Bing retired; Gentele was killed in July in a motor accident together with two of his children; and Chapin ran the Met under curious conditions. For ten months he was kept in a pro-tem status while the board quite openly looked for somebody else. When he was reluctantly given title and contract it was with such bad grace that it made him an underdog and, ipso facto, well supported by the press. Neither this support nor increasing attendance and success seemed to be of much real help, though, because after three seasons he was let go for no apparent reason.

Bing during his final season as general manager had spoken quite unreservedly about the coming regime, which brought him censure for jealousy and lack of tact. History proved the substance of his critique more than accurate, but he could not do anything to help, though he offered his services after the sudden death of Gentele. There is a terrible irony behind the entire misadventure, because it all could so easily have been avoided.

The falling out between Bing and Anthony Bliss after 1966 led to the latter's withdrawal as president and brought in his place a man, George Moore, whose principal aim became to replace Bing. Chapin led Moore to Stockholm and Gentele. The new organization of the opera company could never be tested due to that tragic accident, and when by 1974–1975 the Chapin-Kubelik team had broken down, Bliss emerged from the shadows after more than eight years, took the helm, and fired nearly everybody from the post-Bing administration. In the meantime Bing himself had joined an agency, Columbia Artists Management, and as a representative for singers and conductors the former boss of the Met must have had many second thoughts.

Mine are quite clear. Had Bing seen the necessity, as I and many others did, to appoint a music director in 1966, all might have turned out better and the terrible, dragged-out crisis might have been avoided or greatly lessened. Perhaps I am prejudiced in favor of trained musical professionals, yet I must repeat that a musical theater has to have in the very top command a musician of authority. The ability to *read* music is irreplaceable.

We learned of Gentele's death in Sardinia on July 19, 1972, when my wife was listening to the early morning news on the radio. We were then living for a few weeks near Bayreuth.

## The Wagner Shrine

Cosima, Richard Wagner's second wife, survived him by forty-seven years and ran during that time the festival at Bayreuth. Her son, Siegfried, died only four months after her, which brought the management of that daunting inheritance onto the shoulders of his thirty-six-year-old widow, Winifred. She was most ably and faithfully assisted by Heinz Tietjen, a conductor and stage director, but more important for the future of Bayreuth and of the entire Wagner family was the aide of another enthusiast, Herr Hitler. He helped by getting the new superhighway (the autobahn) to run through Bayreuth, making the festival city more easily accessible. Following the war Bavaria was under the rule of the United States Army, which declared Frau Winifred, because of her friendship for the dictator, unfit to hold sway. She was banished into an annex of Villa Wahnfried, the home Wagner himself had built, and there she has lived unrepentant and vigorous, highly critical of the newfangled ways that have brought the festival so much publicity.

Winifred's sons, Wieland and Wolfgang, took the festival into their untainted hands and reopened in 1951. The brothers complemented each other well. Wieland was the more artistic and Wolfgang the more administrative and technical, but the team was suddenly short-circuited by Wieland's death in 1966. He had in fifteen years taken the spotlight with productions of his grandfather's works that were by turns imaginative, untraditional, sometimes contrived, sometimes absurd, but always full of ideas and never dull. His avowed aim was to take the Teutonic overtones out of the works, to denazify them, and to establish their psychological all-human validity. His disregard for specific directions of the author influenced and encouraged other producers to do likewise, albeit without as much talent and without Wieland's means of correcting every aberration through the availability of unusual means at the Bayreuth theater. Whatever blunder he might commit one year, the next summer he would erase and correct it. He also had the knack of publicizing his intentions and ideas in such a manner that a dutifully brainwashed intelligentsia bowed low and propelled him in less than a decade into a fully grown genius.

Whatever anyone's verdict or reservations, his death left Bayreuth in sole charge of Wolfgang, who was very good at many things, but staging was not one of them. He had presided over an occasional production, but now he needed help and, fortunately, knew it. In 1971 he engaged August Everding — who staged our Met *Tristan* — for *The Flying Dutchman*, which was successful but failed to produce what Wolfgang looked for most keenly — a sensation. Determined that Bayreuth should not fall into any conventional or traditional rut, Wolfgang picked as producer for a new *Tannhäuser* in 1972 Götz Friedrich, a disciple of Walter Felsenstein's and then still a resident of East Berlin. In hindsight I doubt that Wolfgang ever invited me out of any conviction but rather as an American passport holder who would be a welcome counterweight should the East German person cause him political troubles. Bavaria subsidized the festival significantly, and its very Catholic government and population might not have taken the appearance of an "Easterner" lightly.

Of course I might have been wrong. Wolfgang could have asked me because not one person in the cast knew the opera. When I arrived a year before the première to meet with Friedrich and the designer, Jürgen Rose, it was crystal clear that both had glanced through the libretto without grasping any deep knowledge of the text or the thought behind it. Neither had ever produced Wagner before. It was like a theater asking a director to stage *King Lear* because he is unacquainted with Shakespeare. The calculating dishonesty behind such a decision is the expectancy that sensational results will be more readily forthcoming the fewer the inhibitions of the producing team. Wolfgang had reckoned accurately. Friedrich, given to diligently searching for social significance, found it in the romantic opera too and let us have it in fullest measure. In the ten months that elapsed between our first meeting and the staging rehearsals in June 1972 Friedrich must have reread the whole opus of Marx, Engels, Trotzky, Liebknecht, and the lot. What he did not read up on was Wagner. When in the Venusberg Music the three graces ought to appear, we got three death skulls carried across the stage on very long poles. When the hunting party came on stage, the class struggle between the downtrodden employees and the Landgrave was made manifest by the subtle device of using a sedan chair to carry the basso. The pilgrims had to carry a cross of such (real) weight that the usually faultless Bayreuth chorus sang three out of four passages flat. They were helped in this by the stage director's insistence that they disperse in small groupings of three and four, which is absolute musical murder for a chorus and especially one of these chromatic complexities. That moment reminded me of Wieland's staging of the same scene, when the group of men were not only close together but also slowly marching in a stylized manner, pictorially reminiscent of a medieval painting and musically most helpful to the vocal and intonation problem.

Whatever happened in act one was child's play to the next scene, the great hall where the singers' contest takes place. It begins with the jubilant aria of Elisabeth, who on this occasion had to express her joy not only in Wagner's grand final phrase but also by lowering herself first onto her knees and then all the way to the floor, which she had to kiss in anticipatory joy of Tannhäuser's return. After Elisabeth fell to the floor, Tannhäuser comes in and he, by Wagner's directive, must kneel down to greet her. In this case people did not kneel, they went all the way to the ground. When in the dress rehearsal both singers scrambled around the floor I heard a good deal of merriment, not a usual reaction of the public in Bayreuth.

The entire setting of act two was a platform placed above fourteen steps, to symbolize that the party in the castle takes place "upstairs" socially. Therefore all the invited guests climb those fourteen steps until they can greet their host. The climbing was an ever so subtle hint of social climbing and snobbishness. What the designer and the unsnobbish director forgot was that from that dizzy height all the voices went up and away into the flies instead of going out into the auditorium. It was perhaps the first time that social criticism had ruined the perfect acoustics of the Bayreuth Festival theater. In this instance Wolfgang interfered, as I have mentioned, and ordered a concert ceiling from the warehouse to be hung on top of that set to give the voices a chance to be heard. The third act had Elisabeth leave the stage after her prayer by crawling on her belly all the way. It was a long way, but Friedrich had great luck in the person of Gwyneth Jones, who liked the idea. I didn't. Barely had she crawled out and Wolfram sung the "Evening Star" than Tannhäuser crawled in, coming from Rome. By then I began to wonder if I had missed somewhere in my reading any special predilection Wagner had for reptiles. Perhaps an undecided liberal could still call these nuances legitimate interpretation. The end of the opera was, however, turned completely around. Every Tannhäuser tells in act three, usually with only a shred of his voice left, how the Pope in Rome condemned him in the severest terms: "Just as this staff in my hand will never blossom forth again, so will you never be redeemed from the fires of hell." Wagner, at the height of the final scene, has the younger pilgrims enter chanting and carrying with them the greening staff of the bishop of Rome; the unheard-of has happened, the sinner has been redeemed. So much for Wagner, but none of that for Friedrich. Perhaps he feared for his own safety on returning to East Berlin if he staged anything as Christian as all that. The younger pilgrims never appeared but sang their lines unintelligibly from backstage over microphones. Tannhäuser died without having learned that the Pope had erred or that he was forgiven.

The day between dress rehearsal and performance I went to visit Wolfgang and asked him to relieve me of my earlier promise to conduct nine more performances in 1973. He was not really surprised but attempted to see if I would postpone my decision, asking if "we shouldn't await the returns," to which I replied that I had come exactly before any returns were in, because my refusal to continue was based on total incompatibility with the director and my total rejection of his way with the work.

The story of the person who sang the lead is a sad tale. All the members of the cast were new to their roles. How else could they have taken that kind of stage direction? The tenor, Hugh Beresford, had given five performances of the role in a small German house but was, which I did not know then, only recently converted from baritone to tenor. I only noticed that he forced his voice mercilessly, so much so that I often feared he would bust a gut. He was no youngster anymore, and when my five performances with him were done I heaved a sigh of relief. In 1973, I was told by one of my assistants that Beresford was so hard-pressed vocally that after the first act of the first performance that year he was taken out of the cast and never returned. One of his tenor colleagues thought that Beresford had later had a total breakdown and was in hospital. This reminded me of a very curious parallel in 1930. Then Wolf-

gang's father had also discovered a brand-new singer for Tannhäuser, a Hungarian named Pilinski, who was brought to Bayreuth and strained himself badly while performing the role under
Toscanini. He also disappeared permanently after that period of
glory.

My refusal to return in 1973 was neither the first nor the last
time I confirmed my new freedom; it was, however, the most
famous place to which I said, "No thank you." To assert one's
convictions and independence is a lot easier when there is no
board of directors back home watching like Big Brother.

I did have great satisfaction with the truly festival-caliber
orchestra members, who were kind enough to send me roses and
an affectionate letter when learning of my decision. The orchestra manager came in during the second interval of my final
performance with the flowers and the letter and tried to get
me to change my mind, which I promised to do if he could find
me a music drama without a stage director. That was August
14, 1972. The next day I flew to New York.

No dramatist could have thought up a bigger contrast than
the days that followed. It was from a Midwestern tour with
the New York Philharmonic that I single out one of the most
wondrous and most unlikely evenings of my musical life.

On a very hot August evening we played Madison, Wiscon-
sin. The concert took place in the Stock Palace. That is the
name of the place and that is exactly what it is in daytime,
a place where cattle are auctioned off. It consists of an arena
covered by a dirt floor on which the cattle are paraded for the
buyers who sit on benches arranged amphitheatrically around
the dirt oval. For the concert the parade ground was furnished
with hard narrow benches, for the orchestra an ample platform
had been moved into the arena, just off center but still giving
the feeling of a theater-in-the-round. I have always liked to be
surrounded by the public, since it makes for a different and
better contact and lacks that divisive footlight element. The

thermometer was in the low nineties and management agreed that the players could be in shirt sleeves. I put on a white roll collar and also went on without a jacket. The public, which by eight-thirty filled every available space, was in various stages of undress, fans were wiggled in an attempt to create some air current, the doors were left open to assure at least some minimum of circulation, and it is quite natural that we did not expect to do better than a decent professional job under these conditions. From the first moment of the *Figaro* overture I noticed the very good warm sound and the acoustics that make ensemble easy. Whether it was the oval shape or the dirt floor, the musicians were happy, as they always are when their playing makes sense and they can hear themselves. We fared nicely; I had no concern with keeping things together and felt free just making music. We followed the overture with four pieces from the Klee settings by Gunther Schuller. Toward the end of one entitled "Abstract Trio," a distant locomotive blew a long whistle, which was heard clearly through the open doors. It came nearer and nearer, and by the time the short selection ended a freight train passed just outside the doors on the right where the railroad tracks ran by the hall. Quite logical for the loading of cattle. In our case the clangor and rattling and blowing obliterated all sounds from the music. Rather than pretend to have noticed nothing I turned my head and said, "This was not part of Schuller's orchestration," which was applauded and followed by some giggling. I continued: "I stress the point, because in this style of musical composition it might have been." More laughter and an intimate contact with the audience was established instead of my putting on a dignified, phony frown disapproving of the whole business. It was our good luck that this had been the last train for the day. No further comments were necessary. After a concerto played by an attractive Korean girl to the evident pleasure of the public we sweated through an intermission and then got ready for Beethoven's Seventh Symphony.

Nothing had prepared me for what happened. That performance scaled the heights in a way reserved for a few special occasions.

For some reason the sound of the Philharmonic catapulted me back to their era with Toscanini. Perhaps it was the tympanist, Sol Goodman, who played in those years and who was now in the summer of 1972 closing his final active season with the orchestra, but no detailed analysis could hope to nail down in words the atmosphere and the spirit of those forty minutes. Even the heat, which usually bothers me, was of mysterious help that night as all seemed to add to a total collective dedication where only the music counted for anything.

As if that had not been enough, the hotel refused to accept payment for the suite that had been placed at my disposal. This was to me important not for the saving of a few dollars but for the spirit of hospitality extended to the strolling player. We had most certainly looked that evening like strolling, perspiring, unkempt, overheated, and intensively devoted players. That was a night when I knew precisely what this profession of mine is all about and why it is sometimes necessary to put up with so much annoyance. This feeling of oneness with the music and with the public for a one-night stand is so much more to my taste than the stance of the music director with the chauffeur-driven limousine and the other emoluments of position and prominence.

The green wagon is more beautiful than the finest Rolls-Royce.

## Music, Manners, and Fashion

While in Madison nobody had dressed for our concert, the audience in Bayreuth on equally hot days could be seen at three in the afternoon walking toward the festival theater in heavy dinner jackets and velvet gowns. Theirs is a kind of purpose-fully unfashionable elegance, marking the wearers as the middle-class elite, which sports ancient styles of dress but splurges on wildly overpriced admission tickets. Compared to this reminder of what the nineteenth century was like in upper bourgeois Germany, the United States has moved into the present day and age with determination. Summer festivals combine music that ranges all the way from the best to the humdrum with the in-formality of the audience. This relaxed atmosphere was part of my affection for Tanglewood. It also spurs me to wage an un-ending and not very successful battle against other ritualistic leftovers from earlier eras.

Clothes serve only one purpose, and that never changes: pro-tection from the natural elements. The only other reasons for wearing apparel are communication and conformity. When we wear black to a funeral we show our attitude as mourners. Wearing black is most important to those who feel no sadness or sense of loss since it is a symbol of conforming with those who are sad and who have lost a dear person. I believe that the more you feel the less you need appropriate clothes.

It is quite the same with the attire for concerts and opera, which was established as the norm by a middle-class society, for a long time quite unsure of itself and its position in the social hierarchy. Today it is not only superfluous and old-fashioned to pursue these rules of proper clothes, it seems to me even counterproductive, alienating unnecessarily many young people who are neither in possession nor in the habit of wearing formal attire.

There is no sense whatsoever in the members of an orchestra wearing tails. They sit, which produces wrinkles in a suit, which was designed not to sit down in. They cannot wear the proper starched shirt if they have to hold violins and violas between cheek and collarbones, and the soft shirt with the turned-down collar looks messy and most inelegant. Yet with the exception of the New York Philharmonic, where short jackets are the rule, in every other orchestra this absurd frock is still official uniform. A few soloists of the younger and more free-thinking generation have made a stab at finding new outfits, but not all of them persist.

Clothes alone don't tell the whole story. We surround our doings with a set of outdated manners and even mannerisms, some of them detrimental to the best and most natural enjoyment. At the top of my list is frowning on applause between the movements of a symphony or a concerto. When Henryk Szeryng played the Brahms Concerto with me in London it was quite clear that people wanted to applaud after the first movement. As the clapping started the soloist, in all his dignity, with his instrument always under his chin, raised his right arm and held the bow in a gesture of such peremptory shock that no high priest in whose inner sanctum a sacrilege had been committed could improve on it. What utter nonsense. The notion, once entertained by questionable historians, was that an entity must not be interrupted by the mundane frivolity of hand clapping. The great composers were elated by applause, wherever it burst out. Mozart even wrote with glee on an occasion when the Parisians, surprised and delighted by a turn in composition, applauded in the middle of a movement.

The young pianist André Watts once thanked me for what he called "the best advice he ever got." I was not immediately aware of having dispensed such wisdom and wanted to know the particulars. "When we did the B flat Brahms at Carnegie you turned to me after the first movement when the public applauded and I remained seated, hissing at me to get off my arse and thank the audience," he replied.

Truly bad manners are shown at the end of operatic acts when the eager beavers cannot wait until the music has ended to crash in with their bravos. Many final passages in opera, such as the last bars of the *Otello* love duet, are so tender and lyrical that loud shouting is a barbaric act. I am convinced that the spontaneity of public reaction should not and need not be controlled or curbed and that excesses appear only when prearrangements by a claque are involved. This has led me to believe that the famous scandal at the première of *Le Sacre du printemps* was a staged and arranged act of hostility.

My travels have shown me that attitudes and styles are hard to change. In Vienna the lighting of concert halls has recently become an issue. For as long as I can remember, the chandeliers have remained fully lit, which I, a student, welcomed, as this made the printed scores I brought along easy to read. In America I found the dimming so great that the atmosphere was that of a funeral parlor rather than of a festive occasion. The overhaul and modernization of symphony and other concerts need to be done by a brilliant stage director, who should also teach musicians how to look for the newer medium of television, on which most appear ill at ease, either with inexpressive poker faces or forced smiles that freeze into masks.

Attempting to do my own bit for defossilization, I have since 1970 dispensed with the full-dress suit, although I do not sit down and mine never wrinkled. A tailor and my wife decided on a loose jacket at once comfortable and elegant. No matter where I wore it, it was admired by professional colleagues, and many of my dressing room preconcert visitors have been conductors inspecting it at close quarters. Yet nothing, except for Pierre Boulez's short dinner jacket, has done away with the old-fashioned garb.

The one negative comment I know of was made in Madrid. Concerts there start at seven-thirty and the public, as in most Latin cities, is of superlative elegance. My wife, who was brought up in a Spanish-speaking country, was sitting in her place at the Teatro Real when she overheard the end of a conversation behind her: "But after all, he could have afforded to rent one."

Nineteen seventy-three was a year for flying. To go to Hong Kong and to the Australian continent within nine months was the best payoff for my wanderlust. The musical reason for the Hong Kong trip was a newly created Fine Arts Festival, in reality a promotional ploy by a British airline to bring the Far Eastern public to Hong Kong. My part consisted of three uneventful concerts with the London Philharmonic and many far more memorable Chinese meals. Most gratifying of all were the new friends we made on the trip. The singular combination of English and Chinese civilizations has made some of the natives most engaging and attractive to our taste, and we have rarely come back from a short visit with so many personal attachments. Our only regret about the journey is that the continuation onto mainland China was a strictly British affair for which the orchestra had to limit its staff to English conductors.

The fall voyage to Honolulu, New Zealand, and Australia was grand in all respects, especially musically. Traveling with the Cleveland Orchestra made all the concerts a joy, some in good halls quite outstanding, others in dry places worthy and dignified.

In Honolulu both Stanislaw Skrowaczewski, the alternate conductor, and I received at the close of our programs beautiful leis presented by a charmingly attired native lady. In Auckland we were received by a Maori family and a Maori challenge. This had been arranged by Michael Maxwell, manager of the Cleveland Orchestra, himself a native of Auckland. As soon as we were through the nominal examination by the authorities we faced in the arrival hall an aboriginal family of three generations. The head, a stocky athletic fellow who was bare to the waist and barefoot below his grass skirt, performed a ritual dance climaxed by his dropping a small object on the floor. Before I had to pick it up as a sign of our peaceful intentions he swung a wooden spear in front of our noses, mainly mine, as I was delegated his counterpart. As visiting chieftain they probably thought of me as a Cleveland Indian. I later attempted to imitate the whole ceremony but succeeded only in making the most awful grimaces, surely as wild as the chief of the clan. As soon as I had bent down and collected the little symbolic token, the family began a short recital of native songs with percussion accompaniment and we were welcomed by friends and the local press. The steward of the Qantas charter had given the astonishing report that the orchestra members consumed more beer than had been done on any flight of similar length, which prompted me to pass this on to the local journalists. I thought that such intelligence if told with the wrong emphasis would make the musicians appear as sots, but I turned it around and said: "Isn't it wonderful that they drink only beer. Imagine, some others do the same with whiskey." All the papers wrote what a moderate and civilized bunch of people the Clevelanders were.

In barely nine hours from Honolulu, we had skipped a day. We were in the Southern Hemisphere, and everything was turned around in a double dislocation of time and space. In flight there had been some debate between the more and the less sophisticated as to whether we would notice the date line and the equator. Some members of our group distinctly felt one bump as we crossed the date line and a double bump at the equator, less sensitive members were unaware of either.

The old town halls in Auckland, Wellington, Brisbane, and Melbourne were better for our music-making than the newer halls, with the exception of the one in Adelaide, which was highly spoken of by the orchestra. Stan was there, so I could not witness it myself. Judging by the heartwarming reception from the public, there hadn't been a concert in a decade. We played encores, another one of the strange folkways of our professional mores, as this spontaneous thank you to the public remains reserved for tours only.

After our day of rest we rehearsed all morning and went en masse to another part of the Town Hall building complex, where the lord mayor gave a reception, with lunch to follow. On a separate scheduled flight many orchestra wives and several board members had come along, and we were a hungry crowd of at least 150 when the lord mayor of Auckland, with a magnificent chain of office around his neck, mounted a small rostrum to say welcome. We stood and stood, since the gentleman had found his captive audience for a major statement of politics, philosophy, and a thorough dissertation on music appreciation. His historic statement referred to American culture with reservations, to our program selection with general approval except that we should not have brought anything by Aaron Copland, and finally to the personnel of the orchestra, the roster of which he had examined thoroughly for Jewish names. He himself was Sir Dov — which made me understand his particular hang-up — but the whole performance was put on against a background of people standing on their feet and getting increasingly impatient for a meal. To hear at such a moment what Brahms has meant to His Honor tries the patience of the fullest stomach. Finally it was Maxwell's turn to give thanks for the welcome, which he did very briefly but politely. He then called on me to speak, for which I was totally unprepared. I thought faster than ever before, stepped onto the small rostrum, and spoke three sentences: The first expressed our thanks, the second our appreciation for having learned about music appreciation, and the third, my own appreciation at the moment was the loud noises made by my colleagues' stomachs, with a final Cadence of Good Appetite. Of all my many little speeches this one was most sincerely appreciated.

In Brisbane a few musicians had misread the thoughtful travel hints in their itineraries and walked into a highly recommended Chinese restaurant with a name like "Lotus." Their error was in mixing the town up with Canberra where we ate every one of our magnificent meals in a "Lotus Bowl." The Brisbane Lotus was a brothel and their menu was of a different order. We fed kangaroos and I was photographed with a koala bear. In Canberra we met Prime Minister Gough Whitlam at an after-concert party, and I found four men with whom I had gone to school in Vienna forty-five years earlier. In Melbourne another lord mayor spoke more briefly, eschewing music appreciation and sticking to the usual expressions of good will. There were gate crashers on that occasion, one a local zealot who was trying to round up, once again, the Jewish members of the orchestra to lead them into private houses for the impending High Holidays to share in the celebrations. Birgit Nilsson attended but left early in a huff. She was on a concert tour, and we were happy to run into one another. I didn't notice her departure from the party, as my wife and I were being escorted to a private supper by charming people. Where else could it happen that a letter from a casual acquaintance in New York brings to the fore two people in Melbourne who take us in tow after a reception, arrange to keep the kitchen of a most elegant restaurant open, and treat us to a fine late evening meal? That kind of hospitality I have not found elsewhere.

Returning to the hotel from that outing my wife found a note from Birgit, who explained that she had precipitously left the party because an impostor had appeared, a woman who had given Nilsson's name as her credit endorsement in various parts of the world while running up sizable bills in stores and hotels.

Courtesy of officials in both New Zealand and Australia outdoes anything I ever experienced. Every time we were taken from or to an airport there was not only a car with a chauffeur, an executive of the broadcasting corporation went along to be sure that everything was as it should be. Our escorts never left departure lounges in airports until the aircraft had actually taken off. Then they phoned the next town the precise time of departure to make sure the expecting functionary would be there. On our return to the States we had to put up with an unscheduled change due to a slowdown of radar operators at Sydney airport. Given the details, we flew from Melbourne on a domestic flight to Sydney and there to the intercontinental terminal on the other side of the airfield. For that brief trip there was a limousine with a chauffeur and the ubiquitous executive of ABC to look after us. He remained in the departure lounge until he was sure that our flight to Honolulu would take off as planned.

After this red-carpet treatment it was a double blow to arrive in Honolulu for a thirty-hour rest without our luggage and to be informed by phone and cable that my concerts in New York had been struck. The Philharmonic and their management were in an insoluble contract negotiation, which closed the schedule for a total of ten weeks, my own concerts included. That I should more than make them up was not yet written in the stars.

The one regrettable story of Australia was the failure to build a better opera house in Sydney after a protracted sequence of misjudgments and miscalculations. It still looks very unusual and beautiful from the outside, but this does not give a true picture of the many inside failures. The saga as we heard it is probably far closer to the truth than the official embellishments. The winning design for this project was at first among the rejects and pulled out of the wastebasket by Eero Saarinen. When construction was to commence, it appears that the design was merely a beautiful picture without any chance of standing up. The necessary technical jobs to correct this took many years and caused overruns quoted as high as 1500 percent. The outcome has been an opera auditorium seating 1400, an absurdly small number, no close parking facilities, no elevators for ailing people, long walks to and from the halls, and a concert hall of indifferent acoustical properties.

## Intermission

I spent the unplanned vacation in New York, benefiting from beautiful weather in early October for long walks and longer thinking. It was now a little over four years since I had first embarked on the free-lance vessel. Concentrating on my own music-making had liberated me tangibly and significantly, in many subtler ways. I felt that not only had my own situation changed for the better but that the whole musical landscape was much improved. I have always had an emotional resistance to exhorting the "good old days," which gives me perhaps an overly positive outlook on the present. The position of musicians has surely improved not only economically but, more important, in their relation with conductors. I could still recall the time when conductors would use rehearsals to learn their scores, holding musicians for long sessions because they had to make up their own homework.

When I first came to America it was considered a tough country, where no social security or job safety existed, where the head conductor of Radio City Music Hall could signal in a moment his discontent with a musician by merely holding up two fingers of his left hand. This meant the musician had two weeks' notice with no chance of appeal. Now in 1973 it was London's turn to be merciless on musicians. Dependent as the English players are on recordings and other electronic media, efficiency is the first necessity, and I had witnessed new faces come and go with cruel frequency. Brass wind players, whose slightest mishap can cause a take to be useless, are examined and discarded with a cold impatience that was hardly matched thirty years earlier by the so-called materialistic United States. Now, of course, America is an easygoing welfare state compared to the slaughterhouses of London's record studios.

I had the added satisfaction that in my constant travels certain changes, not evident to the distant observer, were very real and almost measurable to me. I made up my mind to by-pass in the future many of the forty orchestras I had visited, not only the handful that were below par but, of more consequence, all the organizations that worked on an overly tight schedule where the feeling is always to stand with the back to the wall.

This schedule had unfortunately proved most rigid in London, which both of us love so much that in 1970 we almost decided to make it our residence.

In 1968, when I passed through London for a rehearsal with the New Philharmonia, the manager told of a press interview that quoted George Szell as stating "that it would be better for two orchestras to be excellent than for four to be mediocre." This was a classic summary of a widely shared professional opinion. Yet only resentment by the unnamed mediocrities is caused for anyone who, like Szell, has tried to prod the English music establishment into reform. The most recent exchange I had observed involved none other than Prime Minister Edward Heath, who was rebutted and actually rebuffed by the managing director of the London Philharmonic. I had been going to London so many times for concerts and for recordings that it had amounted to twenty-five separate trips in the preceding two years, and my personal review during that October liberty in New York made me decide to reduce the frequency of my visits. I still thought that there was something quite unique about the public and the atmosphere and I hoped to keep a continuous, though looser relationship.

Such decisions had to be made for two years thence, and one resulting shift was to bring me more frequently into the German-speaking orbit.

## Faust

I go back to my first season in Boston and my discovery that each program had to have a fifteen-minute intermission. Planning performances of the Brahms Requiem I came face to face with the contractual necessity to find something for the first half of the program. It was absurd and musically too much to stuff in another fifteen or twenty minutes of music before such a mighty work, but this was the reality of the Boston Symphony. Just then I had read in a magazine an article on musical symbolism in Schumann's *Scenes from Goethe's Faust,* a work I did not know. Leonard Burkat borrowed a score from the Boston Public Library, and together we pored over it. A wonderland opened up to us. Why had this been totally neglected?

To test our enthusiasm and judgment I asked the baritone for the Requiem, Hermann Prey, to learn the sixth part of the work, the scene of Faust's Death. We performed it before the Brahms, and I had the pleasure to have in Prey another member of our small club of enthusiasts who considered this a masterwork. We lost no time planning then and there performances of the entire work, which is a full evening. In 1966 my labors bore fruit in the shape of four performances, two in Boston and two in New York. They came and went, but except for two or three people who felt as I did, there was no "shock of recognition." I had become very deeply involved during the long preparation for these concerts, and my disappointment was correspondingly keen and not without some bitterness, because it also involved Goethe's text, which is next to holy writ to me.

My confidence, if it had been shaken, was restored when I performed the work in Frankfurt, Berlin, and Munich during my free-lance years. Not only were most comments in accord with my estimate of the score, I myself became known throughout Germany very rapidly, since two of the three productions were for broadcast systems, which meant frequent replays all over the many cities of the land.

When I looked back on the comparative merits of the performances themselves I found some strange facts. In Boston I had a far better choir than in Frankfurt where every participating group was below the Boston level. Yet the Frankfurt version became the event of rediscovery, from which all the others resulted. I commented jokingly that they even made ready an honorary grave for me next to Goethe's. The fate of Faust was typical of a deeper difference between countries and

their musical culture. Not only in Boston, but in most orchestras in America I — and my colleagues — find that choral works
are roundly detested, not only by the players, who feel themselves degraded to accompanists, but also by most subscribers.
Of course management dislikes anything so costly and so clumsy
to produce. It has either escaped the notice of all these disparate
members of our society, or they do not care, that works where
music, poetry, religion, and philosophy are merged happen to be
more than great scores, they are at their best the milestones of
our Western culture.

In my years in Boston, every time one of those monumental
works was planned I had to hear from the orchestra committee that they did not want evening rehearsals — the only time
choirs can be counted on. I also had to find inexpensive solo
singers, lest the management find the nonspecific budget over-
run; I had to accept the repeated assurances that the public did
not fancy "choral works," the generic term for all the masses,
oratorios, and sacred or profane pieces; and I had to receive
messages from the clergy accusing me of cultivating anti-
Semitic compositions.

The real reason behind all these difficulties was simpler, but
I did not discover it until I had left Boston far behind me: the
American symphony orchestra is a magnificent accomplishment,
which has not been incorporated into the intellectual life of the
community served. Perhaps it is not entirely accidental that the
stage of Symphony Hall was too small from the day it was built
to accommodate Beethoven's *Missa Solemnis*.

Not only has Goethe very little meaning for the subscriber of
a United States symphony orchestra, but the Faustian motiv is
as little known as Greek mythology. And yet "Manfred," also
a Schumann score, is a poem by Byron, composed to a German
translation.

My personal conflict has always been my noncomprehension
of the terrible paralysis of the intellectuals in Central Europe,
where all that interplay existed, to no practical avail when the

political chips were down. Is that a reason why musical organizations must exist in a curious isolation from the rest of our culture in America?

Another intensely personal satisfaction in the year 1973 was my return to Vienna after not having appeared there in public for twenty-six years.

The Vienna Symphony Orchestra, an autonomous club, invited me to do a short German tour with them, followed by a pair of concerts in Vienna's Konzerthaus-saal.

I could fill a hundred pages describing my conflicting emotions as I stood on that stage at the end of the music program, engulfed by a veritable storm of cheers and my ears full of the thunder caused by stamping feet. This may be boring to read but most assuredly not to write. It may be the acme of vanity to say, as I do, that such a moment makes up for many longer time spans of my youth when I could not get the work for which I was prepared. Once again the melancholy conclusion came to my mind that survival is the trick that counts in the end.

If one is allowed to wait long enough everything seems to fall into place. Goethe again says it better: "Wes man in der Jugend begehrt, des hat man im Alter die Fülle" (What one covets when young, one has amply when old). As always with a great thinker, there is the implied meaning that by the time we receive what was so much desired in youth, it does not so much matter anymore.

Since that date in May 1973 I have returned regularly, but with long intervals, to Vienna, which I enjoy for brief sojourns more like a foreigner than as a prodigal son, a role I cannot assume.

## Return of My Not-So-Fair-Lady

The final performance of our new *Tristan* production was a matinee on December 18, 1971. My wife and I spent the evening party-going, ending up at a late affair, with an almost entirely Russian cast, in honor of Sol Hurok and Mstislav Rostropovich. One of the most charming ex-Russians present was Kyra Gerard, wife of the scenic designer, who told me how dreadfully sorry she was not to have been as yet to her favorite opera, our fabulously successful new *Tristan*. When was my next performance? When I replied "On January eleventh, nineteen seventy-four" she thought I was pulling her leg.

When making peace with Gentele I also settled my return for the revival of *Tristan*. When we spoke of casting, Gentele said to me — quite reasonably — that it was not possible to count on "Birgit forever" and therefore he planned to have Catarina Ligendza do six of the eight projected performances as Isolde. I had heard and liked Ligendza at La Scala and went in 1972 to several of her dress rehearsals in Bayreuth, where we also met and chatted pleasantly about our forthcoming collaboration. In the summer of 1973 she was reported to be pregnant, having canceled a few appearances, but otherwise no alarming news was heard. When we ran into Nilsson in Melbourne she asked me in her straightforward manner "if I had made sure of Ligendza for Isolde." "How," I asked, "does one make sure in September if an artist will or will not honor a contract for January?"

The schedule called for rehearsals to commence on December 26. The play — was it comedy or farce? — began innocuously enough on the twenty-second when we were still in Switzerland and a call from Charles Riecker, artistic administrator of the Met, with the news that Jon Vickers, our Tristan, was exhausted from too many performances of *Otello* and would arrive a few days late. The second portion of that call informed me that Everding, the stage director, had been injured in an accident and would also arrive late. Considering that the working plans gave us only eleven days to get this complex production revived with new principals, this was very serious and alarming.

On the twenty-fourth we flew to New York and were not yet fully unpacked when a call from Chapin informed me that he was exhausted and off for a holiday vacation on doctor's orders. No sooner had he hung up than Riecker rang with the next scene. This was a local call, costing less than his earlier one to Switzerland, yet in the end far more expensive to the Met. Miss Ligendza had cabled that on account of a bad case of the flu she had to cancel her entire Met engagement. An inquiry as to why an illness on December 24 had to nullify two whole months of performances brought the reply that Ligendza's flu bouts took three weeks to pass and three more for convalescence, at which point I interrupted to say that she would need three more years to get over her fear of New York, referring to a similar last-minute defection of hers when she had been expected to sing Leonore in *Fidelio*.

This was a major mess for the obvious reason that the Isoldes of this world can be counted on the fingers of one hand and, less obvious, that the hired understudy had never sung the role before. This was not a prank but a result of management's false economies and false optimism. One year earlier Chapin and Riecker had, without benefit of any musician's advice, engaged an otherwise excellent lady, Doris Jung, after she had given a fine audition of the *"Liebestod."* That this greatest of all final pages in opera is only six minutes long and was all of Isolde's role that Jung had known and sung did not bother the two gentlemen who hired her to understudy a notoriously unreliable Ligendza. And, indeed, by December 26, Jung had declared her willingness to do what she was hired for, stand in, stand by, rehearse, and help, but when asked to do the première on the eleventh her answer was No. What the inexperienced Chapin and Riecker had overlooked was that experience had always been the principal ingredient for a cover. It takes nerve and great familiarity with a role to replace a star on short notice. With Vickers, Everding, and Ligendza out for the time being or for good, I had little to do except have some time-killing checkups of the smaller roles and their understudies.

If I am asked to pinpoint the most confused, maddening, and puzzling day of my professional career I must select without any close second December 31, 1973. The day began with a phone call at 10:15 A.M. It was Carlos Moseley, president of the New York Philharmonic and a good friend. After the amenities were out of the way, he told me that the first rehearsal of the orchestra for next Thursday's program had begun, but an assistant conductor was reading through a new score because the announced guest had not appeared, was not in his hotel, had apparently never arrived in New York, and could not be located by his own agent. In this calamitous situation, with another holiday upon us and telephone service erratic, would I — being a friend and having a good relation with the Philharmonic — consider doing the four concerts, Thursday, Friday, Saturday, and Tuesday, just in case there was no change in the unaccountability of the guest conductor. I was so sure that there was nothing but a minor misunderstanding that I agreed lightheartedly and even made a program with Carlos, perfectly certain that the guest had thought that the Philharmonic's usual pattern of free Mondays, with Tuesday-morning rehearsals, would prevail, perhaps forgetting New Year's Day. I could not conceive in my wildest dreams that a thirty-two-year-old man, making his Philharmonic debut, would simply not show up. I like Carlos and wanted very much to calm his nerves and settled that by some late-afternoon hour the next day I should be called to get a progress report.

Soon after finishing this new emergency call there was my
friend from the Met on the wire with news of a candidate for
the Irish princess flying at that very moment from her home in
Arkansas to sing for us at three in the afternoon. For one week
I had been present at intercontinental searches over the telephone for Isoldes willing, able and available to step in, without
results. All first-line choices were unavailable, and of those who
were perhaps free, none would accept, as they were offended at
not having been invited originally. Time was running out since
any suggestion of postponing the première had been rejected as
inadmissible. We were down to six working days, if we could
start with a cast on the second of January.

I shall call the soprano who was to be heard Norma Jonas.
When I arrived at the Met auditorium I saw sitting there every
secretary from the many offices, several of the assistant conductors, Charles Riecker, and his assistant, but not the general
manager, or the music director, or his deputy. While this
critically important and urgent audition was going on the
troika responsible for the opera company was absent. Miss
Jonas came on stage, carrying a vocal score, muttering after
my "How do you do" that she really could not understand why
she was being compelled to sing for a role she had not learned.
This was a bombshell of absurdity, and I wanted now to clarify
who in this case was mad, I or somebody else. While I had a
short question and answer period with Miss Jonas, my wife
overheard the artistic administrator say, "She is pulling his leg,
I know she has sung the role."

Considering the flight and the effort and the professional
reputation of the singer I invited her to do something that was
in her repertoire, and she sang portions of the Immolation
Scene. Then she read a few pages of Isolde, which convinced
me that she had either never studied the part or that she forgot
more quickly than any professional I had ever met. I left the
Met somewhat disgusted, and we spent New Year's Eve and
part of the next day discussing with a mixture of amusement

and amazement the two detective stories being enacted by the
two major musical organizations of this big city: "A Search
for Isolde" and "The Missing Guest Conductor." When by
noon on New Year's Day the second mystery was still a mystery, Carlos cut the ribbon and asked me officially to do the concerts, with three rehearsals on Wednesday and Thursday.
Around such an emergency and the attendant changes there are
many details and constant phone ringing to absorb. Every department called: "How many seats does Mrs. Leinsdorf want?"
"In what order will you rehearse the selections?" "Which edition of the Bruckner symphony?" "Do you want doubled
woodwinds in the Schubert symphony?" The Met had vouch-
safed permission for this little stint, which was granted, perhaps
in the hope that I would become less insistent on getting a first-
class Isolde.

Wednesday I had two rehearsals, divided by a one-hour break
for lunch that was filled with telephone calls coming right into
the dressing room. Chapin, back from his health cure, informed
me that Klara Barlow was flying from Munich to New York
and would sing for us the same day, as soon as I was free from
my second rehearsal in the afternoon. Why, I asked, could
Barlow not have done her audition in Munich for Rafael Kubelik, the music director, who was right there in the same town?
That was evidently the wrong question to ask because there was
no coherent answer. I had registered the first seismographic
indications that not all was well in the inner sanctum of the
Met. I knew Barlow, who had been nonperforming understudy
to Nilsson in 1971. By five in the afternoon we had gone
through a ceremonial audition, with every indication that this
was a typical case of Wiener schnitzel. There really was nobody
else — the financial comptroller of the Met was breathing
heavily down Chapin's neck about the financial disaster of
changing a sold-out première to another work with resulting
money refunds so Barlow was engaged. The hassles and acid
exchanges, during which I asked to be relieved of my contract,

were merely the outline of a deep-seated problem. Everding, who had arrived earlier on the second, tried unsuccessfully to talk Chapin out of Barlow, but also to no avail.

My small comfort was that Thursday the first staging rehearsals with Vickers, Barlow, and Everding would find me busy next door at the Philharmonic. I would not be missed since the complexity of the stage mechanism in that production needed a good full working day to be tried, explained, and repeated. Friday the fourth was another red-letter day. At ten-thirty I had my first full rehearsal with orchestra, stage, and singers. At two in the afternoon I did the matinee concert at the Philharmonic. By that time the spirit of gamesmanship had got the better of me and I treated the whole excursion as some kind of a marathon contest. The Met orchestra gave me great pleasure by playing, for the first time since December 18, 1971, the score of *Tristan* as if we had adjourned four weeks ago. In an excellent mood I went at intermission to my room, where I was visited by Jon Vickers. He is a superlative singer, but, like most people in our realm, full of the strangest contradictions and complexes. Now he sat down heavily and declared with a truculent expression: "Maestro, I want out." He probably expected and hoped to get into a fight with me, but I disappointed him by calmly admitting that I myself had wanted to get out but was unable to do it gracefully so I would see it through. He had no choice but to leave my room without a fight. The second part of the rehearsal consisted of corrections and at one we concluded so I could have the luxury of an hour's rest before the matinee concert. When that was finished at four I phoned the Met to hear that Vickers had left and was back in his home in Bermuda. Jess Thomas, who was not due to sing until later in the run, graciously helped us with the première and several of the other performances that had been scheduled for Vickers.

Thirty-five years earlier I wistfully thought many times what a rare privilege it must be to conduct the Met and the

Philharmonic during the same season. On January 4, 1974, I had done it on the same day and, continuing throughout that month, I shuttled back and forth for a total of five performances of *Tristan* and eleven symphony concerts, including a four-day tour in Florida. For the busy days in New York it was most convenient that both organizations are in the same Lincoln Center with underground passages, making taxis superfluous and bad weather immaterial. I dashed to and fro, even managing to pilot Barlow through four Wagner evenings without overt mischance. The end of my marathon run on January 30 was worth every bit of trouble. Nilsson's return had always been planned for that night, a nonsubscription performance, for which Vickers too joined us, graciously leaving Bermuda for Amsterdam Avenue.

It is of no purpose to attempt a verbal account of an evening such as this one turned out to be. I am sure that in every diary this date will have a special place. Everything smiled on our endeavor, and I am glad to have been part of it. So glad that I insisted on a minimum of three years until I would venture into the opera house again.

The difficulties preceding the première became known to the press, partly through Vickers' "flight from Egypt," partly through my shooting off my mouth in a salvo of uncomplimentary epithets to a newspaperman. I spoke of Wiener schnitzel, of musical direction by Teletype, and of commissars for optimism. These slogans were widely circulated and held responsible, or partly responsible, for the eventual downfall of the regime at the Met. It was, of course, not so, since in reality a house of cards needs only a soft blow from thin lips to be toppled over. In contrast to Bing's methods, the Met organized by his successors tried to resemble a German provincial opera house, which could never work out in New York. Between dismissing the lieutenants of the previous administration and relying on an entirely green crew and the sudden death of the general manager, all piled on top of basically wrong concepts, no interview or words of any kind were needed to produce a collapse. My epitaph is that the Met management after Bing fell by its own weightlessness.

## Conclusion

After so much unvarnished description of my troubles, of shenanigans, pranks, and great incompetence, it may appear that things are in bad shape. How does such an impression tally with the beginnings of this book and the mention of our Golden Age? Is that crass contradiction, or forgetful author, or only an inattentive proofreader? None of the above. Our world has been more or less the same and the difficulties encountered by our greatest masters were much more severe than they are today. The musical career was never a bed of roses and if anything, in the present world the sheets and blankets of the bed have at the least rose color and often even petals for the sleeper.

Our disarray is social rather than artistic. In the United States especially there is among musicians a restlessness caused by the much oversold fiction of an egalitarian society. What our Establishment does not do is put social advancement behind the professional accomplishment. Nothing is done to make the splendid orchestra players feel their distinction within the community. Hence the perennial grating negotiations for more money as the one and only mirage of personal success. Europe has done better with calling every member of the symphony Herr Professor and making such achievement into a model for the young to admire and emulate. The American conservatories subject too many gifted students to such an intensive training that only the virtuoso career could satisfy and justify the effort of many years. Instead of this the vast majority land at best in fine ensembles and frequently scrape by making commercial jingles for television. Perhaps the balance between Europe and America lies in the higher price we pay for our superior musical organizations, a price not of coin but of personal maladjustment to the realities.

When I graduated from the Music Academy in Vienna at twenty-one I could not find employment and had to shift from odd job to odd job for four years until I could emigrate to the United States. As assistant to a few of the most famous conductors of the thirties I observed the backside of glory and glamour.

From the days of my studies I ran for much of the time on parallel tracks with my highly gifted colleagues, many of whom have disappeared without trace. The final paragraph of Goethe's autobiography closes with lines from his *Egmont*, which I have tried to translate, because they move me so much.

> *Whipped as if by invisible spirits — the sun horses of time run amok with the light carriage of our fate and we have no choice but to hold firmly to the reins, courageously resolved to keep the wheels away from the boulders on the right and the cliffs on the left. Who knows whereto it goes? He, who barely can remember wherefrom he came.*

Having never lost my awareness of how close the boulders and the cliffs were I feel gratitude to the forces that kept me going. As the sun horses raced on I also felt more and more in proportion to the totality of the world. I looked long and hard for a word other than "humility"; my resistance comes from hearing every two-bit politician use it when accepting nomination for dogcatcher. Not having found anything better I let it stand with a little blush, but it is true.

My many years as a performer convinced me that music is a fundamentally honest profession. This is not wide-eyed naiveté nor the glib assumption of a Polyanna. I find it an honest profession because all long-range decisions are made by the public.

It may be fickle, or lowbrow, or swayed by a phony for a while but there is an all-important but.

It is incorruptible. My real employer, no matter whose name appears under my contracts, has been from the first day the public, and I shall be on stage only as long as it wants me there.

When I performed on two successive nights with the New York Philharmonic and the Met before sold out houses it was thirty-eight years and a few days since I had first stood in front of a large crowd in that same city, where careers were made and broken.

If I dedicate this memoir to anybody it must be to the public of New York, without whose favor over such a long period no publisher would ever have looked at

> *the story of my life*
> *And the particular accidents gone by*
> *Since I came to this isle.*

*INDEX*

# Index

# CADENZA
## A MUSICAL CAREER
## ERICH LEINSDORF

Erich Leinsdorf is one of the best-known conductors of opera and symphony in the world. Born in Vienna, he served a conducting apprenticeship in Europe and first came to the United States in 1937 to serve under Arthur Bodanzky as assistant conductor to the Metropolitan Opera. Within a year, he became principal conductor of the German repertoire.

He then moved on to work with the San Francisco Opera and later became music director of the orchestras in Rochester and Cleveland. In 1962, after having rejoined the Met, he was appointed music director of the Boston Symphony Orchestra. His account of all these years is packed with anecdotes of famous personalities — Arturo Toscanini, Vladimir Horowitz, Ezio Pinza, Birgit Nilsson, Rudolf Bing, George Szell, and many others. An entire chapter is devoted to his relationship with Arturo Toscanini. Leinsdorf's experiences as an international musical celebrity reveal the complex scope of the conductor's